CHILD POVERTY
Aspiring to Survive

Morag C. Treanor

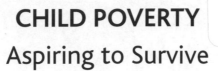

First published in Great Britain in 2020 by

Policy Press
University of Bristol
1-9 Old Park Hill
Bristol
BS2 8BB
UK
t: +44 (0)117 954 5940
pp-info@bristol.ac.uk
www.policypress.co.uk

North America office:
Policy Press
c/o The University of Chicago Press
1427 East 60th Street
Chicago, IL 60637, USA
t: +1 773 702 7700
f: +1 773-702-9756
sales@press.uchicago.edu
www.press.uchicago.edu

© Policy Press 2020

British Library Cataloguing in Publication Data
A catalogue record for this book is available from the British Library

Library of Congress Cataloging-in-Publication Data
A catalog record for this book has been requested

ISBN 978-1-4473-3466-8 (hardback)
ISBN 978-1-4473-3468-2 (paperback)
ISBN 978-1-4473-3467-5 (ePDF)
ISBN 978-1-4473-3469-9 (ePub)

The right of Morag C. Treanor to be identified as author of this work has been asserted by her in accordance with the Copyright, Designs and Patents Act 1988.

All rights reserved: no part of this publication may be reproduced, stored in a retrieval system, or transmitted in any form or by any means, electronic, mechanical, photocopying, recording, or otherwise without the prior permission of Policy Press.

The statements and opinions contained within this publication are solely those of the author and not of the University of Bristol or Policy Press. The University of Bristol and Policy Press disclaim responsibility for any injury to persons or property resulting from any material published in this publication.

Policy Press works to counter discrimination on grounds of gender, race, disability, age and sexuality.

Cover designer: Gareth Davies/Qube Design
Cover image credit: Getty/Johner Images
Printed and bound in Great Britain by CMP, Poole
Policy Press uses environmentally responsible print partners

This book is dedicated to my mother, also Morag Treanor; to my children, Saorsa, Mairi and Luke; and to my grandson, Maximus.

Contents

List of figures and tables

Figures

Tables

List of abbreviations

ACE	adverse childhood experience
AHC	after housing cost
BHC	before housing cost
BME	black and minority ethnic
DFLE	disability-free life expectancy
DLA	disability living allowance
ESA	employment support allowance
IMF	International Monetary Fund
NEET	not in education, employment or training
OECD	Organisation for Economic Co-operation and Development
SMD	severe and multiple deprivation
UNCRC	United Nations Convention on the Rights of the Child

Acknowledgements

I would like to thank Policy Press for giving me the opportunity to write this book.

I would like to thank Adrian and Dorothy Sinfield for reviewing the book chapter by chapter as I wrote it, for guiding and informing my thinking, and for providing tea and biscuits as we went along.

I would like to thank the Joseph Rowntree Foundation for helping me to compile the ethnicity statistics in Chapter 8.

I would like to thank Child Poverty Action Group in Scotland for having me as their researcher on the Early Warning System research that has enabled me to speak to the same families each year since 2013. In many of the quotes I use throughout the book, it is these families' words that you hear.

I would like to thank the families themselves, who have allowed me into their homes year after year, since 2013, and who have shared the highs and lows of their lives and experiences with me. I always come away feeling invigorated and fired up. They are amazing.

I would like to thank one of my oldest friends, Jane Williamson, for coming up with the title of the book.

I would like to thank my loved ones – you know who you are – for your kindness and patience with me while I wrote this book. When I forgot to feed my (almost grown-up, to be fair) children, they fed me.

Preface

We are living through an era where 'fake news' can seem as authentic as 'real' news and people do not know what to believe. We are in a time when it can suit governments to actively promulgate myths and misinformation about those most in need, for example the disabled, refugees and asylum seekers, children and families living in poverty. This allows governments to enact damaging policy initiatives that usually seek to reduce income and other resources to those most in need. Even where governments may genuinely have believed in what they were doing at the outset of austerity, after the Great Recession of 2008, they are now wilfully ignoring the impacts of their actions on children, families, communities and societies. Governments are not acting alone, however. They have willing partners. The negative stereotypes and vitriolic attacks on certain groups of people persist because our media are cheerfully complicit in spreading sensationalised stories, irrespective of the truth, if it sells newspapers and maintains friendships with governments and the powerful. This makes it especially difficult for all of us to ascertain the truth.

My intention was to write a book called *The Truth About Child Poverty* with the aim of setting the record straight; however, in this post-truth era, public trust in 'experts' has been eroded and academics can be considered part of an untrustworthy 'elite'. One of the successes of the 'fake-news', post-truth drive has been to define 'elites' in the minds of the public as academics and experts and not as billionaires and global corporations. Who has more power? Power, lack of power, empowerment and disempowerment are key factors in a book on poverty and inequality. It is not I, an academic, who is powerful; but I feel the need to justify what gives me the authority to write a book such as this, a book that aims to set the record straight and flip the thinking on child poverty while keeping children at the heart of the argument. I have asked myself the same question because I believe I have an ethical duty to the children and families living in poverty, who most likely do not have the same opportunity as me to write this book, to explore what I think qualifies me to do so. Essentially, what gives me the right to speak on behalf of children and their families living in poverty? The answer I have come up with is twofold. The first relates to my own experiences of poverty, and other adversity, in childhood and in adulthood, and the second relates to my work, for close to 20 years, with children and families living in poverty.

I grew up the youngest of five children in a seaside mining town in Scotland and I received free school meals during my entire time in primary and secondary school. Due to other problems in my family, in particular domestic abuse, I lived in numerous refuges before becoming formally homeless at the age of 16. I lived in a hostel for my final two years of school before going to university. At university I struggled to understand the middle-class culture of academia and soon fell pregnant with my first child. I went back to my home town, got a flat from the local council, and worked out how I could finish my degree and what I could do next. I did finish my degree. The following years were spent trying to access even higher levels of education, and employment, with varying degrees of success. I confronted the massive barrier of not having childcare, of having no family support, and faced the impossibility of finding two months' nursery fees upfront. Life did improve but then there were poverty-related setbacks such as my mother being diagnosed with terminal cancer in her early 50s and my decision to stop working to care for her. Now pregnant with my second child I was back living on benefits and feared I would never escape. After my mother died, I did a master's degree, became a researcher and had a third child. Life was smooth until I separated from my partner in my mid-30s and decided I was going to be a single parent and do a PhD on the subject of child poverty. Although I now have a good wage, and life is easier, it has not always been so. I know from trying to escape poverty myself that it is like quicksand, clutching at you and dragging you down further. It makes clawing your way back out increasingly difficult. It drags you deeper: into debt, into petty criminality such as bumping a catalogue, into minor fraud such as faking a job reference, into making decisions that may not be in your own best interests in the long term but can get you out of a short-term fix. I think that this gives me my drive to understand poverty, especially child poverty, as it currently affects families and it also gives me the drive to advocate for those to whom society does not listen: the poor and the young.

This drive to understand and communicate child poverty is the focus of my research. My first project in 2001 was with people who had become homeless due to mortgage arrears. I then did a qualitative longitudinal study with children living in disadvantaged areas making the transition to secondary school. I have since carried out two further qualitative longitudinal research projects with families living in poverty. In 2008, when presenting research evidence at a UK government event, the value of my research was questioned due to the small number of families involved. I decided to learn how to do statistics and the focus of my PhD became the statistical analysis of a large birth cohort study of more than 5,000 children. I continue to use statistics and large datasets, often using situations I find in the lives of the families with which I do qualitative research, to explore whether the issues my families living in poverty face affect lots of families, and whether these issues are systematic and systemic, or whether they are, as is often believed in government and media circles, self-imposed and self-perpetuating.

It is the combination of the personal and professional experience that has brought me to the point of writing this book now. It is important not to rely on my experiences alone but to bring to life the experiences of those who have been part of my own and others' research over the years while setting the issues in the society and context in which they occur. It is vital any consideration of child poverty represents the views of those currently living in poverty and that it keeps the child at the centre of the analysis/argument. So, rather than my trying to convince the readers of this book of absolute truths about child poverty that only I can truthfully convey, instead I invite you to come on a journey with me. In this journey I will present to you what I have seen and learned and will offer interpretations and ideas. I will invite you to 'flip your thinking'; to think about alternative explanations to those you may encounter in the everyday media.

1

Introduction

> The child should be fully prepared to live an individual
> life in society, and brought up in the spirit of the ideals
> proclaimed in the Charter of the United Nations, and in
> particular in the spirit of peace, dignity, tolerance, freedom,
> equality and solidarity. (Convention on the Rights of the
> Child, 1989)

How do children view poverty?

Children are aware of their family's poverty despite the best efforts of
parents to shield them. Children exercise agency in the consumption
of their family's scarce resources. Even at a young age, children are
already active in trying to mitigate their family's poverty by not asking
for the everyday consumer items that their peers enjoy. As children
grow towards adolescence, they employ further behaviours to support
the family's finances, often taking on adult roles and responsibilities
and missing out on key aspects of childhood. At this age, older
children often take responsibility for the care of younger children,
allowing parents to go out to work. This is more often the case in
countries that have prohibitively expensive and inaccessible childcare,
such as the UK. At this age too, older children often find part-time
employment to offset their family's poverty, both directly, by at times
handing money over to their parents, and indirectly, by paying for
the things they need by themselves. Such precocious responsibilities
reinforce the disadvantages poverty brings to a young person's capacity
to participate fully in their education and in the social and leisure
activities of their peers. Some children are particularly vulnerable in
this regard; for example, the children of lone parents who may lack
wider family support.

What we know about the experience of poverty for children comes
from research undertaken *with* them. It is vital to include the voices
of those living in poverty, and of children, in the poverty debate. Too
often policies are made about them without them. In this book, I draw
on my own long-term studies of families living in poverty, and on
the research of others, to provide an understanding of child poverty

that keeps children and their families at its core. This book cannot address every policy that affects child poverty in this country, nor can it address the policies of every country it mentions. Instead, within each substantive chapter it addresses one or two relevant policies to illustrate key points or to emphasise an important point. As much as I would like to be able to address policies pertaining to child poverty more extensively, space does not allow. Therefore, the policies discussed are selected for illustrative purposes and are not an encyclopaedic overview of all policies.

Why child poverty?

Key questions in a book about child poverty in wealthy societies are these: 'What is child poverty?', that is, is child poverty any different to the poverty experienced by adults individually or families collectively; 'Is child poverty going up or down?'; and 'Why does child poverty persist in wealthy societies?' The first of these – on what is child poverty – is addressed in this chapter, the second question on the incidence and prevalence of child poverty is addressed in Chapter 2, and the third, why does child poverty persist in wealthy societies, is considered throughout the book. These questions are important in a book about child poverty, as there is no agreed definition that distinguishes it from adult or family poverty, yet it generates a great deal of attention. If there is no formal distinction between child and adult/ family poverty, why do we focus on child poverty and why should we aim to prevent or eradicate it?

Child poverty is distinct from adult poverty and, therefore, important for a number of reasons. The first is that a child living in poverty for even a relatively short period by adult standards could easily be impoverished for a large part of their childhood. This is critical as poverty adversely affects many aspects of child development, resulting in children accumulating disadvantage throughout their childhoods and beyond. Poverty shapes growth and achievement in, for example, pre-natal and peri-natal health and development, child health, mental health, family stress and wellbeing, participation in peer social and leisure activities, participation in family and cultural celebrations, in school life, in access to suitable housing and nice places to grow up, in education, in transitions to adolescence and adulthood, in access to post-school education and to employment. The National Equalities Panel in the UK found that 'economic advantage and disadvantage reinforce themselves across the life cycle, and often on to the next generation' (Hills et al, 2010: 1).

A second reason child poverty is distinct from adult poverty is that children control few of the levers that govern their families' financial situation (although they are by no means passive) and so rely on the adults around them for sustenance and support. The United Nations Convention on the Rights of the Child (UNCRC) intends that 'children are no longer envisaged as mere recipients of services or beneficiaries of protective measures. Rather, they are subjects of rights and participants in actions affecting them. They need to be respected in their individuality and in their evolving capacity to influence decisions relevant to their lives' (Santos-Pais, 1999: 5). However, in the children's rights approach there is a tension in the duality of the role of children as rights-bearers but also as dependent on their families (Bradshaw et al, 2007). Jans (2004: 27) calls this an 'ambivalent reality' for children, where 'on the one hand, children are surrounded with care; on the other hand, they are stimulated to present themselves as individuals with their own rights'. This tension is never entirely reconciled in studies of children as, in order to have a full set of adult-equivalent rights, children would need all the freedoms and responsibilities that adults possess. This goes against children's fundamental right to protection, and the role of adults and governments to protect them, as set out in the UNCRC.

A third distinction is that children often have little control over the distribution of resources within their own families. How resources are shared in a family, irrespective of whether that family lives in poverty or not, is likely to increase or decrease the prevalence of child poverty. A fourth distinction is that children have traditionally been viewed as blameless, as innocent bystanders of their parents' material conditions and, as such, deserving of society's care and protection from poverty (although this is arguably changing). It is the blend of these ideas, that children are blameless even if their families not, and that poverty poses a far greater threat to the life chances of a child, that have made governments keep child poverty on the policy agenda, even if, as we shall see later, some governments, such as the UK, erode and degrade efforts to prevent and reduce child poverty.

Childhood comprises transitions: from infancy to nursery, primary school and on to secondary school; from compulsory education on to, hopefully, employment or further study. As a result of poverty, every single transition a child will make is made more difficult and more problematic. These difficulties in transitioning gather pace throughout childhood, especially where the experience of poverty is persistent. Without support or intervention, a child living in poverty who experiences difficulties making the transition to secondary school is more likely to have difficulty making successful transitions post-secondary school. Transitions can continue into adulthood. Many adults who live in persistent poverty, and who experienced adversity in childhood, have often made unsuccessful, unsupported transitions to adulthood. At every transitional stage of childhood is a risk of making a worse transition if you live in poverty. For this reason, focus should be on children across the whole of childhood, with special attention given to key transitional stages.

The state of child poverty

Child poverty is rising across affluent Western societies. Child poverty is not inevitable and, even in times of deep recession, is avoidable. What governments choose to do matters. Whether child poverty increases or decreases depends on how countries respond to economic instability and insecurity. Across many wealthy societies, austerity measures were put in place after the Great Recession of 2008. In the UK, severe cuts to in-work income supplements, delivered via the tax credits system, out-of-work benefits for those not in paid employment, and help with the cost of childcare for working parents, has had a harsh impact on those living in poverty.

In the UK, the Child Poverty Act 2010 was rescinded and the definition of child poverty was replaced with one of 'life chances'. Relatively commonplace characteristics such as family 'breakdown', ill-health, lack of skills, inadequate housing, 'poor' schools and parental 'worklessness' were presented as the causes of poverty and the new legislation proposed to remove the income-based targets of the 2010 Act. This was intended to downplay the importance of income to child poverty. However, an amendment that passed in the House of Lords requires that the UK government continue to publish data on how many children live in poverty using the income definition. The new legislation also publishes data that focuses narrowly on educational attainment and parental 'worklessness' as the government's preferred way of measuring child poverty. By massively downplaying the importance of income on (rates of) child poverty, the UK government can justify a position of providing families with less money in the name of austerity. Such a move has increased the rate and severity of poverty in the parts of the UK governed by this legislation. In Scotland, one of the UK's four nations, under devolution and increased powers to the Scottish parliament, the Scottish government has developed its own legislation to replace the 2010 UK Act: the Child Poverty (Scotland) Act 2017. In this Act the income-based measures and targets of the 2010 UK Act are not only retained, but are strengthened. Furthermore, attention has been paid to particularly vulnerable groups, such as lone parents, and it has a focus on children's circumstance and outcomes, in relation to, for example, housing and education. Under this Act, community planning partnerships – comprising local authorities, health boards and other public bodies such as the police – have to report every three years, both prospectively and retrospectively, on what they are doing to tackle child poverty. One of the cornerstones of this new Scottish Act is that respect and dignity must be afforded to all. This is greatly at odds with both the rhetoric and the practice in the rest of the UK, which, as Marsh et al (2017: 234) note, 'requires a proper explanation of why it should be different in England and Wales'.

Across affluent Western countries, much is being said about child poverty, particularly in political and media discourses, with an increasingly disparaging focus on perceived parental shortcomings. Common questions include: Which children live in poverty? Why? Is it real? What does child poverty look like? Are parents to blame? Is there a culture of poverty? Do children learn how to be poor from their parents? Is poverty transmitted between generations? Is poverty caused by parents being unwilling or unable to work? Do parents have too many children that they cannot afford? These questions and more form much of the public understanding on child poverty today. With the roots of child poverty being fiercely debated, the outcomes of these debates are likely to lead to (further) negative changes to how child poverty is understood and tackled by national governments, and by extension, on programmes and initiatives to prevent or eradicate it. At present, the social, political and economic landscape is in flux and low-income children's lives and wellbeing are particularly vulnerable to marginalisation and misrepresentation.

Governments, when they are responsive to the issue of child poverty, often view it through a predominantly economic lens. They understand that child poverty will affect a child's potential as a fully functioning, future taxpaying member of society. Child poverty brings great economic costs (Hirsch, 2013); yet, few governments view child poverty as a fundamental source of inequality, a social injustice, a breach of a child's rights under the articles of the UNCRC and a source of national shame in a wealthy society. When governments do not fully understand or accept the causes of child poverty they turn to blaming parents – especially lone parents, ethnic minority parents and parents who are underemployed or unemployed, even if this is a result of poor physical or mental health – for their children's poverty.

In so doing, they shift the focus from the actions of government to the behaviours of individual families. As previously noted, child poverty is not inevitable, and it is within the gift of national governments to prevent and eradicate it. Yet when governments get involved badly the situation for children becomes increasingly perilous.

In addition to the austere economic responses post-Great Recession, in Europe there is an escalating migration catastrophe that is testing human rights and social cohesion to their limits. In these contexts, it is children who are bearing the brunt of failures in economic and social policies and yet their lives and experiences remain largely hidden or misunderstood and misrepresented. This book places children at the centre of a critical examination of contemporary policies and political discourses surrounding the causes and consequences of childhood poverty in wealthy societies. It looks at received wisdoms and pejorative assertions in relation to child poverty and presents arguments to show that individual characteristics do not distinguish between poor and non-poor people but result in a highly stigmatised and distressed group. Finally, this book asks the reader to consider an alternative, to 'flip their thinking', and to ask questions from a different perspective, to consider the issues through the eyes of a child living in poverty.

So, what is (child) poverty?

When discussing child poverty in today's societies, when thinking about what children today should or should not be entitled to have, people tend to draw on their own experiences, or received wisdoms, often of a different time and place. But the lives and experiences of today's children cannot be measured against the standards of the past. Poverty involves gauging the average standards of any given society at a certain point in time and making comparisons against them (Alcock, 2006). When people lack the resources (income) to obtain what is required to be able to function and participate fully in the norms of that society they can be said to be impoverished (Townsend, 1979). Such comparisons require that the social standards in which people live be taken into account, an exercise that can involve subjective value judgements. This idea of poverty is centred on the tenet that people are social animals with social and familial roles, responsibilities and obligations (Townsend and Walker, 2010). Such social responsibilities require people to participate in family and cultural life course events such as births, marriages and deaths and celebrations such as birthdays, Christmas and other religious festivals (Townsend and Walker, 2010).

To be prevented from participating in events and activities of the family and society that a person belongs to due to a lack of income, according to Townsend, was unacceptable and constituted 'a state of observable and demonstrable disadvantage' (Townsend, 1987: 125). Using Townsend's concept, people can be said to be in poverty if they lack the resources to live a life free from deprivation:

> Individuals, families and groups in the population can be said to be in poverty when they lack the resources to obtain the types of diet, participate in the activities and have the living conditions and amenities which are customary, or at least widely encouraged or approved, in societies to which they belong. Their resources are so seriously below those commanded by the average individual or family that they are, in effect, excluded from ordinary living patterns and activities. (1979: 31)

Townsend's idea uses a measure of both 'income poverty' and 'material deprivation': the former pertains to income and resources available (1987) and the latter refers to 'conditions or activities experienced' (1987: 127). Based on Townsend's ideas, the measure of income poverty now used across all Organisation for Economic Co-operation and Development (OECD) countries, and beyond, is income at 60 per cent median equivalised income and material deprivation as measured by a set of individual deprivation indicators that together form an index of material deprivation.

Income and material deprivation

The threshold used to measure income poverty is 60 per cent of median *equivalised* income. When income is equivalised it is adjusted depending on who is in a family, that is how many adults and children. It is understood that more people living in a family will require more resources and the adjustment, or equivalisation, takes this into consideration while making modifications for economies of scale. The equivalisation process is often criticised for not taking into account circumstances that will make a family require greater resources, such as disability. As such, the rate of child poverty for those experiencing disability in the family may be underestimated.

The advantages of using income as a measure of poverty are manifold. Income confers an objective, well-defined, measurable gauge that provides information about the extent of poverty and inequality within a society and allows for comparisons with other advanced industrial societies (Alcock, 2006). The use of material deprivation as a measure of poverty would be incomplete in itself, as it is only when material deprivation is imposed by a lack of income that it constitutes a measure of poverty. Lister (2004) warns of the danger of downplaying income when defining poverty for fear that it be used to justify a policy stance opposed to raising the incomes of those living in poverty, a prescient sentiment as will be discussed in the following chapter.

A problem with using income to measure poverty results from the power adults have over income, expenditure and consumption, and the lack of power children may have. This power over income is not just a function of the adult–child relationship, it is also a function of the gender of the income-earning adults. Intrafamilial transfers of resources can be uneven, with women (and children) often exercising less control over the distribution and use of family resources, leading to higher levels of deprivation for these two groups (Pahl, 1989, Pahl, 1999, Goode et al., 1998). However, in such families it is usually mothers who experience the highest levels of deprivation as they are shown to subjugate their own needs to safeguard those of their children (Middleton et al., 1997, Magadi and Middleton, 2007, Harris et al., 2009, Ridge and Millar, 2011). Income, therefore, while imperfect, is still the necessary and defining aspect of poverty and usually forms the basis of any multidimensional measure.

Material deprivation is an index comprising 11 indicators for adults and ten for children consensually agreed by the public to be necessities. The index of material deprivation thus distinguishes between child and adult poverty. Across societies these indices show that parents are more deprived than their children because they sacrifice their own needs to protect their children (Treanor, 2014). How material deprivation has changed over time is explored in Chapter 2. A problem with material deprivation as a measure of poverty for children results from who decides what the child-centred indicators of material deprivation are. The children's items on the index of material deprivation currently in use have been consensually agreed by adults. There has been meagre attention paid to children's voices in the selection of deprivation indicators thus far, which is a loss to the understanding of child poverty and a missed opportunity to allow children to inform and enrich the debate on deprivation.

A new child-centric measure of material deprivation, using children as informants, was developed by Main and Bradshaw (2012). To ensure the resulting measure of deprivation was caused by a lack of resources, the data were linked to income data the parents had provided. In the analysis, this child-informed index explained more of the variation in children's subjective wellbeing then parental income poverty did. Interestingly, it also showed that subjective wellbeing was lower for children who were deprived but not in income poverty and higher for those who were in income poverty but not deprived. This shows the importance of material deprivation to the concept of poverty, including child poverty, and the importance of measuring child deprivation from a child's perspective.

Income inequality

Although the agreed income threshold used to measure income poverty is 60 per cent of median equivalised income, there are other thresholds in use across the OECD, for example, being below 50 per cent of median equivalised income (severe poverty), and other measures in use, such as the poverty gap and the relative income gap, among others (Hudson and Kühner, 2016). This book will focus on poverty as 60 per cent of median equivalised income. It will also address another way of looking at unfair income advantage and disadvantage: income inequality.

As a framework for studying poverty, income inequality is of increasing interest and growing concern. Income inequality refers to the gaps in income (and wealth) between the highest and lowest paid in society. Some governments view poverty as a mere artefact of inequality. Furthermore, among right-leaning governments, income inequality has been seen as a precondition of economic growth, as 'necessary for creating competition in the free market' (Ridge and Wright, 2008: 288). This is because it is through maintaining low wages that businesses can maximise profits and retain a competitive edge over others. Thus, some commentators would say that 'inequality is acceptable, even desirable in an economy requiring strong incentives for people to work hard' (Marsh et al, 2017: 15). Walker and Walker (1997) argue that the right-leaning Conservative Governments (1979–97) in the UK had a deliberate strategy of creating inequality to stimulate competitiveness.

Income and wealth govern people's access to capital, goods, services and functions. Those at the lower end of the income (and wealth) inequality spectrum have lower levels of influence and control over the conditions of their and their children's lives. Income inequality perpetuates advantage and disadvantage, leaves the poor trailing behind, and negatively affects progress across all wealthy nations (Wilkinson and Pickett, 2010). In fact, income inequality negatively affects almost every facet of life (Wilkinson and Pickett, 2010). In very unequal nations people are less healthy than they are in nations where everyone is more equal, whether they are equally rich or equally poor (Marsh et al, 2017). Inequality matters because what happens in the upper deciles of the income and wealth spectrum also negatively affects children living in poverty. This is a consequence of those at the upper end striving to protect the social position of their children and ensuring they do not slip down the ladder of social mobility. In so doing, their actions serve to block and exclude poorer children advancing up the social scale. This is most notable in relation to the family, education and employment, and will be further discussed in Chapters 3, 4, 5 and 6.

Political will usually focuses on the impacts of poverty and socioeconomic disadvantage rather than on the impacts of wealth and socioeconomic *advantage*. For children, income inequality brings unequal chances, opportunities and outcomes. The reasons why looking at the experience of children living in poverty through the lens of inequality is illuminating is twofold: firstly, its relational nature allows us to make comparisons in the experiences and outcomes of children living in poverty compared to all other children. It does not isolate children living in poverty as a separate group to be fixed, but engages with the experiences of all children. In so doing, it allows us to see the distance travelled and how far we have yet to go as a society to try to equalise children's experiences and outcomes. Secondly, it allows us to focus on what is happening at the top of the socioeconomic scale and analyse the impact of social policies on them. As the income gap widens, so too does the experiences and outcomes for children and young people living at the lower end of the socioeconomic spectrum. In order to understand the gaps, child poverty ought to be compared to the corresponding experiences of children living in the upper strata of society. This is in keeping with the central request to the readership of this book, to flip their thinking, in this instance to introduce the idea of focusing on the problems with the rich and wealthy rather than the problems with the poor.

There has been disproportionate attention paid to people living in poverty, and the problems associated with them, and almost none paid to people living in the upper strata of society and the problems they may bring. As Tawney (1913: 10) said: 'what thoughtful rich people call the problem of poverty, thoughtful poor people call with equal justice the problem of riches'. Over a century has passed since Tawney made this observation and little has changed in the intervening period. Even then, the behaviours and character of individuals were blamed for their poverty. Tawny (1913) understood this and wryly noted that the behaviours and character of the wealthy should also draw attention: 'improve the character of individuals by all means – if you feel competent to do so, especially of those whose excessive incomes expose them to particular temptations'. Given the short-lived focus on the behaviour and character of bankers in the aftermath of the 2008 Great Recession this is vatic counsel indeed. This book will have reminders in each chapter to flip our thinking on who we should be focusing on; those with the least or those with the most. While there is little research on the advantaged and the ways in which they perpetuate their advantage, a reminder of this gap and what it could mean for children living in poverty recurs throughout the book.

While some commentators have sought to downplay the importance of inequality, divorcing it from the problem of child poverty, analysis shows that societies with high levels of inequality also have high levels of child poverty and, furthermore, rates of child poverty historically have tracked those of inequality (McKnight et al, 2017). Thus, income inequality is a structural cause of child poverty, and previous attempts to reduce child poverty have been criticised for explicitly avoiding any focus on income inequality (Lister, 2011, Stewart et al., 2009). To achieve the goal of reducing poverty it has been argued that inequality of income and wealth must be tempered (Giddens and Diamond, 2005).

What causes child poverty?

The risks, causes and consequences of child poverty are frequently conflated in the UK and internationally. They are often misunderstood and misrepresented. How a government understands the causes of child poverty is key to the steps it would be willing to take to mitigate and prevent it. There are increasing policy and media discourses on parental attributes and behaviours as causes of child poverty. This erodes government and public support for child poverty initiatives and also damages the wellbeing of children themselves. This lack of understanding extends to the general public too: in 2014 a quarter of the Scottish public thought that child poverty was mainly caused by parents' alcoholism, drug or other substance use (McKendrick et al, 2016: 68). The current UK-level political and media narrative that attributes child poverty to parental behaviours has created a political backlash and led to those not in poverty blaming those in poverty for their situation. Both have weakened support for the maintenance of

Figure 1.1 Change in negative attitudes to unemployment and benefit payments

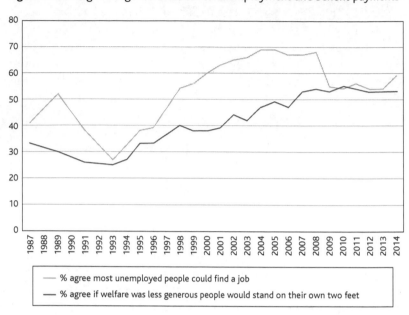

Source: British Social Attitudes Survey, 1987–2014[1]

anti-poverty strategies. In Figures 1.1 and 1.2, the change in positive and negative attitudes to unemployment and the receipt of unemployment benefits in Britain is tracked from 1987 to 2014. In Figure 1.1 it can be seen that there is between a 30 and 40 percentage point increase in the number of people who believe that most unemployed people could find a job and that if welfare was less generous people would 'stand on their own two feet'. In Figure 1.2, we see that there has been a decrease in positive attitudes to benefit receipt over time. Here, the percentage of people who agree the government should spend more on welfare and who think unemployment benefits are too low has almost halved. Why have these attitudes changed and why do pejorative ones now prevail? These are questions that will be posed throughout the book; however, it is safe to say that one reason is that the public are constantly being told that it is so.

Contrary to common misconception, child poverty is caused by a complex blend of structural and personal issues relating to macro-economic, political, social and individual factors. Macro-economic factors, such as the structure of the labour market, the housing market, low pay, irregular hours and insecure employment cause child poverty. Political factors, such as the level of social security payments and the recent social security cuts for families both in and out of work, are

Figure 1.2 Change in positive attitudes to unemployment and benefit payments

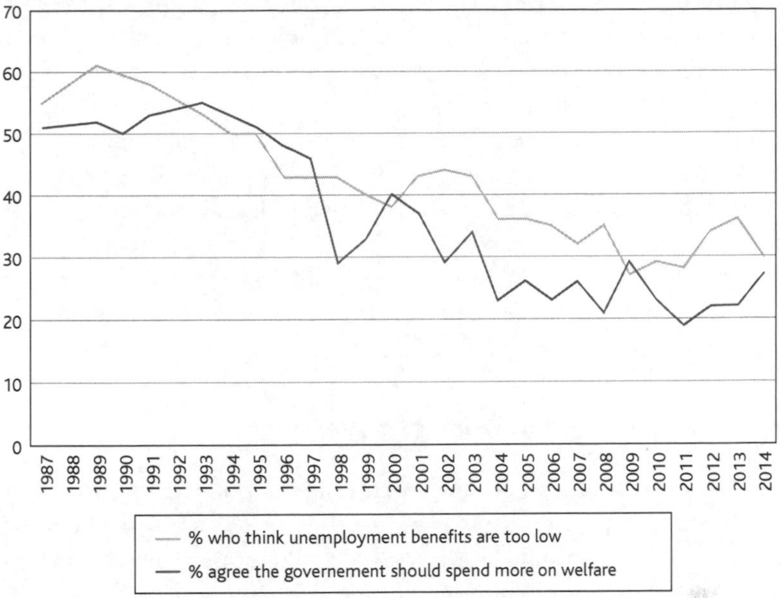

Source: British Social Attitudes Survey, 1987–2014

another cause. Social factors, such as gender, lone parenthood, disability, age and race/ethnicity result in a heightened risk of living in poverty, although this is not inevitable as will be seen later in the book. And, finally, individual factors in relation to capacities and choices play a part too, although arguably 'what appear to be individual level factors often reflect underlying social and economic processes' (McKendrick et al, 2016: 60). These risks and causes will be discussed further in Chapter 2.

Consequences of child poverty

The consequences or impacts of child poverty start before birth and accumulate across the life course. Poverty has negative impacts on children's health, cognitive development, social, emotional and behavioural development, friendships, self-esteem, relationships, experience of education, educational outcomes and access to employment, amongst other areas (Treanor, 2012). Poverty does not just impact on children's future outcomes. Poverty has detrimental effects on children during childhood itself, providing a compelling case for action to address it.

More rarely, children living in poverty are at increased risk of growing up with additional adverse experiences, such as substance misuse, domestic abuse or involvement with the criminal justice system (Bramley et al, 2015). Despite public belief, these are a minority of cases (approximately 3 per cent of all people living in poverty); however, where these issues do occur they have highly devastating consequences for children and require dedicated and specialised input from services (JRF, 2016). In fact, it is such adversity in childhood in addition to poverty, rather than the experience of poverty in isolation, that can lead to children developing complex needs in adulthood. Adverse childhood experiences will be explored further in Chapter 9.

The children at greater risk of poverty

Risks and disadvantages cluster together and amplify each other and it is through this clustering that we are able to see who are the most disadvantaged (Wolff and De-Shalit, 2007). There are groups who are at particular risk of poverty, such as women, ethnic minorities, refugees/asylum seekers, the sick and disabled, the young, the unemployed, those with larger families, and those with lower levels of education and social class. These are also some of the people in society who are more likely to experience prejudiced attitudes and behaviours in the first place. This compounds the disadvantages experienced by these groups in society and adds to their marginalisation, stigma and shame. These groups will not be the primary focus of the book but will be considered throughout.

There are also groups of young people who are especially vulnerable, including children in/leaving care, teenage parents, children with a parent in prison, children with disabilities or disabled parents, children who are carers, migrant children and refugee/asylum-seeking children. Not only are these groups more at risk of poverty, the experience of poverty for them is often more severe, which, when interacting with their already vulnerable status, can be particularly damaging. For example 'the impact of the recession on children in migrant households in Europe was often greater than it was on children from non-migrant households ... in the two countries where child poverty increased the most, children in migrant households suffered disproportionately' (Fanjul, 2014: 22). Chapter 8 looks at children of higher risk of poverty who are especially vulnerable.

The following chapters will address common understandings and misunderstandings, and the impacts of child poverty on children in relation to: Context, Family, Lone parents, Education, Employment, Health and Children at particular risk. It is important to note that these areas are not free from intervention; there is much policy governing them. The following chapters will discuss why it matters *how* we address them.

The rest of the book

Chapter 2 looks at the profile of child poverty, as measured by both income and material deprivation, within the UK and beyond and explores whether its rates are increasing or decreasing. It looks in depth at the misunderstandings, causes and consequences of child poverty and how government (mis)understandings of child poverty affect how it is perceived and tackled. It looks too at the profile of child poverty as regards who lives in poverty and describes how child poverty is a dynamic phenomenon with different groups of families cycling into and out of poverty across time. The chapter emphasises the importance of income to child poverty and concludes by describing a small number of policies that help to increase family incomes.

Chapter 3 takes a critically informed look at the role of families, and children's position within families, in understanding child poverty and disadvantage. It looks at the role of social support and gendered relationships and examines how families are not value-free environments. Family life under conditions of disadvantage tends to be pathologised and denigrated: parents who are 'poor' are frequently situated as 'poor parents'. Low-income families are particularly vulnerable to categorisation as 'troubled families' or troublesome families (Ribbens McCarthy et al, 2013). This chapter looks at the myths and realities of family life at the bottom of the income structure, how children understand, negotiate and mediate poverty in family life and their experiences and agency within the family.

Chapter 4 explores the importance of, and relationship between, family formation, or 'breakdown' and lone parenthood in the context of childhood poverty. Few subjects excite the public and political imagination quite as much as the issue of lone parents. It is an area with strong connections to poverty, disadvantage, gendered inequalities, and the supposed breaching of normative values and expectations. I engage with myths and assumptions about lone parents and reveal the corrosive effect of demonising lone-parent family life on children's lives and wellbeing. I show that relationships are dynamic, that lone parents are not a homogenous group, that a large proportion of children will spend time in a lone-parent formation, and that how a government responds to lone parents in policy terms directly relates to how impoverished their children will be.

Chapter 5 explores the importance of understanding child poverty and its relationship to children's education. It takes a child-centred perspective to situate children in the context of their peer relationships, pupil–teacher relationships and parental relationships to explore their wellbeing and achievement at school. Education has the potential to be a vital passport for low-income children, but many children are unsettled, undervalued and underachieving at school. This chapter will explore the importance of education, of school social and academic life to children living in poverty, of educational transitions, of examinations and achievements, and of wellbeing, participation and inclusion at school. It looks at how school culture and the misunderstandings of teachers on the causes and consequences of poverty can present a barrier to the full participation of children living in poverty in their schooling.

Chapter 6 explores the complex relationship between child poverty and families being in and out of work. It looks at the role of employment in lifting families out of poverty and how low quality, low security employment poses a threat to children and families rather than a route out of poverty. The chapter examines poverty and employment from the perspective of the child, exploring the implications for children of parental employment, unemployment, worklessness, low pay, and insecure employment. With the increase across the developed world of labour market activation, and the dominant status and values attached to employment, this chapter draws on research from children and low-income working parents to highlight the challenges faced by children and families situated at the insecure, fragile end of the labour market.

Chapter 7 focuses on health. The subject of health can encompass disability; however, the subject of disability is addressed in Chapter 8 as well as being a cross-cutting thread that runs throughout the book. This chapter, then, explores how poor health can be a risk, cause *and* consequence of poverty. It illuminates the ways in which poor health has particularly strong consequences for children and young people. There is a strong association between health and poverty with poor health being a universally accepted predictor of poverty across time and place. What is less well known is that the association is bi-directional, that is that poverty also causes poor health. Even short-term falls in income increase the risk of ill health (Smith and Middleton, 2007: 58). This reverse causal relationship is strong and is also seen in people with disabilities: those who become disabled are more likely to have been poor beforehand. Another facet of health that is important to the study of children living in poverty is whether the health condition is physical or mental. Poverty is strongly related to poor mental health in adults and children. Furthermore, children are increasingly presenting with poor mental health themselves. Chapter 7 focus predominantly on mental health as an increasing risk to the wellbeing and outcomes of children living in poverty now and in the future.

Chapter 8 looks at two groups of children who are at increased risk of living in poverty: those from an ethnic minority background and those who are disabled or who live in a family with a disabled family member. For those from an ethnic minority background the conscious and unconscious racism and discrimination they face affect many areas of life from education to employment and health. Those with a disability experience higher levels of poverty, personal and social disadvantage and are more likely to experience deprivation, debt and poor housing than children without disability in the family. This chapter explores the issues that affect children from these groups and emphasises the need to have policies that help to overcome the discrimination they face.

Chapter 9 looks at the children who are particularly vulnerable and who are at increased risk of living in poverty. Some of these children are living outwith the protection of family and community, for example looked after children and refugee/asylum-seeking children, which enhances their risk of poverty and lack of support. There is also a (relatively small) proportion of children who experience trauma and adversity in childhood, sometimes called 'adverse childhood experiences' – such as parental mental health issues, domestic abuse or a parent in prison – that put them at particular risk. These adverse circumstances can also make children more likely to experience complex needs in adulthood, such as homelessness, imprisonment, addiction or mental health issues. It is often the case that these particular adversities are confused with poverty, and there is often the assumption that all children living in poverty are exposed to adverse experiences. This chapter shows that, while it is the minority of children who experience additional adversities in childhood, they comprise a group of children in great need of dedicated services and a dedicated policy response.

Each of the chapters has a section on 'flipping the thinking', an entreaty to encourage the reader to think about child poverty in a way that deviates from the current dominant discourse. At present, what people know or think they know about child poverty and its impacts derives from received wisdom, common sense ideas, what they hear and what they read in the media. Even many professionals working with families living in poverty do not necessarily appreciate the nuance of its risks, causes and consequences. This is especially the case with those professionals who work at the sharp end of family and community life and who come into contact with high levels of adversity. Their understandings of poverty can be skewed to the experiences of particular families, which can make individualised and behavioural accounts of poverty seem most reasonable. This book offers an understanding of child poverty, situated within families, with children at the core that, hopefully, generates more light than heat, unlike the current dominant media and policy discourses. Each chapter also presents details on one or two policy responses that are particularly helpful or unhelpful to the incidence or experience of child poverty. As this is a short book to get a broader understanding of child poverty in our society, I cannot address all of the policy issues that govern child poverty, no matter how much I wish to, so I am having to be selective. These concise policy reflections, and the entreaties to 'flip the thinking', are picked up and discussed further in Chapter 10, the conclusions chapter. In this chapter questions are asked such as 'What could be done? What should we do? How do we respond to thinking about child poverty differently?' The aim is to encourage all of us to 'flip our thinking' and allow alternative ideas and explanations to guide us on a path that might actually prevent and eradicate child poverty.

2

Context

One must recognize the crucial role of structures in producing injustice, even in cases where individual actors may be going about their business in a normal way and not intending to do any harm. (Nussbaum, 2011: xiii)

Introduction

Taking 60 per cent of median equivalised income and material deprivation as the measure of child poverty as outlined in the introduction, this chapter looks at the state of child poverty nationally in and within the UK and internationally across affluent nations. It explores whether child poverty is increasing or decreasing and, in so doing, looks at the convergence and divergence of policy responses to child poverty to assess what impact they have on its incidence and prevalence. The chapter investigates the risks, causes and consequences of child poverty, the misunderstandings between these, and the effects of such misunderstandings on, for example, government responses. While there are many factors related to child poverty at its root is a fundamental lack of income. This chapter explores the importance of income in understanding child poverty and its effects on children's outcomes.

When we talk about what percentage of children live in poverty, it is easy to think that the same children are in poverty each year. In fact, poverty is dynamic and, while there is a group of people who live in poverty across many years, known as being in persistent poverty, the majority of people living in poverty exit poverty, and each year new people enter into it. This chapter looks at the factors that lead people to fall into poverty, such as a low-wage economy, unemployment and insufficient benefits. This can lead to a low-pay, no-pay cycle that churns different groups of people into and out of poverty over time. The chapter emphasises the importance of income and considers how poor people experience a lack of income, for example in being exposed to financial vulnerability and the poverty premium. It concludes by considering initiatives that maximise family incomes and prevent/

reduce poverty asking the reader to flip their thinking on the causes and consequences of child poverty.

Profile of child poverty internationally

Between 2008, the year of the Great Recession, and 2012, rates of child poverty rose in 23 of the 41 most affluent countries, including the UK, the US, Denmark, France and Luxembourg (Fanjul, 2014). In 18 countries, including Norway, Finland and Australia, child poverty rates decreased over the same time period (Fanjul, 2014). The principal reason for the increase or decrease in rates of child poverty post-crisis was that some governments curtailed financial support to children and families whereas others increased it. This shows that, at times of deep recession, increases in child poverty are not inevitable and government investment makes a difference (Fanjul, 2014), The countries' differing responses to the Great Recession reflect that policies are being generated in very different social and cultural contexts and are informed by different values and expectations. This has a very real impact on children's lives. At the start of the Great Recession, some countries were in a stronger economic position than others and had stronger social protection policies in place for children and families (Fanjul, 2014). This had an impact on how they fared afterwards. Others may have been in a weaker position prior to the crisis but their response during the crisis protected children to some extent. The policy choices that some governments have made since then has once again changed the profile of child poverty internationally.

In Australia after the Great Recession policies were enacted to protect families' income and to sustain consumption among poorer families (Fanjul, 2014). The analysis of the Australian approach suggested that cash transfers targeted directly at poorer families with children had the strongest positive effect on preventing families falling into poverty (Fanjul, 2014). While Australia protected family incomes for a time, reducing its rates of child poverty, a new government since then has reversed this position and child poverty is rising again. New Zealand has experienced the opposite trend. Child poverty had been increasing under a right-leaning government until a new administration was elected. This New Zealand government is choosing to focus on reducing child poverty and is succeeding in decreasing its incidence and prevalence. These fluctuations in rates of child poverty across affluent societies post-2008 crisis show that the ways in which countries respond to recession, instability and economic insecurity directly increases or decreases child poverty.

After the Great Recession, in Europe, countries, under pressure from financial markets, cut budgets and introduced programmes of austerity. As a consequence, 'there was a fall in social spending on children and families' (Fanjul, 2014: 3). High levels of austerity have had devastating impacts on children overall, but especially on more vulnerable children such as migrant children and the children of lone parents (Fanjul, 2014). In the UK, austerity policies and the associated cuts made to services disproportionately affect families with children with lone parents. In November 2018, the Special Rapporteur on extreme poverty and human rights, Professor Philip Alston, undertook a mission to the UK. His report, published in April 2019, was excoriating in its condemnation of the actions and austerity measures of the UK government. He says,

> Austerity policies have deliberately gutted local authorities and thereby effectively eliminated many social services, reduced policing services to skeletal proportions, closed libraries in record numbers, shrunk community and youth centres, and sold off public spaces and buildings including parks and recreation centres. It is hardly surprising that civil society has reported unheard-of levels of loneliness and isolation, prompting the Government to appoint a Minister for Suicide Prevention. The bottom line is that much of the glue that has held British society together since the Second World War has been deliberately removed and replaced with a harsh and uncaring ethos. (Alston, 2019)

Using the latest data available at the time of writing, my analysis of the Eurostat data, presented in Table 2.1, gives the current state of affairs with child poverty rates across the EU. It presents four measures of child poverty and one of inequality to give a comprehensive overview. Column A gives the child poverty rate when it is measured at below 60 per cent of median income, the standard measure in use in the UK and across Europe. The data here show that in the UK, child poverty rates are around the EU average. It shows too that, generally speaking, Scandinavian countries have lower rates, former Soviet bloc countries have higher rates and Mediterranean countries also have elevated rates. As this table is for the EU only, it does not show that the affluent society with the highest child poverty rate is the US, the richest country in the world (Marsh et al, 2017).

Column B gives the child poverty rate when it is measured at below 50 per cent of median income, a more severe measure of poverty. This

Table 2.1 Key indicators of child poverty and income inequality in Europe, 2018

	Below 60% of median income %	Below 50% of median income %	Deprived on 3 or more essential items %	Deprived on 4 or more essential items %	Income inequality 80/20 ratio[n] %
European Union (28)	20.3	12.5	16.1[a]	7.1[a]	5.1[a]
Belgium	20.6	12.4	14.3	7.0	3.8
Bulgaria	26.6	20.9	28.0	19.1	7.7
Czech Republic	11.0	6.1	8.6	3.4	3.3
Denmark	11.0	5.3	8.5[p]	4.3[p]	4.1
Germany	14.5	7.6	8.0	2.7	5.1
Estonia	15.2	9.2	11.1	3.5	5.1
Ireland	15.8[p]	7.0[p]	19.1[a]	6.8[a]	4.6[a]
Greece	22.7	16.2	35.3	18.6	5.5
Spain	26.8	19.1	15.4	6.5	6.0
France	19.9	9.6	14.5[a]	5.1[a]	4.2
Croatia	19.7	14.3	21.9[p]	7.6[p]	5.0
Italy	26.2	18.4	16.3	8.1	6.1
Cyprus	17.3	11.1	32.2	12.6	4.3
Latvia	17.5	12.7	19.7	8.3	6.8
Lithuania	23.9	17.0	21.2	10.0	7.1
Luxembourg	22.7	15.1	5.1[a]	1.2[a]	5.7
Hungary	13.8	10.8	28.4	15.2	4.4
Malta	21.4	13.3	10.7	4.0	4.3
Netherlands	13.1	7.6	5.8[p]	2.3[p]	4.1
Austria	19.2	11.3	8.3	3.6	4.0
Poland	13.0	7.2	9.0	3.6	4.3
Portugal	19.0	12.8	16.3	5.7	5.2
Romania	32.0	24.0	35.2	19.7	7.2
Slovenia	11.7	5.1	7.5	2.2	3.4
Slovakia	20.5	11.2	17.8[a]	9.1[a]	3.5[a]
Finland	11.1	4.2	8.8	2.7	3.6
Sweden	19.3	12.3	6.8	2.3	4.1
United Kingdom	24.1[p]	14.7[p]	17.4[a]	5.8[a]	5.4[a]

Table 2.1 (Continued)

	Below 60% of median income %	Below 50% of median income %	Deprived on 3 or more essential items %	Deprived on 4 or more essential items %	Income inequality 80/20 ratio[n] %
Iceland	10.4[b]	4.6[b]	7.4[b]	2.5[b]	3.3[b]
Norway	13.2	7.2	5.0	2.7	3.7
Switzerland	19.0	11.5	7.0[a]	2.0[a]	4.5
Montenegro	31.7[a]	23.4[a]	-	-	7.6[a]
North Macedonia	29.9[a]	25.0[d]	50.8[a]	34.4[a]	6.4[a]
Serbia	28.8	22.5	27.5[a]	16.3[a]	8.6
Turkey	33.0[a]	23.2[a]	48.2[a]	34.6[a]	8.7[a]

Year: 2018 (except at a. and b.)
a. 2017 data
b. 2016 data
n. not specific to children
p. provisional
- no data available

Source: Eurostat (https://ec.europa.eu/eurostat/web/income-and-living-conditions/overview). Latest available data 30 November 2019. Author's own analysis.

is the OECD's preferred measure. Those countries with high rates on this measure have children who are particularly impoverished and those with low rates are likely to have a safety net in place that does not allow children to fall too far into poverty. The proportion of children who fall into the gap between 60 per cent and 50 per cent gives an indication of whether their government has policies to protect family income.

Column C gives the percentage of children who are materially deprived on three or more items, with column D giving the percentage of those deprived on four or more items, a more severe measure of material deprivation. The UK has high proportions of children who are materially deprived compared to other EU countries with the same poverty profile, for example Sweden. This suggests that children in Sweden have not been as poor for as long as those in the UK, as a high level of material deprivation is associated with more persistent levels of poverty (Treanor, 2014). When thinking about rates of material deprivation, it is worthwhile to consider what numbers these proportions translate to. In 30 European countries '1.6 million more children were living in severe material deprivation in 2012 (11.1 million) than in 2008 (9.5 million)' (Fanjul, 2014: 3).

In the UK, between three and five per cent of children lack basic items such as a good diet, good shoes and new clothes (Marsh et al, 2017: 56). Furthermore, around 100,000 children lack three meals a day or a warm winter coat because their parents cannot afford it (Marsh et al, 2017). When parents are asked about how poor they feel, those who say they feel 'poor all the time' are 21 times more likely to say they cannot afford to give their children three meals a day (Marsh et al, 2017). There are increasing levels of poverty and material deprivation in adults due to 'greater wage inequality, the rise of zero-hours contracts and wage freezes' (Marsh et al, 2017). These employment factors are exacerbated by austerity measures that manifest in cuts and freezes to benefits. When poverty is sustained and severe people can become destitute. It is estimated that 1,550,000 people, including 365,000 children, are destitute in the UK (Fitzpatrick et al, 2018). Reasons for the crossover from severe hardship into destitution include debt, benefit problems, health issues, unaffordable housing and, for some migrants, either extremely low levels of, or absolutely no eligibility for, benefits (Fitzpatrick et al, 2018). What makes these rates of child material deprivation in Table 2.1 so alarming is the fact that we know parents prioritise the material needs of their children to their own detriment (Treanor, 2014). This suggests that parents in poverty, especially those at increased risk of more severe poverty, for example lone parents, are likely to be far more materially deprived than their couple parent counterparts.

Column E gives a measure of income inequality for these countries that is not specific to children. It gives a ratio of the total income received by the 20 per cent of the population with the highest income (the top quintile) to that received by the 20 per cent of the population with the lowest income (the bottom quintile). Column E shows that, in the UK, the richest 20 per cent of the population has five times the income of the poorest 20 per cent of the population. Once again, the UK compares to the average across the EU. However, it fares poorly compared to other northern European countries, such as Norway, Finland, Sweden and the Netherlands. Instead, it has a profile more akin to former Soviet states, such as Estonia, and states in south-eastern Europe, such as Croatia. The countries that do most poorly in terms of income inequality are the former Soviet bloc countries, such as Bulgaria, and those in southern Europe that have suffered since the Great Recession of 2008 and have needed intervention from the International Monetary Fund (IMF), such as Greece. Income inequality has grown fastest in the countries that reversed their earlier, more redistributive fiscal regimes, for example, Sweden (Marsh et al, 2017). Countries like France, which made greater efforts to retain their earlier levels of social protection, have seen little or no increase in income inequality (Marsh et al, 2017: 151).

Profile of child poverty in the UK and its four nations

Table 2.1 presents a profile of child poverty in the UK and its four nations. In the UK, child poverty rates are given on a before housing cost (BHC) basis but also on an after housing cost (AHC) basis, on the understanding that housing costs can be high and can push families into poverty. The AHC measure is preferred by many organisations working with poverty in the UK and is the measure preferred by the Scottish government. The UK government, however, uses the BHC measure although it reports on both. Table 2.2 presents my analysis of the latest data available from the UK government's Households Below Average Income (2019) series on the BHC and AHC measures of poverty in the UK and its four constituent nations.

Around 4.1 million children in the UK are living in poverty on an AHC basis and 2.7 million on a BHC basis. This is 30 per cent of all children. In the UK, there has been a modest growth in real incomes (that is incomes adjusted for inflation) in recent years, triggered by a growth in employment, real earnings and low inflation (McGuinness, 2018a: 9). For the whole population of the UK, including adults,

Table 2.2 Profile of child poverty in the UK and its four nations, 2017/18

Geographical area	Child poverty rate 60% BHC%	Persistent poverty rate BHC[ab]%	Child poverty rate 60% AHC%	Persistent poverty rate AHC[ab]%	Material deprivation and low income[c]%
United Kingdom	20	11	30	17	12
England	20	11	31	18	12
Wales	20	13	29	20	12
Scotland	20	9	24	10	11
Northern Ireland	21	16	24	16	8

a. The persistent poverty rate gives percentage of children from 2012/13 to 2015/16.
b. The persistent poverty rate data are from Understanding Society.
c. A family is in low income and material deprivation if they have a material deprivation score of 25 or more and a household income below 70 per cent of contemporary median income, BHC.
d. The totals for all children are shown for the UK for 2017/18 (the latest year) and are not three-year averages.

Source: Households Below Average Income, 2019. Poverty rates are averaged over the three-year period 2015/16 to 2017/18. Author's own analysis.

this has not had any effect on the relative poverty rates. For children, in spite of this increasing employment and modest growth in real incomes, their rates of poverty continue to increase across the UK. Reasons for this UK pattern are that: the increase in employment is not of the level or quality to reduce poverty; the UK government's austerity measures are hurting families; and, increasing rents, lower levels of home ownership, coupled with less financial help for low-income renters, mean that people are struggling to meet their housing costs (JRF, 2017). Austerity in the UK has resulted in major cuts to in-work and out-of-work benefits, which is having the most severe impact on families living in poverty. Even though there have been tax cuts and minimum wage rises, they have had a limited capacity to improve child poverty, as any gains have been far outweighed by the reductions to in-work and out-of-work benefits (JRF, 2017). As for the wealthy, in the UK 44 per cent of wealth is now owned by just 10 per cent of the population – it is the fifth most unequal country in Europe in terms of income (IPPR, 2018).

The rates of child poverty in Scotland and Northern Ireland are lower than in England, on an AHC basis, in part due to the lower housing costs in these countries. In Northern Ireland, the rate BHC is higher than those in Scotland, Wales and the UK as a whole, showing that it is not housing costs that are pushing families into poverty but other factors. In Wales, the rate is particularly high AHC compared to BHC, suggesting that housing costs in Wales are pushing families into poverty. The persistent poverty rate for children in Wales too is significantly higher than in the rest of the UK. Scotland is the part of the UK that is doing best: Scotland's persistent poverty rates are the lowest in the UK for children and for adults on a BHC and AHC measure (rates for adults not shown). As well as Scotland's lower housing costs, there are other initiatives taking place that are likely to further improve its rates of child poverty. These are discussed further under the section 'Causes of child poverty'.

The trend in the UK is that child poverty is increasing and will continue to do so with perhaps either the exception of, or a slower increase in, Scotland. It has been forecast by the respected Institute for Fiscal Studies that child poverty will increase by 50 per cent between the years 2015/16 and 2020/21, from 18 per cent to 26 per cent BHC (Browne et al, 2016). They predict a sharp rise in poverty among families with three or more children solely as a result of planned tax and benefit reforms (Browne et al, 2016). Other groups for whom poverty is projected to rise are lone parents in general, but 'especially lone parents in work, particularly in full-time work' and 'couples where parents work but where there is not at least one full-time and one part-time worker' (JRF, 2017: 22).

Causes of child poverty

The structure of the labour market and its ability to provide secure, quality employment is a key factor in child poverty. The structure of the labour market has changed since the 1980s, when people with relatively low levels of education could gain well-paid secure employment in heavy industries. In a post-industrial era, labour that requires a lower level of education has been monetarily devalued (Marsh et al, 2017). The majority of jobs are now in the service sector, which asks for different skills of its employees, for example cognitive and social skills. Those who are less strong in these skills are now in increasingly marginal positions, the social effects of which have been dramatic (Marsh et al, 2017). In addition to the changes to the nature of the types of jobs available to less-educated people, there has been a massive growth in flexible employment as demonstrated by the rise in zero-hours contracts, temporary, part-time and self-employed work. There are now almost a million people in the UK on zero-hours contracts and 15 per cent who are self-employed (IPPR, 2018). Many businesses that would previously have been large-scale employers now require their 'staff' to work on a self-employed basis. This is explored further in Chapter 6 on employment.

Another of the key drivers of child poverty is the low pay of their parent(s). The children of parents working for low wages are very involved in helping their parents to work by providing help in the home, for example childcare for younger siblings. This is particularly the case for the children of lone parents and is discussed further in Chapter 4. Low pay does not always lead to poverty as the majority of low-paid workers live in households with other earners such as parents or partners (JRF, 2017). This means that the household does not have a low income overall and, consequently, the children of that household will not live in poverty (JRF, 2017). It is sometimes the case that mothers in couple families choose to take on low-paid work on a part-time basis if it allows them to prioritise childcare. These women and children are unlikely to be living in poverty. On the other hand, employment that is not considerate of people's childcare needs can mean that people, usually women, especially lone mothers, are not able to take on employment or work fewer hours than they would wish. This too is discussed further in Chapter 4.

The UK currently has a historically high rate of employment and a rising minimum wage, yet low pay remains endemic (JRF, 2017). Furthermore, the UK ranks 'poorly against other developed economies in terms of the prevalence of low pay' (Hurrell, 2013). For more than a decade average earnings have stagnated, despite economic growth, and 'the 2010s are forecast to be the weakest decade for average real earnings in 200 years' (IPPR, 2018). Rather than be a starting point on the employment ladder, people often get stuck in a low-paying job. Three quarters of low-paid workers are still in low pay after ten years (Hurrell, 2013). There are some groups at particular risk of remaining low paid based on their gender, full-time/part-time work status, age, region and particular type of occupation (Hurrell, 2013). Women and older people are at greater risk of remaining in low-paid employment. Furthermore, if you are a woman aged between 41 and 60 years old you have a 57 per cent risk of remaining on a low income compared to a man of the same age who has a 35 per cent risk (Hurrell, 2013). Once again, it is thought that women undertaking the majority of childcare play a significant role in this and that one of the ways to prevent children living in poverty is to support parents (mothers?) to balance childcare with employment.

Another factor that drives child poverty is the work intensity of the household; that is, the number of workers in a household and the number of hours they work. How much paid work the adults in a family are able to undertake varies according to their health and whether they have to care for young children or disabled family members (JRF, 2017). Childcare is often cited as the main reason for one member of a couple, usually the woman, not to be in paid work (JRF, 2017). Figure 2.1 gives the percentage of children living in poverty by family type and work status in the UK in 2017/18. As can be seen by Figure 2.1, work will only protect against poverty for couples with children if the family has two full-time positions or one full-time and one part-time position. Again, in couple families, having one or more part-time workers, or a single full-time worker in a household does not protect against poverty very well. This means that every family needs a high work intensity in the UK, if they have a low-income job, in order to avoid their children living in poverty. This makes it particularly difficult for lone parents, of whom 23 per cent in full-time employment are living in poverty. The poverty rate for lone parents working part-time is 35 per cent, even though many lone parents need to work part-time to enable them to look after their children. Childcare for lone parents is discussed in Chapter 4. Furthermore, after the 2008 Great Recession, work intensity for lone parents reduced and did not recover at the rate

Figure 2.1 Percentage of children living in poverty by family type and work status, 2017/18

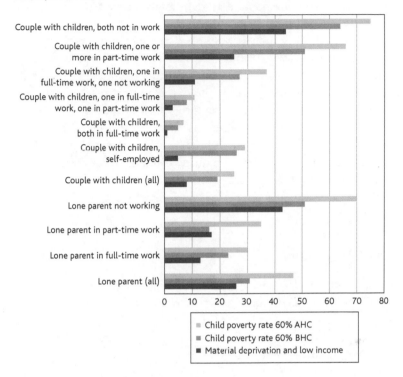

Source: Households Below Average Income, 2019

at which it did for couple families (Treanor, 2018b). As can also be seen from Figure 2.1, not being in work leads to exceptionally high rates of poverty at 75 per cent for couple families and 70 per cent for lone-parent families.

Historically in the UK, the benefit and tax credit system had the dual role of supporting people who were out of work and topping up the incomes of those in low-paid work (JRF, 2017). This is what led to massive decreases in child, adult and pensioner poverty in the UK throughout the 2000s. With retrenchment of the benefit and tax credits system in the UK, this is leading to renewed increases in child poverty rates. With record levels of employment and increasing minimum wage, the UK is (worryingly) still not preventing increases to child poverty.

In addition to low income and work intensity, the rising costs of living in the UK are contributory factors to child poverty. For example, of families living in low-income households, 47 per cent spend more than a third of their income on housing (JRF, 2017). These rising housing costs are partly due to large increases in the numbers now living in the private rented sector, by increases to the costs of social rented housing and by reductions in the benefits to help low-income families pay for housing (JRF, 2017: 14).[1] There has also been a dramatic fall in levels of home ownership, which is predicted to cause great problems in the future as people age without owning their own home. Lastly on housing, there has been a huge growth in property values, which will price many of today's young people out of the housing market: children and young people in the UK today are set to be poorer than their parents (IPPR, 2018). Other increasing living costs that contribute to child poverty are: childcare costs, which disproportionately affect lone parents and families with three or more children; food costs, which are increasing in the UK and are set to increase further should Britain leave the EU; and fuel costs, which have also increased over recent years (JRF, 2017).

Poverty is dynamic

The risk of poverty changes over the life course, with the need to rely on social policies, including those that financially support children, increasing or decreasing accordingly (Hills, 2015). Life course transitions, such as having a child, becoming ill, retiring or splitting up with a partner, can all increase the risk of falling into poverty for a time (Rigg and Sefton, 2006). In the same vein, getting a new job, a child leaving home, or a new partnership may lift people out of poverty. As well life course transitions, people's employment changes, including insecure contracts as discussed earlier, can also mean that there is a degree of 'churning', with people being vulnerable to repeated spells of poverty (Jenkins et al, 2001; Shildrick et al, 2013).

Thus, the population of those living in poverty is not fixed but fluid, with a larger proportion of people experiencing poverty in their lifetime than cross-sectional snapshots would suggest. Furthermore, 'almost everyone will claim a social security benefit at some point in their lives' (Marsh et al, 2017: 4). It has been suggested that this dynamic aspect of poverty is not completely negative as it means that those who experience poverty will not always do so (Ridge and Wright, 2008b); however, 'volatility in income can have a profound effect on those at the bottom of the income distribution' (Marsh et al, 2017: 148–9). The experience of poverty over time leads to an accumulation of deprivation that is more extensive than that experienced by those who only briefly go without (Alcock, 2008: 49–50).

The fact that poverty is a dynamic phenomenon is critically important. When people assume that the same fifth or so of people are in poverty each year, it lends credence to the political and media portrayals of poor people as a fixed 'underclass' of 'skivers', 'shirkers' and 'scroungers'. It feeds into the misunderstandings that fuel negative stereotypes and so badly damage children and their families who live in poverty. If people understood that half of the people who are living in poverty this year will not be living in poverty next year and that new people will be in poverty next year who are not in poverty now (Marsh et al, 2017: 140), then they would understand that there is a large swathe of the population at risk of at least a temporary experience of poverty, perhaps including their own kith and kin.

Compared to other European countries the UK has high entry and exit rates for poverty (Marsh et al, 2017: 142). This is consistent with the UK's relatively low persistent poverty rate and average overall poverty rate compared to the rest of the EU (Marsh et al, 2017: 142). It is also consistent with the UK's high proportion of zero-hours contracts, temporary, part-time and insecure jobs. It 'means that while people in the UK have a fairly high risk of falling into poverty, they also have a high chance of escaping it' (Marsh et al, 2017: 142). In the UK, there has been a 60 per cent increase in the number of people moving repeatedly between work and unemployment since 2006 (Marsh et al, 2017: 67).

In my qualitative longitudinal study of families living in poverty, there are lone parents who cycle between employment and unemployment, often as a result of a lack of affordable childcare. This brings additional difficulties, as the switch between earning a low income and earning no income also means a loss of key benefits, such as free school meals. One of the lone parents in my study, Jennifer, who had been on benefits, then became a student, then obtained a job, then had to leave the job because her autistic son was struggling in after-school care, and who was paying for school meals for her three sons on a daily basis, found that

> 'There's still days when I say, maybe on a Friday, I often say to [her middle son], "I've not got any change", this sounds terrible, "I've not got any change. Just say to the teacher that I'll pay two on Monday" and he'll say, "Yeah, that's fine". He thinks it's normal because I do it all the time. The teachers probably know I do it all the time but that means on Monday – I get money on a Monday morning – I can go into the office and say "[My son] never took his dinner money on Friday". It's because it saves me money.' (Treanor, 2018a: 504–5)

This highlights another important aspect of the behaviours parents, and particularly lone parents, use to mitigate the shame associated with poverty: they try hard to mask it, including from their own children, and they feel ashamed (Treanor, 2018a).

Children at increased risk of poverty

There are certain groups of children who are at increased risk of poverty depending on their family circumstances. Some individual and social factors that are associated with a child being in poverty are whether they live in a lone-parent family, the number of children in the family, the ethnicity and migrant status of the family, whether anyone has a disability and the work intensity of the adult(s) in the household. Despite what may be portrayed in the media, these characteristics are not causes of poverty per se but, rather, the wider societal factors such as gender inequality and structural racism mean that a higher proportion of these children are at risk of living in poverty (Marsh et al, 2017: 132).

Where children live in a house where there is disability, whether it be their own or a family member's, they have a higher risk of poverty. In families where someone is disabled 26 per cent have a low income compared to 20 per cent of those in families with no disability (Marsh et al, 2017: 173). Child poverty is also patterned by ethnicity and migrant status. In the UK, white British people are the least likely to be living in poverty with a rate of 19 per cent (Marsh et al, 2017). In contrast, Pakistani, Bangladeshi and 'other ethnic groups' are more than twice as likely as white British people to be living in poverty. However, it should be noted that while the *rates* of poverty for non-white communities are higher, their absolute *numbers* are far lower due to the small size of their overall populations. This means that, despite their lower poverty risk, 9.7 million people of white British origin live in poverty compared to 240,000 people of Bangladeshi origin (Marsh et al, 2017). This is further explored in Chapter 8 on the increased risks of poverty associated with ethnicity and disability.

As previously discussed, low work intensity is a poverty risk, although it should be noted that in the UK two thirds of children living in poverty live in a house in which at least one adult is in paid employment. However, where children live in a house in which no-one is in paid employment, the risk of poverty is exceptionally high, and the poverty is likely to be more severe and prolonged. Risk factors do not operate in isolation. Lone parenthood is a risk factor for children to live in poverty: partly due to the often part-time, insecure and temporary nature of the employment available to them; partly due to there only being one adult contributing to household finances; and partly due to the lack of supporting systems in place, for example childcare. However, where a child lives in a lone-parent household that also experiences disability or the systemic racism experienced by ethnic minority populations, the risk of living in poverty multiplies. That lone parenthood is constituted of 90 per cent women, means that gender inequalities also come strongly into play. The situation for lone parents is explored further in Chapter 4.

As well as children being at particular risk of poverty due to their family circumstances and composition, there are also groups of children who are especially at risk of poverty, but who also have additional vulnerabilities. This is especially the case if the situation that leads to their being vulnerable coincides with the incidence of poverty, for example children in care, children leaving care, children with a parent in prison, children who are carers, asylum seeker/refugee children, Traveller/Gypsy children and children with additional family adversities, such as domestic abuse or the poor mental health of a parent. Not only are these groups more at risk of poverty, the experience of poverty for them is often more severe, more persistent, and requiring of dedicated service support. This is explored further in Chapter 9.

Money

In market societies, such as those in the most affluent countries, money is essential to everyday life and livelihoods. In this book about child poverty, the principal theme that weaves throughout is that money, while not the only defining aspect of poverty, is absolutely core to its definition, measurement and initiatives to prevent or mitigate it. It is money that 'determines whether people in the UK are able to compensate for other shortfalls in their lives' (Marsh et al, 2017: 18). Across affluent societies generally, countries with higher income inequality 'tend to have lower levels of overall child wellbeing' (Hudson and Kühner, 2016: 162). Large gaps in income inequality are not inevitable; policy makers have the tools at their disposal to reduce them and make life better for all children (Hudson and Kühner, 2016).

As well as income inequality, income poverty itself causes the reduced wellbeing of children. Money has been shown to make a difference to children's cognitive, social, behavioural and health outcomes irrespective of money's correlation with other household and parental characteristics such as parental education or attitudes (Cooper and

Stewart, 2013). It was calculated that while increases in household income would not eliminate differences in outcomes between low and high income children altogether, it would contribute to substantial reductions in these differences (Cooper and Stewart, 2013). There are two principal pathways through which a lack of income adversely affects children's outcomes. The first, and strongest, is the Family Stress Model, which comprises maternal mental health, relationship conflicts and parenting behaviour. The second, less strong factor, is the Investment Model, which includes learning in the home environment (Cooper and Stewart, 2013). Put simply, an increase in income to families reduces stress, leads to improvements in maternal mental health and stimulates investment in children. Stewart (2016: 11) explains that 'an increase in income changes the nature of what happens in the household, creating a calmer environment and enabling better engagement from parents'. Furthermore, as parents receive more income, it has been shown to be spent on child-related items, such as footwear, fruit and vegetables, clothing, toys and books, with a concomitant reduction in expenditure on alcohol and tobacco (Gregg et al, 2006).

There are other aspects of money that impact negatively on families such as problem debt, financial vulnerability and the poverty premium. Debt can mask the severity of poverty as a person's income may differ greatly from their disposable income due to debt repayments. In the UK, 20 per cent of families living in poverty report having 'problem debt', which is defined as being behind with any household bill or credit commitment, excluding debt incurred on store cards, mail order payments and informal loans from friends or family (JRF, 2017). It is also often the case for those living in poverty that the debt owed is to local authorities or central government as a result of the non-payment of bills or the overpayments of benefits, such as tax credits (Harris et al, 2009). A working lone parent in my research, Pauline, says of her debt,

> 'There's been quite a few times towards the end of the month that I've had to borrow money off my mother in order to get the petrol to get to work. Wednesdays, the day before tax credit days, we really are sort of pulling the scraps together to eat. Basically [her teenage son], he's 18 and six feet two and he eats like a horse, so yeah, it's been hand to mouth, it's been completely hand to mouth.'

Financial vulnerability pertains to issues of debt, money worries and managing on current income (Harris, 2009). We know from our qualitative research that children are aware of and adversely affected by the financial vulnerability experienced by their families even when parents make great efforts to protect children from this vulnerability (Ridge, 2002; Treanor, 2016a). We also know from our quantitative research that financial vulnerability has the largest negative effect on mothers' emotional distress, greater than that of income per se, which, in turn, has an adverse effect on child wellbeing. (Treanor, 2016a). When increasing financial vulnerability hits families, due to insecure employment and income, housing and environment, increasing costs and increasing strain, children reflect this stress and vulnerability in their own wellbeing. Children are highly attuned to circumstances affecting their parents; they are like barometers gauging the pressure experienced by their parents. Financial vulnerability then becomes something that the children themselves try to manage and alleviate. Children and young people try to manage money flows that pertain to them, for example by not sharing information that will incur a cost, by not accepting pocket money, by trying to earn (and share) their own income and by engaging in their own self-sacrifice. This leads to children and young people's withdrawal from social and leisure activities with their peers and from participation in school and community events.

Money is critical to the experience of living in poverty, not just through levels of adequacy, but also through the systems put in place in everyday expenditure that benefit the better off. One such example is known as the poverty premium. The poverty premium is a financial penalty paid by families living in poverty due to their exclusion from: short-term overdraft facilities; discounts associated with direct debit arrangements (for example for gas and electricity); interest-free purchase schemes (for example for furniture and white goods); bulk purchases and multiple purchase offers in supermarkets; and bank loans at affordable interest rates (Harris et al, 2009; Stewart, 2009). Families' exclusion from standard financial facilities and their inadequate income can result in their using non-standard credit, such as doorstep lenders, to meet socially defined minimum living standards for social inclusion, such as buying Christmas presents and birthday presents for their children. The excruciatingly high interest associated with such non-standard borrowing leads to debts and arrears in other areas, such as utility bills. Such exclusion from standard financial facilities and exposure to high interest financial risks is problematic for children's wellbeing and security.

For those living in poverty, family and friends are the most valuable additional resource, especially when income loss is short-term (Marsh et al, 2017). Family and friends help financially, help to look after children and provide other benefits, such as holidays (Marsh et al,

2017). However, help from family and friends is not always given freely without judgement, and power relations within families can be unequal. This is especially the case for women and children and is explored further in Chapter 4.

Government policies that affect child poverty

Across affluent nations national rates of child poverty are reduced by social transfers such as the benefits and tax credits paid to families, working and non-working, to increase their incomes. Where a country has a high level of child poverty pre-tax and transfers, the tax and benefits system will have to work hard to lift families out of poverty. The UK is one such country where the tax and benefits system works hard to mitigate child poverty. The UK cuts a relatively high pre-transfer child poverty rate by about 60 per cent once taxes and transfers are taken into account (Marsh et al, 2017). Unfortunately, 'the real value of social transfers to UK families has fallen recently and will continue to fall sharply under the new universal credit benefit regime' (Marsh et al, 2017: 161). In the 1980s and 1990s in the UK, child poverty experienced the most rapid increase among OECD countries (Marsh et al, 2017). Then, in the 2000s, it also experienced the most rapid decline in child poverty, illustrating how policy targeted at reducing child poverty rates is effective (Marsh et al, 2017). The UK's initial child poverty rate before transfers is among the very highest in Europe and is driven mainly by low wages. Thus, government policy aimed at raising the incomes of those living in poverty will have the greatest impact on rates of child poverty and on child development and wellbeing.

In the UK, it is argued that benefit rates are kept at poverty levels as a disincentive to those who might otherwise be disinclined to work (McKendrick et al, 2016: 63). The argument goes that by so doing they will encourage claimants to find work in order to escape poverty. While this may or may not be the case, what is undeniable is that benefit levels are historically low, far below the poverty threshold, of lower value compared to wages than at any time in the past 40 years and are, with planned cuts to in-work and out-of-work benefits, projected to fall further. Furthermore, as previously discussed, more than two thirds of children living in poverty are in a family where someone works.

As well as the general inadequacy of benefits, there is concern about the uptake of benefits. There are people in low-income working families with children who are entitled to certain benefits who do not claim them. For example, UK government statistics for 2015/16 show that the child tax credit take-up rate was 83 per cent, a decrease of three percentage points between 2014/15 and 2015/16, a change that is statistically significant at the 5 per cent significance level (HMRC, 2017: 6). There are numerous reasons why a family may not claim their full tax credit or benefit entitlement, not least of which is the awareness of their entitlement in the first place. This is especially true of those having their first child, or who may be experiencing a relationship breakdown, who are likely to be negotiating the confusing tax credit and benefit system for the first time. In addition to non-take up of benefits there is growing evidence that around a fifth of all new claims for universal credit are being rejected due to the complexity of the application process (Savage, 2018).

Scotland is diverging from the rest of the UK in its approach to child poverty. After the Child Poverty Act 2010 was abolished in the UK, Scotland brought forward its own Child Poverty (Scotland) 2017 Act. One of the reasons why Scotland is diverging is that in its new Act there is to be a requirement to maximise the incomes of people living in poverty. It is widely recognised that some people who are entitled to certain in-work and out-of-work benefits are not claiming their entitlement. Income maximisation is a service that looks at people's entitlements and advises on them. In Scotland, there are initiatives to maximise the incomes of people who, for example, are pregnant and may be entitled to more financial support due to the birth of a child. This is often delivered alongside statutory services, such as midwives and health visitors. It is not only health services who offer income maximisation; there are now money advice practitioners embedded within schools and voluntary services in areas of high deprivation in Scotland. There are various reasons why maximising incomes is an increasingly important poverty reduction strategy. The first is that the evidence shows that there are negative effects on maternal and child wellbeing of financial vulnerability over and above the effects of income and poverty (Treanor, 2016a). The second is that it is one of the few initiatives that can help children and families pre-, per- and post-pregnancy. A third is that 'having more money directly improves the development and level of achievement of children' (Cooper and Stewart, 2013). A fourth is that it allows services to identify those *at risk of* poverty and to take preventative action as well as to mitigate against already existing poverty. A final reason is that money generated by maximising the incomes of people living in poverty is spent in the local community, thus benefiting a multitude of services, including local businesses. With a coordinated response across sectors to income maximisation it has the power to improve lives at a relatively low cost.

As well as policies to increase incomes, child poverty responds well to the control of essential costs, such as housing and fuel, and provision of essential services, particularly those services required to facilitate employment, such as transport and childcare. People on low incomes struggle to afford these essential costs even if they are receiving the rather ineffectual subsidies on offer (Marsh et al, 2017). Childcare is discussed further in Chapter 4. Some of the negative narratives towards families living in poverty centre on why taxpayers should subsidise those with children who cannot afford a decent standard of living without tax and benefit transfers. The reasons are manifold, ranging from the moral to the economic. I will focus on three very practical reasons. The first reason is economic in that it is today's children who will pay for the healthcare and pensions of tomorrow's older generation. There is often a misunderstanding that pensions are paid out of funds that people have paid into all their lives whereas, in reality, it is the taxpayers of tomorrow who will cover the costs of our pensions. Therefore, there are sound economic reasons to support children during childhood. The second reason for supporting children financially is that most parents will have spent time working and paying taxes before they had children and, as children bring additional costs, they ought to be supported in this endeavour, given that children benefit society. The third is that, given that children benefit society, it is in the interests of everyone in society to ensure that those children have as secure and stable a childhood as possible. The following chapter explores the family and how life is for the children of families living in poverty.

3

Family

> Families play a key role in the transmission of unfair and unearned advantage and disadvantage. The nature and position of the family a child is born into makes a substantial difference to their life chances. (Calder, 2018: 424)

Introduction

This chapter takes a critically informed look at the role of families, and children's position within families, in understanding child poverty and disadvantage. The chapter begins by demonstrating that family life under conditions of disadvantage tends to be pathologised and denigrated: parents who are 'poor' are frequently situated as 'poor parents'. Low-income families are particularly vulnerable to categorisation as 'troubled' or troublesome families (Ribbens McCarthy et al, 2013). It goes on to look at the myths and realities of family life at the bottom of the income structure and considers how wealthier families, who are held up as the benchmark of the ideal family, reinforce and perpetuate the disadvantage of poor children and families by employing their superior resources to confer advantage onto their own children.

The chapter closes by asking what it all means for children: how do children understand, negotiate and mediate poverty in family life and their experiences and agency within the family. It addresses some of the challenges children face living in a low-income family, such as stigma and bullying, and explores how children succeed in masking or hiding their poverty from their peers. It shows the difficulties children and young people living in poverty face trying to make transitions from adolescence to young adulthood. The chapter concludes by asking how we could flip our thinking on families facing disadvantage.

What is family?

Everyone has their own idea of what a family is and most people, for better or worse, are a member of one. There are many books on what makes a family and there is no agreed definition of 'the family' (Edwards et al, 2012). This book does not seek to explore the conceptual discourses on the family; instead, here, a family is taken to mean any lone, couple or group of people, of any gender, who come together to 'do' family. As this is a book about children, it will consider those families who are together with the intention of bringing up children. There is more than one 'ideal' of the family – we are given different messages at different times as to the proper roles and expectations of a family, which are often heavily gendered (McKie and Callan, 2012). The traditional 'ideal' of family is that of the 'nuclear' family, that is a family with a male breadwinner and a female caregiver, in a married relationship, with children. A more recent 'ideal' of the family, across wealthy societies at least, is one of women having a profession and men sharing in the unpaid domestic and childcare tasks.

The 'family' is the site of many societal expectations. Across wealthy societies, the obligations of a 'good' family are: to be largely self-sufficient, to look after children independently with minimal state involvement (with the exception of standard education and health care), and to experience neither 'unmanageable troubles' nor 'cause troubles for others' (Welch, 2018: 199). The raising of children is the raison d'être of 'good' families and, within them, children are viewed as 'relatively passive and innocent recipients' of parental caregiving (Welch, 2018: 200). Furthermore, in striving to have the ideal family, and to provide the ideal childhood, people no longer recognise that challenges and changes, or what some might term 'troubles', can be a normal part of children's family lives (Ribbens McCarthy and Gillies, 2017). Children are expected to have no troubles at all during the ideal childhood, and so the boundary between troubles considered 'normal' or 'ordinary' and those considered sufficiently 'troubling' such that they warrant intervention, becomes indistinct (Ribbens McCarthy and Gillies, 2017: 220).

Where there is nonconformity to the ideal of the family, and of childhood, parents are held lacking and culpable (Welch, 2018: 200). This is especially the case for parents and children living in poverty, who are not likely to have the resources to conform to the demands of the ideal family, and are likely to be judged not to have the 'right' type of family or the 'right' type of childhood. As well as the extreme social pressure on all parents to conform to the ideal type of family, and the judgement on disadvantaged parents who can only fail by comparison, there are negative consequences for children and young people too. For those whose families are trying to provide an ideal childhood in an ideal family, there are 'unrealistic expectations of a special phase of life protected from troubles', which fails 'to equip young people to cope with the (more or less) inevitable vicissitudes of existence' (Ribbens McCarthy and Gillies, 2017: 224–5). For children living in poverty, they are aware of, and hurt by, the judgements passed on their families (and by association on themselves), and keenly feel the differences in experiences of family and childhood (whether real or performed).

Thus, the idea of 'the family' is not straightforward: it is controversial. It is controversial because families are not value-free environments: they are neither 'context-free' nor 'static' (Welch, 2018: 199). The idea of the family has the ability to evoke more moral and evaluative judgements than almost anything else we come together to do as humans (McCarthy et al, 2018: 154). Families are often described in binary, oppositional terms such as 'functional' or 'dysfunctional', 'healthy' or 'unhealthy' and 'normative' or 'troubled' (McCarthy et al, 2018: 154). Indeed, when the word 'troubled' is used for families, it is often masking what people really mean, which is *causing trouble* or *troublesome* and is usually assigned to families living in socioeconomic disadvantage (Lecture by Levitas, 2013 cited in Shildrick et al, 2016: 831).

Pathologising low-income families

That families facing economic disadvantage are often pathologised and denigrated is not a new state of affairs; indeed it is a discourse that reappears 'in public debates with a regularity that is uncanny' (Macnicol, 2017: 99). Since at least the late nineteenth century there have been concerns about families living in poverty (Welshman, 2013). They have long been deemed problematic; from the 'social residuum' of the 1880s, the 'social problem group' of the 1930s, the 'problem family' of the 1950s, the idea of a 'culture of poverty' in the 1960s, the 'cycle of deprivation' of the 1970s, Charles Murray's 'underclass' of the 1980s, to the 'troubled families' of the present day (Welshman, 2013, Macnicol, 1987, Macnicol, 2017). While these concerns over the decades have not been framed in identical ways there is more that binds than separates them (Welshman, 2013). What is remarkable is that 'these reconstructions have occurred despite a large volume of social scientific research that has found little evidence of a distinct group of poor people with a different culture, separated from the rest of society' (Crossley, 2016: 267).

Macnicol (2017) notes that, throughout this period of history, in times of high employment and economic opportunities, for example, after the two world wars, those families who were previously deemed problematic and unemployable managed to find employment and cease their membership of the 'underclass'. This was even noted in the US during World War II, where the poverty of African-Americans was inextricably tied to their race (and still is): a teacher at a black high school testified thus: 'I'm from Oklahoma and my whole subclass of culture of poverty happened to disappear with World War Two. All of a sudden us dumb Okies were not dumb Okies any more. We were capable of working in defence plants at two dollars per hour.' (Terkel, 1989: 32) cited in (Macnicol, 2017: 103) This leads Macnicol to pose the question 'whether the post-war fluctuations in unemployment – both rises and falls – can be explained primarily in terms of the changing personal characteristics of jobseekers' (Macnicol, 2017: 100). The conclusion here is that when there is a massive stimulus to jobs, the idea that poor families' individual characteristics or behaviours are making them poor becomes redundant. Yet, despite the historical and contemporary evidence that families' poverty is a function of the prevailing social and economic conditions, and that individual characteristics and behaviour, while not irrelevant, are not its dominant cause, low-income families continue to be categorised as 'troubled families' or troublesome families. The modern attack on low-income families derives from a contemporary anxiety about anti-social behaviour, where specific families are singled out by the media and dubbed, for example, 'families from Hell' (Gillies, 2011: 7). Such depictions of low-income families are not neutral but are, in fact, profoundly prejudiced. They are both 'deeply classed and are sometimes explicitly racialised' (Gillies, 2011: 7). In this stigmatising public narrative about low-income families, the UK government and the media influence each other. The Conservative Party minister, Iain Duncan Smith, played an important role in courting the media to report on his and his Centre of Social Justice's pejorative views of those living in poverty and in receipt of benefits.

It is not just the media that recycles the discredited 'culture of poverty' thesis. Recent government policy in the UK reproduces this argument and, in fact, reinforces 'the discursive framing of poverty as cultural in nature or origin' and 'positions the family as the location in which the cultures of poverty are reproduced' (Lehtonen, 2018: 86). By naming the family as the site of their own troubles, 'consideration of competing explanations such as systemic or structural issues, are shut down' (Sayer, 2017: 198). In fact, not only does it shut down competing explanations, the discursive strategy put forward by governments positively feeds vindictive public attitudes towards families living in poverty (Levitas, 2012). For example, in the UK, David Cameron, Prime Minister until 2015, said there are 'the small number of families' that are 'the source of a large proportion of the problems in society: drug addiction, alcohol abuse, crime, a culture of disruption and irresponsibility that cascades through generations' (cited in Shildrick et al, 2016: 822). Furthermore, the concomitant Minister for Communities said the Government approach would be 'more forceful in language, a little less understanding ... Sometimes we've run away from categorising, stigmatising, laying blame' (Chorley, 2012). The UK is not alone in blaming parents and families for the poverty their children face. In New Zealand until 2017, child poverty rates were rising and families faced this familiar condemnation (Berentson-Shaw, 2015; Ainge Roy, 2016; Collins, 2016). A change in administration in October 2017 has targeted child poverty with hopes to greatly decrease it (Mercer, 2018). In the US, where the discourse fiercely blames parents (Garey and Arendell, 1999; Blum, 2015), advocates try to emphasise that poverty degrades parent–child relationships (Barber, 2014) and that poverty is the key cause of parenting difficulties (Russell et al, 2008).

In such scenarios, when the family is explicitly named as the cause of the problems they face, when poverty and material disadvantage are not mentioned, and the electorate holds vindictive views towards such families, it devolves governments of the responsibility to make the required changes to the macro-economic structures, such as the labour and housing markets, and justifies their not increasing or, in fact, decreasing state financial support to families (Lansley and Mack, 2015). It can generate public support for austerity measures, a lack of sympathy for families living in poverty and can be a useful tool for government. That is not to say that families with severe and multiple troubles (for themselves and others) do not exist – they do – just not in the massed ranks that governments suggest they do. Their numbers are often exaggerated and used to justify welfare cuts (Shildrick et al, 2016: 826). Furthermore, in the public consciousness, and in political circles, these portrayals of 'troubled' families become conflated with families living in poverty. In this way, poverty becomes synonymous with troubling, troubled and troublesome families.

These behavioural explanations of poverty continue to prevail not because they shed light on the causes of poverty (Lister, 2004) but because of the 'ease with which they take hold in the public consciousness' (Pemberton et al, 2015: 34). In the behavioural understanding of poverty, the 'structural issues affecting these families, including poverty, poor-quality employment and poor housing conditions' and the failure of the government to address these is not mentioned (Crossley, 2016: 270). Instead, parenting is to be tackled as a root cause of child poverty and family intervention is the preferred solution rather than raising family incomes (Gillies, 2011).

To whom are low-income families being compared?

If low-income families are being deemed as lacking in critical functions and capacities it is important to identify to whom they are being compared and to explore how fair is the comparison. The benchmark against which low-income families are compared is the idealised family and childhood outlined earlier in the chapter that privileges better-off families. Since the early 2000s 'inadequate' parenting 'has been seen as the source of serious social ills, driving a cycle of deprivation and generating crime and anti-social behaviour' (Gillies, 2005: 838). Parents living in poverty have been portrayed as unable to self-govern and as being unable or unwilling to capitalise on their lives (Gillies, 2005: 837). Through such personal failings, then, it is seen as inevitable that parents will 'reproduce their poverty' (Gillies, 2005: 840).

This assumption has strengthened over time among governments across wealthy societies. The modern approach to tackling disadvantage in families, therefore, is to instil in them middle-class values (Gewirtz, 2001, Gillies, 2005). Thus, the yardstick against which poor families are compared is their wealthier, middle-class counterparts and the political aim is to ' to equip working-class parents with the skills to raise middle-class children' (Gillies, 2005: 838).

Parents or mothers?

With the intense political focus of the past 20 years being on parenting, with 'good' parenting being seen as the panacea to all of society's ills, including poverty, it is parents who are charged with ensuring children are turned into responsible citizens (Lister, 2006). Although the political focus has been on the gender-neutral term 'parenting', the intensity of that focus has mainly been on women. There is the assumption that mothers are responsible for looking after children and so have greater responsibility for children's successful development (Shirani et al, 2011). Furthermore, when parenting in poverty, it is working-class mothering practices that are considered to be the antithesis of good parenting and are thought to result in poor outcomes for children (Gillies, 2008: 1080). The result of this is that

> While governments may talk of 'parents', the impact of policies that impose home-school agreements, fine the parents of truants or require the parents of children appearing before the courts to attend parenting classes falls quite disproportionately upon mothers, not fathers.

> In research conducted by one of the authors, for example, mothers were held responsible for the behaviour of their children by the courts even on those rare occasions when fathers were also present. (Scourfield and Drakeford, 2002: 627)

The blaming of mothers living in poverty for the difficulties their children face is common to many wealthy societies. In the US, mothers are often blamed for the country's social ills; in particular, low-income, immigrant, and non-white mothers 'have served as easy scapegoats for tough problems like poverty, delinquency, unrest, and "lawlessness."' (Blum, 2015: no page). In Canada, a country with a strong understanding of the structural elements of poverty, it has yet been argued that the political discourse has served to make the structural causes of poverty less visible, to displace women's issues and women's poverty, and to blame mothers for their and their children's poverty (Lister, 2006: 328). Thus, the brunt of the opprobrium towards disadvantaged parents is usually directed at mothers. As well as being a controversial and value-laden environment, the family is also, therefore, a primary locus of gender inequality.

Living in a family on a low income

Parents and children are part of the same family facing the same disadvantages and, although their experiences have similarities, they also have many differences. Unfortunately, not all of the many deprivations that accompany a life lived in poverty can be addressed in this chapter; for example, some real and critical aspects of child poverty, such as poor quality housing and negative neighbourhood effects, are not explored in this book due to reasons of space (Quilgars and Pleace, 2016). Others are addressed in the remaining chapters, for example: poorer mental health (Davie, 2016) in Chapter 7; poorer physical health and development (Donkin and Marmott, 2016) in Chapter 7; poorer quality of and access to education (Treanor, 2018a) in Chapter 5; poorer quality of employment and security in Chapter 6; and being a lone parent (Nieuwenhuis and Maldonado, 2018) in Chapter 4. Also, the qualitative experiences of living in poverty, such as making the decision whether to heat one's home or to eat, are well-documented elsewhere (see for example Duncan and BrooksGunn, 1997; Ridge, 2002; Green, 2007; Ridge, 2007; Harris et al, 2009; Marsh et al, 2017) and so will not be addressed here. Instead this chapter will look at the effects on parents and children of living on a low income as a consequence of the dominant narrative that pervades wealthy societies, that of blaming the attributes and behaviours of parents personally, and mothers especially, for their poverty.

Two thirds of children in poverty in the UK live in a family where someone is working. This figure is far higher than in other wealthy societies, for example the rate is 37 per cent in New Zealand (CPAG NZ, 2017). Despite this high rate of in-work poverty, and despite sharing the qualitative experience of poverty, poor working families stigmatise those who are not working for being 'shirkers' compared to 'workers', which serves to 'exacerbate existing fault lines within their own communities' (Pemberton et al, 2015: 30). The divisive nature of this rhetoric has created hostility among neighbours and communities and has led to an atmosphere of intolerance and misunderstanding, which has had 'a particularly insidious impact on wider social relationships (Pemberton et al, 2015: 31).

These divisions are not only present between the working and the non-working poor in communities. Increasingly, poor people themselves have absorbed the rhetoric of the deserving and underserving poor and apply stigma to each other, even when they are living in *identical* circumstances, each viewing the other's poverty 'as a consequence of individual ineptitude or moral failure' (Shildrick and MacDonald, 2013: 292). Furthermore, at one time it was the case that the poor blamed themselves for their situations (Gough et al (2006) in Shildrick and MacDonald, 2013). Now, however, the poor reject the idea that they may be to blame and, instead, blame those who share the same circumstances as them (Shildrick and MacDonald, 2013). Although, people living in poverty reject personal culpability for their own situation, they remain aware that they may be perceived this way by those around them (Pemberton et al, 2015: 31). This perception of blame and stigma from others produces strong emotions in people, including 'anger and frustration at being thought of as "lazy" or "not contributing"' (Pemberton et al, 2015: 31). As well as blaming each other for often identical situations, those living in poverty often do not believe themselves to be living in poverty at all, in spite of the most impecunious circumstances. Their rationale, according to Shildrick and MacDonald (2013), is that as they are able to manage in straitened circumstances, therefore they cannot be seen as poor. This chimes with Alcock's (2006: 200) observation that 'to identify oneself as poor is to identify oneself as having a problem and being in need of help' (Alcock, 2006: 200).

It is not just the UK that has seen an intensification of negative attitudes toward poor parents. In the US and Canada, the idea that people should bear personal responsibility for their circumstances has increased as social support to families has decreased, resulting in a punitive approach that demonises parents living in poverty (Russell et al, 2008). Furthermore, the powerfully gendered nature of the parental discourse in North America means that women 'continue to bear the primary burden of parenting, have increasingly been expected to seek employment outside the home, without additional resources to support the dual role as parent and worker' (Russell et al, 2008: 84). This conflict in the role of primary carer and primary worker is explored further in the chapter on lone parents.

For those living in poverty, there are tensions between: those believed to be trying and those seen to be lazy; those who are working and those who are not; those who are perceived to receive disability benefits genuinely or not; those in the same circumstances but who distance themselves from the blame they apply to others; and a complete denial of living in poverty at all. The effects of the modern discourses on families living in poverty are blame, stigma, shame, denial, anger, accusations, social distance and isolation. So, who is vulnerable, not only to poverty, but to the stigmatising blame for that poverty? In Shildrick and MacDonald's (2012, 2013, 2014, 2016) work it is mainly the working class, geographically fixed communities; however, both poverty, and the stigma of blame for that poverty, is more likely to be experienced by migrant families, those of a non-white race or ethnicity, the disabled (explored in Chapter 8), young parents, those with a large family and lone parents (see Chapter 4). The effect of this on children is that they grow up knowing that their families are demonised and internalise the stigmatised identity as shame.

Shame is a factor common in all personal accounts of poverty across time and place. An international study of poverty and shame shows that, across high, middle and low-income countries people in poverty report often feeling ashamed because of the limitations imposed by their poverty; furthermore, they said they were frequently *made* to feel ashamed on a daily basis (Walker, 2014: 183). Walker (2014: 183) says 'that failure to take adequate account of shame has resulted in a distorted understanding of the experience of poverty', which is why this book is premised on the experiences of children and their families living in poverty, including stigma and shame. Walker concludes that, although poverty in the global North and South may look different in regards to material resources, 'the emotional pain and psychosocial consequences for the people affected are much more directly comparable than might previously have been thought' (Walker, 2014: 183).

The cycle of advantage

The cycle of deprivation is a phrase that, although repeatedly discredited, gets recycled every few years (Welshman, 2007). It means that the children of poor parents will themselves be poor in adulthood as a result of deprivation being transmitted from one generation to the next. This is thought to occur for a variety of reasons such as learned behaviours (culture of poverty), poor education, low social capital, inherited dispositions, among others. This chapter does not aim to rake over the coals of old arguments; instead, it seeks to explore that which is much more obvious, but little talked about: the *cycle of advantage*.

The cycle of advantage is where wealthier middle-class parents 'consolidate their advantages and ensure the reproduction of privilege through the generations' (Gillies, 2005: 836). In utilising greater resources to maintain their wealth and social position for their children, middle-class families feel 'entitled' to their privilege, which 'itself becomes a key resource for cementing family privilege' (Gillies, 2005: 842). In sum, feeling entitled to pass on their privilege to their children is in itself a resource used to maintain that privilege. Dermott and Pomati (2016:138) also find that the most advantaged parents are able to maintain their advantage, which suggests that

> a reorientation in thinking about who really is 'different' is in order. Our suggestion is that the most educationally advantaged fraction of the middle class is setting the tone and standard in terms of key markers of educationally 'appropriate' and 'supportive' parenting. Instead of maintaining a focus on the parenting behaviours of those who are most disadvantaged in the mistaken belief that they 'do' parenting differently, it may be time for greater attention on the most advantaged.

Thus, rather than comparing poor parents to all other parents, it may be that the most advantaged parents are the ones who are different to everyone else and should be the focal point of study. There are other reasons why comparing disadvantaged parents to advantaged parents is not fair. In the first instance parenting practice cannot be detached from a family's socioeconomic circumstances as parenting in impoverished circumstances is extremely difficult (Katz et al, 2007; Russell et al, 2008). Furthermore, to then use a family's parenting practice as the reason for their poverty, when their parenting is grounded in that poverty, is paradoxical. Another reason, is that when working-class mothers seek to support their children's education they are not as effective as the middle-class mothers who have far greater material and cultural resources to draw on (Irwin and Elley, 2011). So similar efforts in terms of time and energy will not have the same effects between those with high and low resources.

In fact, the idea that low levels of education and poverty result in poor parenting, or even an absence of 'good' parenting, was found to be unsubstantiated in Dermott and Pomati's (2016) study. In a similar vein, they found no 'evidence for the existence of a group of "delinquent" parents who fail to participate in parent–child activities' leading them to conclude that 'associations made between low levels of education, poverty and poor parenting are ideologically driven rather than based on empirical evidence' (Dermott and Pomati, 2016: 138). Inspired by Dermott and Pomati (2016: 139), we could flip our thinking by: (1) moving understandings of parenting away from a 'goal-oriented, individualised framework' towards acknowledging the 'significance of intimacy, emotionality and reciprocity', which are shown to be in abundance in low-income families, and which have the added advantage of focusing on children in the present rather than in the future; and (2) emphasising that we need to look at elite families as the unusual ones; we need to study their privilege.

What it all means for children

Children living in families experiencing poverty are aware of and adversely affected by society's negative perceptions of their families. Furthermore, the stigma and blame attributed to families extend to children living in poverty – they too are adversely judged as being problematic and troublesome. Children are not excluded from the stresses that poverty brings, they worry about their parents and use their own power and agency to try ameliorate family circumstances (Ridge, 2002). One way children do this is to protect their parents through denial of their own needs and aspirations (Ridge, 2002, Marsh et al, 2017). Children negotiate and mediate poverty in family life not asking for money, or for things required of them at school, and by self-excluding from the social and leisure activities of their peers (Harris et al, 2009, Ridge, 2009b). Children can exercise their agency within the family in other ways too. Older children often take on employment so that they can pay for their own material needs, save their parents the burden of paying for them and also to supplement the family finances. Older children often save families money by providing childcare, especially for lone parents. These issues are discussed further in Chapter 6.

Children often face bullying as a result of their poverty and go to great efforts to mask or hide it (Treanor, 2018a). Children feel shame, embarrassment, and ashamed of feeling embarrassed, by their families' circumstances. Parents hide their poverty too, especially from statutory services such as health or education, often out of shame but also out of fear of unwanted service intervention (Treanor, 2018a). This means that statutory services, who could help children most in their travails with poverty, are often unaware of the difficulties families face. One consequence of this is that, when statutory services do come across families facing difficult circumstances, it is often due to other adverse experiences in addition to their poverty. The outcome of this is that statutory services, such as health, education or social work professionals, often mistake poverty for family problems, or believe poverty to be caused by them. This is why it is important to educate statutory professionals on the causes and consequences of poverty and to supportively challenge them to flip their thinking (Treanor, 2018a).

Children do not stay children forever; they have to negotiate transitions, to adolescence and on to young adulthood. The transition to secondary school is one of the most difficult and stressful periods for a young person (Galton et al, 1999; McGee et al, 2004). It is shown to exacerbate inequality and be particularly difficult for young people living in poverty (Reay and Lucey, 2003, Evangelou et al, 2007). Although for many young people its effects are short-lived (Anderson et al, 2000: 326), negative transitions are found to have a deleterious impact on outcomes, not only in adolescence, but also beyond the school years and into adulthood (Wassell et al, 2007; West et al, 2010). Achieving a successful transition is associated not only with better academic attainment (McGee, 2004), but also with an improved 'general sense of wellbeing and mental health' (Zeedyk et al, 2003: 68). The transition to young adulthood, and on to education and employment, is especially difficult when there are few sources of capital to draw on for children living in poverty. Some children will face almost insurmountable challenges to the transition to adulthood: those facing adversities such as homelessness; those looked after by the state; and those who have asylum or refugee status, among others. When family does not, or cannot, work for children, they often find refuge in the school setting, as discussed further in Chapter 5.

Instead of castigating children living in poverty for what they do not manage to do or achieve, let us flip the thinking, let us admire what families are able to achieve with such few resources and, admire what children manage to do and negotiate, often with great success, that is take on employment, domestic duties, childcare, emotional support to parents, and other tasks beyond the usual responsibility of their years. Let us aim not just to remove the stigma, but also to promote dignity and respect, so that children and young people can gain acceptance in their peer group and pride in their skills and achievements.

Misunderstandings of child poverty

Tackling child poverty involves making judgements about what children need, what they ought to have, who should provide it, and how (Ridge and Wright, 2008b: 3). If this includes increasing resources to parents, who some may hold culpable, then such solutions can quickly deteriorate into judgements on what poor parents and their children *deserve* to have (Lister, 2004). This can fuel public and media discourses on the fecklessness of parents whose children live in poverty.

In every generation public discourse finds ways to shift the blame for poverty onto the poor themselves, even when the evidence does not support it. In recent years, children living in poverty have become increasingly invisible in media, societal and cultural representations of childhood, and a disdain once reserved for their parents now extends to them. How we view children living in poverty depends on what we think of their parents. Thus, when families are seen as problematic, there is less public support for eradicating or preventing child poverty, and the culture of blame then extends to the children themselves. This allows detrimental political decisions and policy measures, such as conditionality in the benefit system, to proliferate.

In the UK today, pejorative descriptions of families living in poverty flourish in the media. The UK Government also portrays families living in poverty in a negative light. These negative discourses between the government and media interplay in such a way as to reinforce the scornful views of families living in poverty. Despite evidence to the contrary these negative beliefs and attitudes towards poor people prevail, even though, for example, two thirds of children living in poverty in the UK have a parent who is working. The public perception of such families remains that they are somehow deficient. A key question arises as to why such beliefs and attitudes prevail? One explanation is that how a government addresses child poverty sets the tone for the media and for the public. If the government and media have a symbiotic relationship on these matters that bombards the public with negative portrayals, such as the case in the UK, then people may believe their views to be accurate and true. Another explanation is given by Lister (2004) when she describes the 'othering' of people living in poverty.

To 'other' someone living in poverty is to treat them as different from the rest of society. Lister describes it as 'a process of differentiation and demarcation, by which the line is drawn between "us" and "them" – between the more and the less powerful – and through which social distance is established and maintained' (Lister, 2004: 101). She describes the line as being 'imbued with negative value judgements that construct "the poor" variously as a source of moral contamination, a threat, an "undeserving" economic burden, an object of pity or even as an exotic species' (Lister, 2004: 101). In this way, the marginalised position of people living in poverty is used against them, to stigmatise them and to exclude them (Marsh et al, 2017). So, people need to differentiate themselves from those living in poverty. This may partly be due to an innate human tendency towards hierarchy. If one looks at one's poorer neighbour, perhaps is it important to be sure that such a fate cannot be yours due to your being different. Perhaps it is difficult for people to appreciate that wealthier circumstances may be due to family background and structural forces and not to an innate exceptionalism. The prevailing negative attitudes are not, however, reserved to those who are significantly better off. Among communities with high levels of poverty, there are increasing instances of poor people othering those in similar circumstances to themselves in their community. For example, if on disability benefits, the nature of their entitlement may be called into question (Shildrick and MacDonald, 2013). If they have children, what they do, what type of parents they are seen to be and what they spend their money on may be critiqued (Shildrick and MacDonald, 2013). In this way, poor people deny being poor and lay the blame at the door of their equally (or more) poor neighbours. That such negative portrayals have been absorbed into the narratives of the poor themselves is testament to the pervasiveness of political and media discourses. That they have become accepted unquestioningly into everyday understandings of poverty, even among those who are poor, is testament to the old adage that 'mud sticks'. Whatever the explanations are for negative attitudes to prevail, the result is that it engenders a lack of sympathy towards those living in poverty and a lack of respect for the efforts they do make to bring their children up in straitened circumstances. This does then permit undignified treatment and public shaming to prevail. And the people who suffer most from these negative beliefs and attitudes, and the attendant treatment, are the children themselves.

There is the idea that too much of taxpayers hard-earned money would need to be handed over to (potentially feckless) parents to eradicate child poverty. Yet, the cost of doing nothing about child poverty is so much more. In 2008 it was calculated that child poverty was costing the UK economy £25 billion annually (Hirsch, 2008). An updated calculation in 2013 put the figure at £29 billion, with the caveat that were child poverty rates to increase by their predicted amount by 2020 the figure would rise to £35 billion (Hirsch, 2013). These costs are incurred by the lower productivity and the higher risk of unemployment of adults who grew up in poverty and by the additional public spending to counteract the social problems effected by high levels of child poverty (Marsh et al, 2017: 11). This is a phenomenal waste of money to the economy and a waste of potential for society.

There is still a widespread lack of understanding on the causes of child poverty, even among those who can help prevent it or mitigate its effects (Simpson et al, 2015). To flip the thinking on the misunderstanding of poverty, consider if all public bodies were to receive training on the actual causes of child poverty. This would prevent and reduce not only poverty but also the othering that it brings. If there were compulsory equalities training in relation to poverty and income inequality, then public services would be better able to identify the early signs that indicate a heightened risk of poverty. This would also reduce stigma and shame. In some areas of the UK, and in Scotland in particular, this type of work is currently being rolled out and I have been fortunate enough to play a part in it. Some of the policy and practice initiatives discussed later in this chapter, in relation to income maximisation, results from this type of professional awareness training.

Beyond individualised accounts of poverty

Political poverty analysis concentrates on the behaviours and characteristics of the poor and political leadership puts greater emphasis on ending welfare 'dependency' than on fighting poverty and its root causes (O'Connor, 2001: 292). However, if we shifted the focus from dependency to the political actions and institutional structures that govern social and economic practices, then a new poverty knowledge could emerge – one that would focus on poverty rather than the poor (O'Connor, 2001). Such a new poverty knowledge would, argues O'Connor (2001), recognise class, gender, and race as legitimate units of analysis and not simply as demographic variables to be isolated and controlled for (O'Connor, 2001: 292). This would enable an understanding of the social and economic stratification that govern the inequalities based on class, gender and race. When poverty is understood at the individual level you get a psychological resolution: when you address poverty at the community level you get a community-based resolution that targets the structural causes of poverty.

There are several problems with identifying and addressing poverty from an individualistic perspective. One, is that individual accounts of poverty neglect social relationships and context (Brady, 2009). As Tilly (1998) cited in Brady (2009) notes: 'Instead of reducing social behavior to individual decision-making, social scientists urgently need to study the relational constraints within which all individual action takes place.' The inequality in social relations is discussed later in this book. Another problem with the individual account of poverty is that the characteristics widely seen to 'cause' poverty, for example lone parenthood, do not have the same relationship with poverty across all affluent Western societies. Such characteristics are linked to poverty through their social context and the extent to which they are associated with poverty varies dramatically across countries (Brady, 2009). In this way the characteristics themselves cannot be held responsible for poverty, rather, 'societies make collective choices about which insecure labor market and family situations will not be protected. If certain characteristics associate with poverty only in some contexts, it tells you at least as much about that context as it does about poverty' (Brady, 2009: 18). In sum, we choose which families, and therefore which children, we will allow to flounder and those we will protect.

Impacts of poverty on children and families

The consequences of living in poverty include social exclusion, social divisions and isolation, and its impacts extend beyond those living in poverty to their families and the wider community (Asenova et al, 2015). Poverty brings intolerable levels of stress to families, relationships and children. The higher levels of stress poor parents experience can inhibit their ability to plan for the future, adopt calm parenting strategies and develop their own or their children's wellbeing (Schoon et al, 2012; 2010). It is important to recognise that good parenting is achieved in families regardless of income, but that 'living in poverty does make it undeniably more difficult' (JRF, 2016: 31). The impact of poverty on relationships should not be underestimated: children in poverty are more likely to say that they argue with their parents and do not discuss important issues with them (JRF, 2017). Conflicted relationships pertain to the adults in the family too: couples living in poverty experience higher levels of relationship distress, which is shown to decrease as incomes rise (JRF, 2017). For this reason, couples living in poverty are more likely to separate than their better-off counterparts (JRF, 2017).

There is real pressure on poor parents to meet standards for their children that their incomes do not support (Marsh et al, 2017: 60). To do this, parents routinely sacrifice their own wellbeing to protect their children; by reducing their food intake, eschewing new clothes or socialising, and working long hours in low paid, low quality employment (Ridge, 2011, 2013; Ridge and Millar, 2011; JRF, 2016). These parental sacrifices can have detrimental effects on children's wellbeing and then children make their own sacrifices. They do not bring home letters from school about activities that cost money, they do not ask parents for money to join friends in social activities, they help out at home caring for younger siblings when parents are working long, unsocial hours, and they hold off on replacing worn-out clothing until their parents can afford it (Harris et al, 2009; Ridge, 2011; Ridge and Millar, 2011; JRF, 2016).

In a modern, technological world, living in poverty means that you can lose access to the streams of communication that fill other people's lives and can be cut off from the common ways of your friends, family and community (Marsh et al, 2017: 1). This is especially detrimental for children as young people almost exclusively communicate via social media and other online platforms, and even their schooling requires access to the online world to complete homework or obtain study materials. There is pressure for young people to have a smart phone so they can be like their peers, but also so they can actually access their education effectively. This is a situation that will only become more critical as more of everyday life is lived in the virtual world. A lone parent in my research, Claire, has three daughters who are currently fighting over two old, second-hand mobile phones, which, she says is making her 'depressed'. She explains how this affects her and her daughters:

> 'The three of them are working off the two phones and the arguments that's causing ... [a second-hand one would cost] only £50, I, I could probably just say, "Right, I'll take that £50 out [the food shopping] money", but I couldn't do that. And every night [they're] like, "I want a phone, I need this phone, you never get me this..." But they don't understand how hard it is. If I was to take that £50 it would take me two weeks to get back on my feet, to manage food-wise, electricity, gas, what have you. But they see what I'm

going through as well but … in a way … I think it's making them more aware of both sides. Like, they see I struggle but they still want the finer things. They still want the phone. My sixteen-year-old, she sort of understands that I can't just pull that money out of thin air. She knows if I get a lump sum of money or money just happens to fall out the sky, she'll get that phone [laughs]. But until that happens she just has to wait and steal her sisters' when they're sleeping.'

An increasing phenomenon among families living in in-work and out-of-work poverty is that of food insecurity. Contrary to the idea of poor families not knowing how to budget, those living in poverty know the costs of everything they need to buy, especially food. It is simply a matter that their income is not sufficient to cover their needs. Oftentimes, people living in poverty need to sacrifice quality over quantity and are acutely aware of this. In one of my longitudinal poverty studies, Janice, a mother and grandmother, explains,

'You can't buy healthy food. I mean I'd love to have fruit and veg every day … and chicken, instead of junk and junk and junk. Like I say, you get five packets of biscuits for £1, what you pay for a melon. So it's just easier but it's not good for your health.'

When not sacrificing the quality of everyone's food in the household, parents deny themselves food to give more to their children. For an increasing number of people, their incomes are just insufficient to meet their families' food needs. In the UK, this has led to vast increase in the use of food banks, which is well evidenced elsewhere (Cooper, 2014; Garthwaite, 2016; Garthwaite, 2017). The main food bank charity in the UK issued 1.6 million three-day emergency food supplies to people in crisis in the year 2018/19, a 19 per cent increase on the previous year.[1] Of these, more than half a million went to feed children. Failures in the benefits system were cited as the main cause of referral. Furthermore, food bank use in this charity's network increased by 73 per cent in the five years to 2019. In a country as rich as the UK (among others), the fact that families, and children, are going hungry and do not have enough to eat is an appalling indictment on its social policy. Children and their families should not have to rely on charity to feed them.

4

Lone parenthood

I don't doubt that many of the rioters out last week have no father at home. Perhaps they come from one of the neighbourhoods where it's standard for children to have a mum and not a dad ... where it's normal for young men to grow up without a role model, looking to the street for their father figures, filled with rage and anger. So if we want to have any hope of mending our broken society, family and par.enting is where we've got to start. (David Cameron, British Prime Minister, 15 August 2011 (De Benedictis, 2012))

Introduction

Few subjects in relation to childhood poverty excite the public and political imagination quite as much as the issue of family 'breakdown'. It is an area with strong connections to poverty, disadvantage, gendered inequalities, and the supposed breaching of normative values and expectations. This chapter takes a critically informed look at the importance of, and relationship between, family formation, family 'breakdown' and lone parenthood in the context of childhood poverty. It engages with myths and assumptions about 'broken families' and reveals the corrosive effect of demonising lone-parent family life on children's lives and wellbeing. It explores the experiences of lone parents and looks at how children and young people often take on additional responsibilities in lone-parent families.

Family separation and divorce is often the point at which many children experience poverty. Poverty can come hard on the heels of breakdown and separation, and children's economic and emotional wellbeing can be particularly fragile as a result. However, poverty and emotional mal-being are not inevitable consequences of separation and divorce. The role of separated fathers in lone-parent families, particularly their financial contribution and involvement in their children's lives, are explored. This chapter looks closely at how the state involves itself deep in the heart of family life in relation to support for children following separation or divorce. Although children are often the centrepiece in relation to policy rhetoric and development, their needs and concerns are often subsumed beneath the interests of the state and the perceived interests of parents. It explores the role of childcare and child maintenance policies in securing equity between children and between parents. Finally, it explores how they can establish financial adequacy and security; fundamental issues for children.

Lone parents are not a homogenous group

Around 75 per cent of children in the UK live in two-parent families and 25 per cent live in lone-parent families (Lansley and Mack, 2015); although, from the disproportionate attention lone parents receive in political and media circles, you would be forgiven for thinking there were far more of them. The incidence of lone parenthood is increasing in many wealthy societies (Calder, 2018), although in the UK the proportion has remained stable for over ten years (Gingerbread, 2018). Lone parenthood is not a fixed state as much as another stage in family life and is usually temporary (Treanor, 2018b, Zagel and Hübgen, 2018), lasting on average around five years in the UK (Lansley and Mack, 2015). The majority (90 per cent) of lone-parent households in the UK are female and only 10 per cent are male, proportions that have not changed in over a decade (Gingerbread, 2018). It is important to note the highly gendered nature of lone parenthood; when we talk about lone parents, we are really talking about lone mothers. From this point onwards, therefore, this chapter will speak of lone mothers, except when presenting statistics where the gender breakdown is not known, in which case it will discuss lone parents.

It is common to hear lone mothers being discussed as though they were one homogenous group, with the same characteristics and situations. In media and political discourses lone mothers are often considered a social problem, as welfare-dependent, as bad parents responsible for raising feral children. Yet, lone mothers are not a homogenous group and there are many, often wrong, assumptions made about them. Contrary to the myth of the young lone unmarried mother, the average age of lone parenthood in the UK is 38 years old for lone mothers and 45 years old for lone fathers (Gingerbread, 2018) and they have usually previously been married (McKendrick et al, 2016). Less than 2% of lone mothers in the UK are teenagers (Gingerbread, 2018) and, in Scotland, only 15% of lone mothers have never lived with the father of their child (McKendrick et al, 2016: 104). Again, contrary to popular mythology, lone mothers are not always poor. In wealthy societies between 70 and 90 per cent of lone mothers have incomes that are above the poverty threshold (Young-hwan, 2018); however, lone mother families are at far greater risk of poverty. In fact, they are more likely to experience multiple disadvantages – the gender wage gap, low incomes, poverty, material deprivation, unstable, low-paid, poor quality employment, and poorer physical and mental health – 27 per cent of lone mothers have a disability compared to 21 per cent of couple parents (Gingerbread, 2018). In addition to being maternal stressors, these multiple disadvantages also have consequences for children and children's wellbeing (Ridge and Millar, 2011; Millar and Ridge, 2013; Treanor, 2016a).

Lone mothers and poverty

Lone parents are disproportionately poor in all countries; however, the highest rate of poverty by far among lone parents is to be found in the US (Brady and Burroway, 2012). In Brady and Burroway's analysis, lone-parent poverty is found to be a function of the 'household's employment, education, and age composition, and the presence of other adults in the household' (Brady and Burroway, 2012: 719). In the UK, although the majority of children living in poverty have two parents, children living in lone-parent families are twice as likely to be in poverty and are three times as likely to experience material deprivation as those in two-parent families (Marsh et al, 2017). In countries where child poverty is declining, for example in Canada and Japan, child poverty rates remain higher for those in lone-parent than for those in two-parent families, which 'underscores the fact that economic conditions affect children in lone-parent families more than other children' (Fanjul, 2014). Across affluent societies, family composition, in terms of both marital status and relationship transitions, is associated with lower socioeconomic status and with income inequality (Kiernan and Mensah, 2009; Kiernan and Mensah, 2010; Schoon et al, 2012).

The current percentage of lone parents living in poverty in the UK is 47 per cent as can be seen from Figure 2.1; however, when the lone parent works full-time the poverty risk for children falls to 30 per cent, which is far lower than the 75 per cent experienced by children in a couple household where neither parent works. Although the political and media discourses see lone parenthood, especially lone motherhood, as a cause of poverty, these data show that it does not cause poverty per se. Instead, it is the way in which the labour market, taxes and benefits operate that increases the likelihood of poverty for lone parents (McKendrick et al, 2016: 99). Poverty is not an inevitable outcome for lone-parent families; it very much depends on the types of policies put in place to support them, for example support with childcare.

The experience of poverty for lone mothers can be a lonely one. The responsibility for doing the right thing by your children, on limited resources, is difficult and can weigh heavily. When you consider that parents often protect their children from poverty and material deprivation by sacrificing their own basic needs, then it is likely that children in lone-parent families have a mother that is far more materially deprived than they themselves are (Treanor, 2018b). In living with poverty, lone mothers take responsibility on themselves for its effects on family life and for its impacts on their children. Despite the difficulties they face, alone, lone mothers go to great lengths to mask their own poverty to protect their children (Treanor, 2018a). In my longitudinal study of families, one lone mother with three sons explains what happens when there is no money for gas or electricity:

> 'The people that make the decisions haven't got a clue... [they've] never experienced hardship in their life. They've never went without food. They've never … there's been times with my kids when I've went to bed and said, "See tonight, we'll light candles, and we'll get our books in bed." And it's because I've no electricity, it's crazy. And when I've run out of gas, and there's no hot water, so we'll be boiling kettles for the bath … and you don't want to tell [eldest son], who's 12, because you don't want him thinking "Oh my god, my mum hasn't got any money"… I'll say, "I can't get that pilot light to light, I'm going to have to phone [the landlord] in the morning." So he thinks I have a problem with my gas but it's because I don't have any money to put in my card [meter], because I've none, so I'm having to boil kettles to give them their bath for school the next day.'

Child wellbeing in lone-mother families

The existing evidence on the impact of family composition on children's outcomes is often contradictory: for example, there is a strong body of evidence from the US that finds that unmarried mothers (both lone and cohabiting) have children with poorer outcomes than their married counterparts (Sigle-Rushton et al, 2005; McLanahan, 2007; Osborne and McLanahan, 2007). However, their analysis uses a sample of families identified as 'fragile': lone mothers and co-habiting parents are considered inherently 'fragile' in the US because the marital status of mothers is more strongly socially and ethnically patterned there than it is in Europe (Garfinkel and McLanahan, 2003). Cohabiting parents in the UK are socioeconomically more like their married counterparts and those in the US are more like lone parents (Kiernan et al, 2011). With these caveats in mind on the use of US data of fragile families, the conclusion that unmarried mothers (both lone and cohabiting) have family types that are inherently worse for children should not be made.

Multiple, often cross-sectional, studies that only look at lone parenthood once as a snapshot in time, blame lower levels of child wellbeing and development on having a lone mother. For example, lone mothers are more likely to experience mental health issues such as depression and low self-esteem, which are associated with lower wellbeing in children (Mensah and Kiernan, 2009). Another factor that strongly affects child wellbeing is the quality of the parent–child relationship (Schoon et al, 2010a); and yet the warmth of the relationship between the mother and child is impaired by poverty (Kiernan and Huerta, 2008). Poverty has devastating direct and indirect effects on child development and wellbeing (Cooper and Stewart, 2013). Schoon et al (2010b) found that mothers exposed to persistent financial and material hardship were more likely to experience continued emotional distress, which was associated with reduced cognitive stimulation for their children and less involved parent–child interactions, which in turn had negative impacts on their children's developmental outcomes (Schoon et al, 2010b: 218).

Often, the lone mother focus is on the differences between married and unmarried parents and not on family *transitions*, that is moving from a couple to a lone-mother family or vice versa. Relationships are *dynamic*, and just as lone mothers are not one homogenous group, nor do people stay in the same relationships over time. My research benefits from annually collected birth cohort data and so has been able to focus on family transitions rather than static snapshots. It has raised several new findings in relation to lone motherhood (Treanor, 2016a, Treanor, 2016b). For example, it shows that family transitions per se are not key to child wellbeing directly, but that they are key to a lone mother's financial vulnerability and their emotional distress (Treanor, 2016a: 691). The transition that was directly linked to higher levels of maternal emotional distress was being part of a couple that had recently separated (Treanor, 2016a). It also showed that being a stable lone mother or having recently repartnered was not associated with maternal emotional distress, showing that the effects post-separation are temporary, suggesting that women may benefit from targeted support at this time. For children of the various family transitions, only having a mother with repeated separations and repartnerings has a direct, negative association with child wellbeing compared to stable couple families, stable lone-mother families, lone mothers who have repartnered and couple families who have separated (Treanor, 2016a). Therefore, it is not the state of lone motherhood, nor separations, nor parents meeting a new partner that is deleterious to child wellbeing but the impoverished and materially deprived conditions that lone mothers find themselves living in (Treanor, 2016b).

Irrespective of whether a child has one or two parents, what parents do with and for their children is more important than who parents are, or how many of them there are (Calder, 2018: 431). While it is instinctively, and almost certainly, the case that, when it works, what couple parents offer each other in terms of emotional, practical and financial support will invariably advantage a child, it does not mean that all couple parenting is good and all lone mothering is bad. There is no evidence that lone mothers are deficient as parents and there are plenty of high-profile cases in the media of neglectful couple parenting (Calder, 2018: 428). Conflict between parents is bad for children in two-parent families and, in cases of parental separation, any potentially negative impact on children's wellbeing is reduced where there is an absence of conflict between parents and where there is a high quality of family relationships post-separation (Highet and Jamieson, 2007).

There are factors that either prevent low levels of, or stimulate high levels of, wellbeing in children who are in poverty. Protective factors are children's social relationships within their families and their inclusion in their peer group (Ridge and Wright, 2008b). When researching children's social connectedness within the family, at school and in the local neighbourhood, each of these milieu had a positive effect on children's subjective wellbeing; however, the connections to family were found to be the most substantial (Eriksson et al, 2012). In my study, when the mothers of children living in poverty had strong social ties and support, their child's wellbeing extended beyond the average of all children, as shown in Figure 4.1 (Treanor, 2016b).

Figure 4.2 shows that for children living in the lowest 20 per cent of income bracket, their mother having high levels of social connectedness was associated with a positive gradient in child wellbeing with the opposite effect being seen for those with the lowest levels of social connectedness (Treanor, 2016b). This highlights that children who are living in poverty with low levels of maternal social connectedness have the lowest wellbeing, which suggests that this is a combination that makes them particularly vulnerable (Treanor, 2016b). This strongly

Figure 4.1 Interaction of social assets and lowest/highest income quintile for social, emotional and behavioural wellbeing

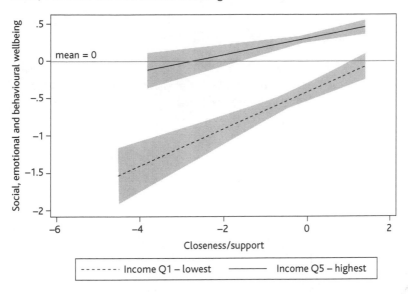

Figure 4.2 Low/high social assets for quintile 1 with social, emotional and behavioural development

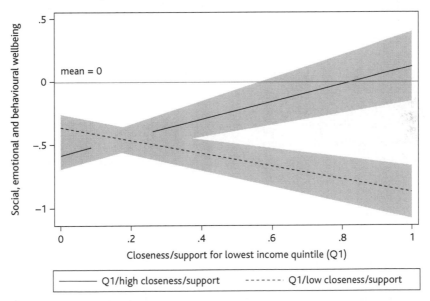

Source: Figures reproduced from Treanor, 2016b. Reprinted by permission of Policy Press.

suggests that relationships are one key aspect to the wellbeing of children living in poverty.

The stigma of lone motherhood

Being a lone mother is one of the most stigmatised positions in UK society today. In the UK, recent governments have placed 'family breakdown' as the root cause of child poverty, with no evidence and to great stigmatising effect (Hancock and Mooney, 2013; Slater, 2014; Mooney, 2011). In today's political discourse, lone mothers are also seen as deficient parents (Dermott and Pomati, 2015) and as 'dependent, underserving, work-avoiding or a threat to the social order' (Calder, 2018: 421). On the political right they are viewed as ' "welfare dependent" and "undeserving" and as being part of a socially threatening "underclass"'; and the centre-left, while they may reject the idea that lone mothers are a 'social threat', have still sought to remedy the 'problem' of lone mothers (Smith, 1999: 313–4). After the riots in 2011 in the UK, mothers in those areas, and in particular lone mothers, were portrayed as 'feral parents', as sexually promiscuous, as wantonly having too many children, and who 'deprive children of a "normal" upbringing through a lack of the nuclear family' (De Benedictis, 2012: 12). Tied into this 'feral parent' discourse is the idea of the lone mother as deliberately denying her children a stable father, seen as essential for authority and stability, 'by selfishly placing her will to parent alone or sexual desire above them' (De Benedictis, 2012: 13). These ideas of lone mothers reinforce and perpetuate disadvantage. Lone mothers, and their children, are aware that they are looked down upon as a family type, which can lead to low self-esteem and self-efficacy.

Shame and stigma are particularly pernicious in poverty discourses today, not just for lone mothers, and have serious negative consequences for people living in poverty. Walker explains that 'institutional stigma, variously manifest in the framing, structure, and delivery of policy is often deliberately imposed as a punishment or deterrent to influence behaviour but is sometimes an unintended consequence of poor policymaking' (Walker, 2014: 49). He is not alone in asserting that shame and stigma has played a deliberate role in some governments' approach to poverty (Mooney, 2011). The negative effects of stigma and shame lead to 'social exclusion, limited social capital, low self-worth, and a lack of agency that could all serve to prolong poverty' (Walker, 2014: 49), which are counteractive to initiatives to mitigate poverty. Taking into consideration the poorer mental health of lone mothers to begin with, then adding the double whammy of poverty stigma and lone-mother stigma, is likely to have a particularly destructive effect on their self-worth, self-efficacy and agency.

Lone mothers and employment

Internationally, around 80 per cent or more of lone parents are working (Nieuwenhuis and Maldonado, 2018). In the UK, the figure is lower (but not outrageously so) at 67 per cent (Lansley and Mack, 2015). This figure is surprisingly high, not at all what one would expect from the dominant notion of lone parents as dependent, work-shy and underserving of support. In spite of relatively high levels of employment, lone mothers remain at high risk of poverty and, even though lone mothers' employment is rising internationally, poverty is not reducing at the associated rate (Nieuwenhuis and Maldonado, 2018). There are many negative outcomes to a lack of employment, as discussed more fully in Chapter 6, and many positive outcomes associated with being in employment. For lone mothers, employment is seen as 'an important outcome in itself – providing independence, identity and an investment in skills and future opportunities' (Nieuwenhuis and Maldonado, 2018: 6). The problem with work in lone mother families is that it is often of the unstable, low-pay, long hours and low-quality variety, and inflexible as regards childcare responsibilities, which can bring more problems than solutions.

When lone mothers are out of work children report experiencing severe deprivation, stigma and (self)-exclusion from school and leisure activities due to low income (Ridge, 2009a). Conversely, when lone mothers enter work young people report a welcome, and valued, increase in income and material goods and increased participation in the life of the school and friends (Ridge and Millar, 2011). When lone mothers' employment is unstable, insecure and low paid they rotate between periods of employment and unemployment. For children, the loss of work can lead to 'the loss of opportunity and dwindling hopes of the improvement that work seemed to promise' as well as a return to severely impoverished circumstances at each transition (Ridge, 2009a: 507). The evidence shows that stable work with standard hours has a positive effect on both mothers and children, but 'unstable employment transitions can threaten wellbeing and result in renewed poverty and disadvantage' (Ridge, 2009a: 504).

Lone mothers' work is more unstable; hours and types of employment change more year after year than for couple parents (Treanor, 2018b). Using data from a birth cohort study, my analysis revealed that only after the Great Recession of 2008 did all families experience a reduction in work intensity. As coupled families recovered, lone mothers continued to experience greater reduction and flux in their working hours and patterns (Treanor, 2018b). Furthermore, looking at lone mothers and relationship transitions across time, the analysis shows that stable lone mothers are more likely to have precarious employment when they have employment, a higher incidence and more persistent experiences of poverty, and far deeper levels of material deprivation compared to all other family transitions (Treanor, 2018b). This shows that the length of time spent as a lone mother 'has an increasingly detrimental effect on employment (as measured by work intensity) and on resources (as measured by income poverty and material deprivation)' (Treanor, 2018b: 93).

Lone mothers experiencing change in their circumstances means that they are often forced back and forth, in and out of employment, often as a result of a lack of affordable childcare. In my longitudinal qualitative study, for Jennifer, who has three sons, studying and finding a job proved to be only the beginning of her difficulties. Her middle son has autism and was well supported in primary school and able to be cared for after school until Jennifer returned home from work. When he reaches high school, he experiences more difficulties in, for example, eating in the crowded, noisy dining room and coming home by himself after school. The responsibility for supporting Jennifer's middle son in school and after school falls to her eldest son, to enable Jennifer to continue working. Now her eldest son is a young carer to her middle son; having to get him to school, through the school day and home again. When the pressure on both boys grows, and her middle son's difficulties become more pronounced, Jennifer puts in a formal request at work to change hours so that they fall during school hours to take the pressure and responsibility off her eldest son. She offers to work weekends instead as she thinks she can get extended family to help at that time. Her request is refused and Jennifer is forced to leave the job she loves. She feels

> 'gutted. I feel cheated. I feel like it's so unfair, because I didn't want to leave and I love my job... And obviously the financial side, it's an issue. So I was thinking, well, what will I do? Because I don't want to – I've been on benefits and everything, and I don't want to go that way again. And I want to work, even if I wasn't that much better off working. For my own peace of mind, mentally, I need to work, because that's just me ... I just feel it's so unfair...

I worked so hard to get to where I got … I just want to work … I just want to work. And I want my boys to grow up knowing that that's what you do. It's normal, it's not normal not to work. It's just so unfair.'

Lone mothers' employment has complex impacts on mothers themselves as well as on their children. In the 1990s the rates of depression among lone mothers was higher than in any other group, including unemployed men, with one in three lone mothers being depressed (Harkness and Skipp, 2013). This rate was the same for lone mothers in and out of work. By the mid-2000s, rates of depression had fallen to the same rate as coupled mothers for lone mothers in work but had *increased* for those out of work (Harkness and Skipp, 2013). In my longitudinal quantitative research, financial vulnerability (measured by coping on current income and debt), income and unemployment are the three factors that have the largest negative effects on maternal mental health and the effects are additive (Treanor, 2016a).

Employment is good for lone mothers' mental health when it is supportive, enabling and allows them to balance childcare, otherwise it can have negative consequences (Harkness and Skipp, 2013). Employment with the absence of support and out-of-kilter with childcare needs is damaging to lone mothers and their children. Being able to balance work and childcare is the condition of employment that lone mothers value most. With the political focus for lone mothers being work activation, it appears that 'policies designed to encourage more lone mothers into work, or to work longer hours, may actually risk pushing up the rate of maternal depression if they are not accompanied by additional measures to help them balance work and childcare responsibilities' (Harkness and Skipp, 2013: 2).

Older children are integral to the employment of their lone mother. They are party to the strains affecting their lone mother and worry about their mothers being over-worked and under stress. It can take the whole family to manage the long non-standard hours that lone mothers have to work (Ridge and Millar, 2011; Millar and Ridge, 2013). Older children facilitate their lone mother's employment by doing household chores, providing childcare for younger siblings and, at times, offering emotional support (Ridge, 2011; Ridge and Millar, 2011). In a previous study I undertook with Barnardos children's charity Jelani is 14 years old and the eldest of four siblings. He shows an understanding and sensitivity to his mother's situation that is way beyond his years. He describes her life as: 'quite difficult … she can't cope. We're always asking for too much … she's asking for loans and debts … she's putting her own life at risk … sometimes I feel like … sometimes I need something yeah, but I see what she's going through and I keep quiet' (Harris et al, 2009: 56). Thus, older children are providing support to lone mothers, but also suppressing their own needs, both material and emotional, to avoid adding stress. Ridge and Millar (2011: 91) explain that this strategy shields the children themselves from disappointment as well as protects their mothers from worry.

Non-resident fathers

In a chapter on lone mothers, of whom 90 per cent are women, it would be remiss not to look at the situation with non-resident fathers. Again, non-resident fathers are not a homogenous group and have varying involvement and input into their children's lives. There are the fathers who may be involved in their children's lives but not contribute financially (perhaps due to their own poverty), or who may contribute financially but have little further engagement, or who may be prevented from having as much involvement in their children's lives as they would like to have, or those who veer between involvement and disengagement, for whatever reasons, with an unpredictability that makes life particularly difficult for children. This chapter cannot give an in-depth analysis of all the various forms of engagement of non-resident fathers, or their impacts, so will present an overview. It should be noted that much of the literature in this area is psychological and so does not take account of the social and structural factors that can have mediating effects on children's developmental outcomes, such as poverty, age, gender, relationships, employment, housing, education and ethnicity.

After a relationship dissolution there remains the idea that children should remain with their mothers because mothers are viewed as the more important parent (Adamsons, 2018). Change in such attitudes is happening slowly, however, and there is an increasing expectation of fathers to have more involvement in their children's lives than just a financial contribution (Adamsons, 2018). There is a relationship between non-resident fathers' financial contributions and his parental engagement. When the non-resident parent pays child maintenance, they are more likely to remain actively involved in their children's lives. This is important to children's wellbeing in post-separation family situations (Highet and Jamieson, 2007; Hakovirta, 2011). Children are shown to benefit both from the non-resident parental engagement and the increase in income as a result of child maintenance. A fuller discussion on child maintenance can be found later in this chapter.

In a meta-analysis of psychological literature on non-resident fathers' engagement with their children, it was found that children's social wellbeing, emotional wellbeing, academic achievement and behaviour were associated with the positive involvement of non-resident fathers (Adamsons and Johnson, 2013). On the other hand, fathers' being uninvolved with their children's lives and having conflict with the child's mother are risk factors for children's development (Pruett et al, 2017). The frequency, quality and presence/absence of conflict in children's involvement with their non-resident fathers is shown to be a function of the contact between their mothers and non-resident fathers (Dunn et al, 2004). This suggests that mothers' relationships with their ex-partners may act as a 'gateway for children's continuing contact with their non-resident fathers' (Dunn et al, 2004: 563).

As previously noted, non-resident fathers' engagement is not necessarily a binary 'sees child/does not see child' situation. Sometimes, non-resident fathers' engagement is varied and unpredictable. Where this is the case, children almost certainly suffer. In my previous study with Barnardos, a nine-year-old girl, Lisa, has separated parents and feels distressed about her father's unpredictability. She describes feeling let down and upset that he 'lies' to her and does not keep his promises (Harris et al, 2009: 54). She retells the story of how he was supposed to see her in her first school play but did not turn up because he 'slept in' (Harris et al, 2009: 54). There is regularity in his unpredictability and, although Lisa believes herself 'used' to it, she says she 'really hates it and wishes he would not do it' (Harris et al, 2009: 54). This has an adverse impact on Lisa's wellbeing, she says: 'I wish he would stop telling lies … breaking promises, I just feel, like, angry … it makes my mum angry that he promises, promises us stuff and then not doing it' (Harris et al, 2009: 54).

Targeting policies at lone mothers

Government policies that are universal for all families lead to lower levels of poverty for all groups (Brady and Burroway, 2012) and lone parents generally 'fare well in a context where *all* families fare well' (Van Lancker, 2018: 241). Where policies are universal they are less stigmatising to those living in poverty, more generous, and they unite the interests of all citizens alike irrespective of poverty status (Brady and Burroway, 2012: 723). Brady and Burroway (2012) find that universal social policies significantly reduce lone-mother poverty and have greater effects than targeted policies and that targeted social policies have no significant effects. Thus, it is debatable whether policies need to be targeted at lone parents specifically or provided more widely to all families in general. As there are a multitude of social policies governing families, lone parents and children, this chapter will look at two in particular – childcare and child maintenance.

Childcare

Two factors that impact on children are whether their lone mother is working and what childcare she has available to her. International research shows that what governments do as regards childcare matter for whether women can access employment (and education) and whether this is sufficient to lift their family out of poverty. In some countries, for example the UK, childcare is primarily market-based and its costs can be prohibitive. Yet, available, affordable, high quality childcare is crucial to lone mothers and their children. When formal childcare is too expensive, lone mothers have to rely on informal childcare from family, friends and older children in the family. This is an insecure type of childcare, which carries an increased risk of in-work poverty and does not support full-time, stable jobs, a pattern that is found across all European countries (Van Lancker and Horemans, 2017). Using informal childcare can result in women having to reduce hours or leave employment altogether (Van Lancker and Horemans, 2017). Also, informal childcare is not necessarily value-free or freely given within families, not all support has a positive effect on mothers (Ghate and Hazel, 2002). Negative effects of support arise when the mothers receiving support feel that they have lost autonomy and have to tolerate interference and loss of privacy in their lives (Ghate and Hazel, 2002). Furthermore, being the recipient of support without the means to reciprocate can leave low-income parents feeling 'bad', 'obligated' or 'owned' (McKendrick et al, 2003: 31).

The difference lies in the provision, accessibility and affordability of formal childcare. This is especially the case for children from disadvantaged backgrounds. Van Lancker (2013: 21), in his study of countries across Europe, explains the importance of governments investing in universal, formal childcare for all social groups:

> [C]hildcare services should be within reach of disadvantaged children in order to be effective in increasing maternal employment rates, increasing children's human capital and mitigating social inequalities. The results demonstrate, however, that in almost all EU Member States childcare coverage is not universal and is socially stratified. Children

from low-income families are enrolled in formal childcare to a much lesser extent than children from high-income families. The only country approaching the child-centred investment ideal of universalising and equalising childcare coverage is Denmark.

Thus, right across Europe the provision of formal childcare is inadequate for mothers to work. Lone mothers face more challenges balancing work and childcare in Finland, the Netherlands and the UK in particular as childcare is just too expensive (Van Lancker, 2018). The cost of childcare and its lack is having a detrimental impact of the ability of families, especially poorer families, to work or take up educational and training opportunities. In Scotland, 25 per cent of parents in severe poverty had given up work, 33 per cent had turned down a job, and 25 per cent had not been able to take up education or training, all because of difficulties in accessing childcare (Save the Children, 2011). We know that when we get childcare right it can make a positive difference to the incidence and prevalence of poverty.

The provision of and access to affordable childcare that has sufficient hours of childcare, so that parents, especially lone mothers, can take up education, training or employment, is a crucial factor in mitigating and preventing child poverty. Childcare that helps parents to balance caring responsibilities with work, including holiday provision that meets the needs of children (especially those in large families) is one of the main barriers to parents, again especially lone mothers, being able to take up work opportunities. Much of the focus on the financial circumstances of lone mothers is on facilitating their access to employment (Hakovirta, 2011: 250). However, there are other facets of lone mothers' potential income that receive far less attention, for example the financial support received (or not) from the non-resident parent (Hakovirta, 2011). The lack of financial support from non-resident parents is a risk factor for lone mothers and, if received, has the potential to reduce child poverty among lone mother families. (Hakovirta, 2011: 250). The next section looks at the issues with the (non)payment of child maintenance.

Child maintenance

Child maintenance is where a non-resident parent regularly makes a payment to the parent with whom the child lives, most of the time as a contribution towards the financial cost of raising a child (Hakovirta, 2011: 249). This is usually the non-resident father making contributions to the resident mother. Most wealthy societies have formal child maintenance systems in place and seek to ensure payment compliance from the non-resident parent (Hakovirta, 2011). Historically, it was the case that these systems targeted support at the post-divorce family, with the assumption that this meant a 'mother with custody of the children and one father who pays child support to compensate for the unequal share of childcare costs' (Claessens and Mortelmans, 2018). More recently, however, two important trends have undermined this model: (1) the increase in shared residential care of children post-separation; and (2) the increasing complexity of family formations with subsequent unions, separations and childbearing with multiple partners becoming more common (Claessens and Mortelmans, 2018). This presents challenges for policy makers because as the 'family' now straddles more than one household, and with increasing complexity in family formations, it is difficult for child maintenance schemes to account for all the different permutations of adults and children across households. What different child maintenance schemes do is to determine whether child maintenance responsibilities are 'based on adults' biological relationships with children regardless of residency, or based on the adults' co-resident relationships with children and with new partners, or based on both biological relationships and co-residency' (Meyer and Skinner, 2016: 82). The complexity of family formations and the primacy of biology versus residency varies from country to country and is excellently explored in Meyer et al (2011) and in Meyer and Skinner (2016).

The impacts of child maintenance

There are several impacts, both negative and positive, that result from the payment and receipt of child maintenance. Firstly, receiving child maintenance reduces overall child poverty rates, albeit by a modest amount (Hakovirta, 2011). The modesty of this reduction in rates of child poverty is not caused by the inadequacy of child maintenance, but by the fact that child maintenance is paid to lone mothers and lone mothers are not the primary cause of child poverty, despite what governments and media portray. Furthermore, it has a modest effect overall because compliance with the paying of child maintenance in many countries, particularly the UK, is low (Bradshaw, 2006; Hakovirta, 2011). For lone mothers who do receive child maintenance, however, the risk of poverty reduces and the poverty gap closes to a marked, but varying, degree. For example, it closes the poverty gap 'quite well in the UK (30%), followed by Canada (23.9%) and the USA (20.5%), indicating that child maintenance is quite an important source of income for those receiving it' and 'it lifts most poor children out of poverty in Denmark and Sweden' (Hakovirta, 2011: 259).

The benefit of child maintenance is demonstrated in my longitudinal study of families with one lone mother really valuing the maintenance she receives from her ex-husband. She feels lucky to have it, as it enables her sons to have and to do things they would not be able to afford otherwise. She says: '[The maintenance] is a massive boost for us but I still feel like I'm really struggling even though I get that. So for people that don't get that, God knows how they cope. Really.'

The potential negative consequences of child maintenance is that it may increase the poverty of the non-resident parent as a result of having to make the payments and that it may change their behaviour by discouraging employment, an increase in working hours or a move to a higher paying job (Bradshaw, 2006). Additionally, little notice is taken by policy makers of the effects on children of having to negotiate money, care and time between separated parents (Ridge, 2017). Children know when their father is not paying money to their mother and become frustrated and worried about it (Ridge, 2017). Furthermore, they express their agency by trying to 'manoeuvre around the ongoing tensions between cash and contact' (Ridge, 2017: 92).

One of the major problems with child maintenance, across societies, is the mismatch between its eligibility and its payment/receipt (Zagel and Hübgen, 2018). The international enforcement of child maintenance is a 'challenging and growing problem' fuelled 'by the demographics of increasing rates of mobility and divorce' (Levine, 2017: 617).

(Non-) compliance with child maintenance

Compliance with child maintenance varies from a low of 22 per cent in the UK to a high of 100 per cent in Sweden (Hakovirta, 2011). Other countries fall somewhere in between, for example Canada 38 per cent, Denmark 94 per cent, Finland 77 per cent, Germany 77 per cent, Norway 56 per cent, the US 30 per cent (Hakovirta, 2011) and Australia 55 per cent (Skinner et al, 2017a). Furthermore, when child maintenance is received it is treated differently in the social security entitlements of different countries. Some countries view child maintenance as a substitute for social security and hold back maintenance payments to reduce public expenditure (Skinner et al, 2017b: 495–6). Others, treat child maintenance as a complement to social security and pass on the full value of child maintenance to eligible families (Skinner et al, 2017b: 495–6). The UK and Australia pass on the full amount to families and disregard it as income for the purposes of calculating social security payments, whereas New Zealand passes on 0 per cent and, in the US, it varies from 0 to 100 per cent according to the state (Skinner et al, 2017b).

In order to improve compliance with child maintenance payments, Australia introduced a new, allegedly fairer scheme with stronger enforcement, between 2006 and 2008 (Smyth et al, 2014). Three years later, analysis was undertaken to see if there were any effects on compliance under the new system and it was found that there was little change (Smyth et al, 2014). Smyth et al (2014: 217) concluded that

> [C]hild support compliance is obviously a much more challenging endeavour because of the leg-work involved in tracking and chasing payments in a large, mobile population of clients, some of whom are challenged by a range of personal issues (including economic and educational disadvantage, housing stress, a lack of social supports, mental health issues, safety concerns, and substance use). The line between ability to pay and willingness to pay can thus sometimes be very blurry.

In addition to inability, rather than unwillingness, to pay, child maintenance is mired in further complexity as many separated households are not well off to begin with. Where it is the case that a non-resident parent cannot afford to make financial contributions to their child's upbringing, they may provide in-kind contributions, such as childcare, to allow the resident parent to work or study. This also blurs the picture for rules governing the calculation of child maintenance. However, there are also situations, not discussed in other literature, where a non-resident parent may not be able to look after his children due to lack of affordability. In my study, Jennifer, who has three boys, has an ex-husband who is not in paid employment. Although he usually takes the children for weekends, especially as she works on a Sunday, it comes at a cost for Jennifer due to his not working. Sometimes, he says he cannot take them because he does not have enough food to feed them. On such occasions Jennifer takes up a bag of shopping to enable him to feed the children so that she can go to work:

> 'I was dropping them off and I said could you be able to have them until six on Sunday. And he said, "I don't know because I've not really got stuff in for their tea", so he had them for the weekend and then I, the Sunday morning

before I went into work, I went up to his house and drop stuff in for their tea. And he doesn't pay anything obviously because he's not working.'

On these occasions, there are unintended consequences for Jennifer as she may also not have enough money and has to resort to asking her family for financial help, which is not always freely given or without judgement:

'There's times he springs it on me, on a Thursday night saying, "You'll need to give me food up for them this weekend." And I might not have the money and I have to say to my mum "Could you give me £20 and I'll give you it back on Monday?". And it's like "Oh, Jennifer, not again." Then, when Monday comes, I'm owing my mum money from then. Or she'll say things like, "I'll give you it but don't tell your dad because he'll really stress out", and that is just more stress for me.'

The situation is complex. There is a need to distinguish been having the capacity to pay versus being unwilling to pay and also feeling unable to have or see children due to a lack of funds. This complexity has raised the question whether some so-called 'deadbeat dads' are really just 'dead broke dads'?' (Smyth et al, 2014: 204). Compliance is higher between parents who were previously married, where the non-resident parent is actively involved with their child, and where there is a good relationship between the parents (Skinner, 2013). In fact, the separated parents maintaining a good relationship is the primary factor in compliance with child maintenance, a factor that is difficult to legislate for (Skinner, 2013).

One solution to the problem of non-compliance is for the state to pay child maintenance to the resident parent and for the state to recoup the cost from the non-resident one, where possible. Some countries, for example, guarantee child maintenance to the resident parent by making advance payments where there is an unwillingness to pay, which is why there is 100 per cent receipt in Sweden. Denmark, Finland, Norway, Sweden and Germany all have guaranteed maintenance systems in place (Hakovirta, 2011; Zagel and Hübgen, 2018), whereas the UK does not. If it did, incomes could increase for lone mothers, reducing their risks of being in poverty. At the same time, children would have more financial security and there would be an increased likelihood that they would have a relationship with the non-resident parent (where this is desirable). This would increase equity in money and childcare between parents and between parents and children.

Flipping the thinking

Lone mothers are constructed in the mind of society as being dependent, undeserving and work-avoiding. What is little considered is that they too are providing society with its future citizens and they desire that their children's lives are stable and secure. They too wish their children to achieve happiness and success in adulthood. To flip the thinking, it is worth considering that 'a lone mother's contribution to reproductive labour and social stability deserves to be more fully recognized' (Smith, 1999: 313). In more extreme discourses, lone mothers are seen as deficient parents, feral parents even, as sexually promiscuous and as denying their children a normal childhood. In flipping the thinking, it is worth considering that this type of discourse, which is without factual foundation, serves only to demonise lone mothers and their children, and perpetuate their disadvantage. By affording them dignity and respect, and securing their and their children's financial wellbeing, lone mothers can be appreciated for the difficult jobs they do in the most difficult circumstances. In flipping the thinking on policies to lift lone mothers out of poverty, it is worth rejecting those that seek to change the behaviours of lone mothers but that instead seek equity with other parents For example, child maintenance is not often used as a social policy for lone mothers but is actually the most useful (Zagel and Hübgen, 2018). Finally, lone mothers are seen as a threat to their own children's wellbeing. Yet, my research shows that it is not the state of lone motherhood that is detrimental to child wellbeing, but the impoverished and materially deprived conditions that lone mothers find themselves living in (Treanor, 2018b). In flipping the thinking, it is worth considering that, rather than being responsible for their children's deprivation, lone mothers actually suffer from the same, or worse, poverty and deprivation as their children and that the experience is felt and shared together.

5

Education

We cannot in our kind of society call an educational system adequate if it leaves any large number of people at a level of general knowledge and culture below that required by a participating democracy. (Williams, 1961: 174)

Introduction

Historically, education sought to pass on the best that had been thought and said and there was the belief that that there was educational value in inherited ideas and culture (Paterson, 2015). Education aimed to develop the intellect of all children; the 'freedom to learn for its own sake' was considered a 'fundamental liberal freedom' (Paterson, 2015). It was thought that education would develop universal values, that it would enhance personal characteristics such as sociability and civility, and that it would encourage democratic participation. Traditionally, education was viewed as a preparation for life rather than a preparation for working life (Paterson, 2015).

Education is a compulsory feature of childhood in all affluent modern societies. The pursuit of education takes up a significant proportion of children's time and forms a large component of their lives. Education is a constant for all children. It is a shared experience that has the potential to provide a space where children are welcomed and nurtured; to enable children to acquire knowledge and skills; to instil confidence and self-esteem; to be an equaliser of opportunities in the present; and a leveller of outcomes in the future. Education is about all of this and more. Education can create active and involved citizens; facilitate democratic engagement; and develop the intellectual rigour and critical capacities that will lead to success throughout childhood and into adulthood. It is through education that social and economic inequalities can be attenuated and gaps narrowed. Unfortunately, however, education can often be yet another seat of inequality, an inhibitor rather than a facilitator of opportunity and outcomes (Reay, 2018). Despite its transformative potential, education continues to fail those who stand to benefit most.

We know that poor children are more likely to fail in school but there is little understanding as to why they fail. When there is no difference in academic ability, poorer children are less likely to gain higher level qualifications than wealthier children (Crompton, 2008). Assumptions about why this is the case often pertain to the personal attributes and behaviours of a child and their family; for example: innate ability, genetic endowment, poor parenting, a poverty of aspirations, a culture of poverty and disaffection. These assumptions lay the blame for educational failure at the door of poor children and their families. They also suggest that such children and families lack the characteristics of success and so are in some way deficient. Such assumptions ignore the role and responsibility that every society has towards their young people and their education. The focus on the alleged deficiencies of the poor denies the actual deficiencies of the systems that create poverty. The study of poverty has often focused on studying, or changing, the characteristics of the poor rather than studying poverty itself (O'Connor, 2001). A change in focus would allow us to understand how the political, economic and institutional structures, such as education, create and perpetuate poverty and how policy decisions shape the distribution of power and wealth in our society (O'Connor, 2001). To flip the thinking on child poverty we need to understand and change the political, economic and institutional structures, outlined by O'Connor (2001), that lead to inequality rather than narrowly focusing on changing the characteristics and behaviours of the poor.

Although school is of vital importance to children living in poverty, many of those children are unsettled, undervalued and underachieving. Access to high quality education is unequal from the outset and poor children often experience difficulties in assimilating. Many children living in poverty find school intrinsically alienating due to the inherently middle-class culture of education, which presents barriers to their full participation (Gillies, 2006). The everyday lives of children living in poverty often differ from those of middle-class children and these differences emerge in school settings (Ridge, 2011). School is argued to be 'predicated on a different set of values, namely, individualism, competitiveness and access to private spaces (rooms to study in and computer workstations to access the internet) and not communal space' (Ivinson et al, 2016). It is a culture that can lead to 'insufferable pressure' on children living in poverty (Ivinson et al, 2016). Yet, children living in poverty do strive to belong in a school culture that may be intrinsically alienating to them.

The adolescent stage of life is critical to support the transition to early adulthood. Where this is disrupted it can become nigh on impossible for young people to get back on track with their education. Being excluded from school is especially detrimental to young people: this is particularly true of boys, and children from a black and minority ethnic (BME) background, who are more likely to be excluded from school. In England, the exclusion rate in schools for African/Caribbean/black pupils was 51.9 per 1,000 pupils compared to 42.2 per 1,000 pupils for white pupils in 2012/13 (EHRC, 2015). Being excluded from school is related to complex needs in adulthood. For example, in Bramley et al's (2015) work on adults with severe and multiple deprivations (SMDs), of those with the following three SMDs – homelessness, offending and substance misuse – almost half had been excluded from school and almost two thirds had truanted. Non-engagement with school through exclusion or truanting should be a warning light that all is not well in a child's life and ought to be a point of intervention in order to prevent a poor transition to adulthood.

Education is of vital importance to poor children and the relationship between education and future income is strong. For children living in poverty a good education can provide opportunities to avoid poverty in adulthood. However, it is an aim that fails to take account of children's experiences of education during childhood and so fails to take account of the factors in childhood that can inhibit or facilitate achieving a good education. How children experience education is important as all children are not treated equally. Yet, despite this, children living in poverty say that school is important to them, for both social and academic reasons, and that their wellbeing in school depends on their peer, pupil–teacher and parental relationships.

The remainder of this chapter begins by exploring the cost of a school day and how education is experienced by a child living in poverty. It looks at some of the parental factors that are suggested to influence a child's education, such as the so-called 'poverty of aspiration'. It also explores popular teacher misunderstandings of the relationship between poverty and education, such as the personal deficiency of children and their families. It concludes by looking at the policy responses of affluent societies, which aim to close the attainment gap between advantaged and disadvantaged children and discusses why we need to flip the thinking on education for children living in poverty.

School costs

Although education is notionally free in most countries there are associated costs to school. Children living in poverty are frequently disciplined for not having the right equipment and teachers often do not recognise the huge efforts poor children make just to participate in school at all (Spencer, 2015). Educational resources such as a computer at home, access to the Internet, a dictionary, a calculator and a fully equipped pencil case are among the increasingly necessary education-related materials that poor children cannot afford to have (Elsley, 2014). The UK has the third highest levels of inequality among 24 OECD countries in access to basic educational resources, with only Greece and Slovakia scoring more poorly (UNICEF, 2010: 6).

In the UK the cost of school uniforms, shoes and bags is significant. Poor parents report that buying these items for their children, especially when they have several children, is very difficult (Treanor, 2018a). Children living in poverty are often not able to come into school at all because they do not have the requisite uniform or right colour of shoes (Treanor, 2018a). Such children are acutely aware of the costs associated with school, more so than advantaged children. They worry about how their parents are going to afford school items and about being bullied by their peers for not having items such as the right clothes (Horgan, 2007, 2009). Children feel ashamed and are stigmatised for not having what is required of them in the school setting. In my longitudinal study of families living in poverty, serendipity in the form of bad weather helped one lone mother to manage the costs of her son's torn shoes without revealing that the only footwear he had in the interim were wellington boots. This was the factor that appeared most important to Fiona, that Robert would not be shamed by having no shoes while she saved for a new pair. She says,

> 'Robert (12) come in, just at the winter, just after Christmas it was, and it was snowing, and he come in with his school shoes with no sole on them … and I was like "How am I going to manage to get his school shoes?" – you can't put money aside for savings because you just don't have any left … there's no way you can go and buy something extravagant … So it was quite good, because, after he lost the sole off his shoes, it was snowing so he went to school in his wellies. So it worked out in my favour, it gave me a couple of weeks to put a wee bit of money back to then buy him school shoes … You can't plan for unforeseen circumstances.'

As well as the costs of clothing and shoes, there are problems for poor children in affording trips and activities. Children and young people's participation in school activities and trips is beneficial to their learning and to their social and cultural development (Hirsch,

2007). Where children and young people cannot afford to access these opportunities, they are disadvantaged on multiple levels, not just in their lack of full participation in school. Parents are often put in the painful situation of not allowing their children to go on school trips, especially larger residential ones, which serves to ensure their children's exclusion. Sometimes, parents tell their children half truths about why they cannot have or do something in an attempt to hide the extent of their financial situation (McKendrick et al, 2003). Often, when parents have not made this difficult decision, children take it for them, exercising their own agency, and either hiding information about trips or being adamant that they do not want to go (Treanor, 2018a). In both instances, children and parents attempt to hide, or mask, their poverty. In my study of families living in poverty, a father of a large family, Jamie, has difficulty in meeting the costs of trips for multiple children. His children pretend they do not want to go on a week-long whole-year residential camp so that he will not feel bad about not being able to afford it. Jamie explains,

> 'For example, the twins ... when they were leaving primary seven and there's a P7 camp, and there was no discount for the fact that we've got two children, so I think for both of them to go it would have cost us about four hundred and odd pounds so it ended up I think, in truth, that the two of them kidded on [pretended] they didn't want to go, because they knew how expensive it was going to be for us. We basically just couldn't afford to send two of them. So they missed out on that.'

When asked how the twins felt about it, Jamie said: 'They made out they were all right about it but they were more gutted when their pals come back and started telling them the stories of things they got up to and things like that and they weren't able to go.' Jamie said he knew that the twins were just pretending they didn't want to go but that there was nothing he could do about it. He did suggest to the school that there could be a discount for multiple children in a family, or that they could do some class activities to raise funds and reduce the cost for everyone, but nothing came of these ideas.

Masking of poverty

The hiding or masking of poverty emerges in other studies. McKendrick et al (2003) report parents attempting to 'mask' their poverty and Patrick's (2016) study gives the example of the benefit claimant seeking to pass herself off as a non-benefit claimant. Patrick (2016) describes this as the 'concealment of a stigmatised identity', a classic strategy for coping with stigma (Goffman, 1990). The hiding or masking of poverty is particularly pertinent to children's schooling as children and their parents make great efforts not to appear poor in front of other pupils, parents and teachers. Furthermore, children and their parents collude in the concealment of their poverty in the school setting (Treanor, 2018a). As well as trying to avoid stigma and shame, parents often hide the reality of their circumstances to schools out of fear of unwanted service intervention (EIS, 2016). For children, such attempts to conceal their stigmatised identity, while trying to fit in at school, can result in difficult and damaging conflicts (Treanor, 2018a).

Such masking or concealment of poverty can add an additional layer of complexity when considering steps to prevent and mitigate the effects of poverty on children's schooling and their parents' engagement with their education. This can result in: teachers not recognising when some families are struggling financially; parents being unwilling to engage with schools for fear of being caught out and exposed; and teachers not understanding the reasons for parental reluctance to engage with their children's education. There may be a multitude of factors that a family is hiding, for example job loss, parental separation or even low levels of parental literacy and numeracy.

Poor children's experiences of education

Children living in poverty are disadvantaged from the time they first start school as they are less likely to have had the same early childhood experiences as middle-class children. Growing up in a middle-class milieu that emphasises early social, cultural and educational experiences privileges middle-class children by making them ready to embrace more of the same in a formal education setting. To children living in poverty, this milieu is entirely unfamiliar and may actually run contrary to what has been expected of them at home. Poor children have to learn a new way of being and doing within this new environment called 'Education' before they can successfully access and negotiate it and this places them at a distinct early disadvantage (Evans, 2006). Middle-class children already have this knowledge and understanding at the entry to formal education.

Younger children living in poverty tend to be more positive towards school, however, as they get older their experiences become more negatively charged (Horgan, 2007). As children grow older, discomfort with the school environment is more likely to manifest as disruptive behaviours that can lead either to exclusion or self-exclusion through truancy. Children as young as ten years old are reported as beginning to disengage from their education (Horgan, 2007). Paradoxically, however, children living in poverty also say that they value school and, for those who experience additional family adversities, such as domestic violence or parental substance misuse, school can be a haven and a place of stability and security (Crowley and Vulliamy, 2007). This makes the experience of school for poor children diverse and conflicted: sometimes they are very good, however, for the majority of poor children, poverty has a corrosive and damaging impact on school careers (Ridge, 2011).

Children living in poverty complain that they are frequently shouted at in school by teachers, whereas more advantaged children do not report this experience (Crowley and Vulliamy, 2007; Horgan, 2009). Children who attend schools in the most disadvantaged areas report the highest levels of shouting by teachers (Horgan, 2007; Sutton et al, 2007). Ironically, poor children are often shouted at for factors relating to their poverty, for example for not being able to afford the costs associated with schooling. The experience of being shouted at in school for poor children is widespread and, although being shouted at in school negatively affects girls' wellbeing, it is boys in particular who say that this makes them hate school and not want to go (Horgan, 2007).

Poverty of aspirations

Children's less successful progress in education is often blamed on their, and/or their parents', low aspirations. This has become known as the 'poverty of aspirations'. Raising aspirations has become a key educational policy driver across affluent societies. It is widely regarded as a critical lever with which to close the attainment gap between children and young people of high and low socioeconomic backgrounds (Zipin et al, 2015). Yet, there is little discussion as to what constitutes a 'high' aspiration. Governments' policies discuss high aspirations within divergent pathways such as higher education, training and apprenticeships, and further education or vocational college; whereas schools and educators tend to assume that a high aspiration means progression to higher education exclusively. Although there is discrepancy in the definition of high aspirations, parents and children are still deemed to be deficient in them.

Children living in poverty do have high aspirations for themselves, although the jobs they aspire to are often of the gendered variety common in their areas, such as hairdressers or mechanics (Horgan, 2007). Often, 'aspirations expressed by young people reflect the expectations and constraints inherent within their setting, rather than a free choice of desired outcome' (St Clair and Benjamin, 2011: 502). Children do not start off with low expectations; when they are younger they have the same hopes and dreams as all children; however, their confidence in their ability to attain their aspirations becomes attenuated over time. Aspirations, even in communities struggling with poverty, are very high – the missing element is the knowledge of how to make these aspirations concrete and obtainable (St Clair et al, 2013). 'The debate on "aspiration" constructs young people from disadvantaged backgrounds as deficient, conflates economic and social equality discourses and individualises structural problems' (Spohrer, 2011). It also ignores and negates the broader inequalities that govern 'who goes where' and, instead, turns (lack of) success into a function of 'individual effort' and 'self-management' (Allen, 2014: 761).

Schools and policy makers put a lot of effort into 'raising aspirations' to increase achievement among disadvantaged pupils; however, this is unlikely to narrow the educational attainment gap because it is based on false assumptions about low aspirations. This creates a problem: if there is misunderstanding of the causes of educational inequality then any measures proposed to mitigate it will be misdirected. It is an approach that promotes 'cultural and psychological explanations and solutions to persisting inequalities' (Spohrer, 2011: 58) and results in measures to boost and raise aspirations that are mainly targeted at changing attitudes (Spohrer, 2011: 57). The real challenge for disadvantaged young people is sustaining their aspirations across adolescence and being supported to achieve them.

The idea that low aspirations on the part of poor parents are responsible for the lower educational attainment of their children permeates political, media and educational discourses (Holloway and Pimlott-Wilson, 2011; Sosu, 2014). This has an effect on how teachers and school staff engage with children and parents living in poverty (Marsh et al, 2017). Yet, parents are repeatedly shown to have high hopes and aspirations for their children; in particular, they desire that their children achieve more than they themselves have (Treanor, under review). While there are differences between the types of aspiration held by parents, for example apprenticeship versus higher education by parental social class, there is no lack of aspiration per se (Treanor, under review). In every study of families living in poverty I have ever undertaken I have never met a parent who did not want more for their child than they themselves had. One lone parent with five children from my 2009 study with Barnardos (Harris et al, 2009) says: 'I try to instil in my kids that school is the most important years of your life, listen to what you're being taught because it will affect your life forever', and 'I would like for her to do really well, to go on to university ... do what I didn't get to do.'

There is the idea that parents living in poverty, when asked about aspirations, give higher priority to their child being happy than to their educational achievement. Unfortunately, most of the existing research does not explore what parents living in poverty mean by 'happiness' nor does it reflect on what children would need in life to be happy. In my study of families, one lone parent who has a son with mental health difficulties equates happiness to freedom and that freedom could be had by material security, in other words by a good job, which arguably stems from high aspirations in education and employment. She says,

> 'I want him to go out and live his life and just experience things in life. I'm always saying to him, "I want you to make the best of your life. If you can get a good job with good money..." I want him to have freedom. I've never had freedom. I've never been able to just say, "Right, I'm going to do this, I'm going to do that." I want him to be able to have that. I want him to have a life. To live it how he wants to live it.'

While poor parents express high aspirations for their children they face multiple barriers arising from structural inequalities, gender inequalities, class inequalities, the relative ineffectiveness of their efforts, and their lack of knowledge of higher levels of education and professions. It is not low aspirations that prevent poor parents from helping their children to succeed in education but an inability to translate their aspirations into reality (Sosu, 2014; Sosu et al, 2014).

Poor parents' experiences of education

Often parents living in poverty had poor educational experiences and outcomes themselves and feel intimidated by, wary of and unconfident about facilitating or participating in their child's education (Harris et al, 2009; Sime and Sheridan, 2014). This does not prevent them from valuing their children's education and having high hopes and aspirations for them, however. In my research a lone parent of three children, Fiona, has been the carer for her disabled mother since she was a child, often missing school because of her caring responsibilities. School was a harsh place for her and she faced bullying from both peers and teachers. This does not mean she does not want the best for her children educationally. She says,

> 'I'd like my own kids to stay on and get an education, but I just couldn't hack it. I couldn't stay in the school because I didn't like it and I didn't like the teachers. I really didn't like the teachers. My kids will never know that, but I didn't like the teachers.' (Harris et al, 2009)

This corresponds to Irwin and Elley's (2011: 493) finding that disadvantage in itself does not undermine hopeful action in respect of education. For parents like Fiona, any contact with school can be stress-inducing and perceived as a judgement on their parenting. Yet, we know that when parents become more involved in their children's education, it improves children's behavioural, social and educational outcomes (Sime and Sheridan, 2014). It can also have a positive impact on parents themselves by increasing their confidence in participating in their child's education and leading to more positive attitudes towards education generally.

Parents living in poverty are more likely to lack the cultural and linguistic practices required to engage effectively with teachers and schools (Lareau, 1987). Parents living in poverty very much feel that their children's schooling is important, but they do not have the skills for optimal involvement (Lareau, 1987, Bodovski, 2010). The culture of education and schooling is unfamiliar and intimidating to parents living in poverty. This lack of familiarity with the milieu inhibits the effective and confident engagement with school. Working-class parents value education no less than middle-class parents, but depend on the teacher to educate their child (Crompton, 2008). Middle-class parents, however, have no such deference to professionals and see education as a shared enterprise (Crompton, 2008). Parents living in poverty are also more likely to have poorer educational skills and therefore to have a lower occupational status, with less flexibility in their work hours and limited time and resources to spend on their children's learning. Poor parents are more likely to have less flexible employment with longer working hours and poorer conditions of employment, including a lack of paid time off to attend school events and consultations (Lareau, 1987). This reduces the time, energy and capacity to engage more fully with school or support their child's education at home.

Wealthier parents, in contrast, are advantaged in that they are skilled in the roles and functions required of them by schools. They are able to take advantage of the education system due to their higher levels of educational, cultural, social, economic and emotional capital. The culture of education is set by the higher social classes for the higher social classes based on higher social class modes of communication, engagement, skills and knowledge. The mothers in higher social class families are more likely to work part-time in more flexible jobs, or not to work at all, which permit them to have a greater focus on their children's schooling (Lareau, 1987). They therefore have more time and resources to make full use of their skills and capacities to engage with their children's education:

> The parents of upper-class children are supposed to act, and usually do act, to make sure that their children are able to maintain their class position. They have income resources to nurture their children in comfortable surroundings, and to provide high quality private or public schools. They have acquired the education and cultural habits through which they supplement the school's education with knowledge, skills, tastes and expectations that socialize their children into what others of the class admire, or find valuable. In their interactions with teachers and local politicians they are treated with particular respect because of the resources they can mobilize, or because of their knowledge, demeanour and position. For all these reasons the road to high status, power and affluence is much smoother for these children than those of a low-income single mother without a high school education. (Young, 2001: 13)

It is argued that governments are failing people living in poverty because the systems that lead to educational success favour the children of educated families (Teese and Lamb, 2007). Governments control the education system, which, across affluent societies, is increasingly marketised, with a focus on parental choice, the quality of individual schools and the outcomes of individual children, as measured by standardised tests and league tables. This marketised, choice-based approach to education sets children living in poverty at an immediate disadvantage as their parents are much less likely to have the knowledge and skills necessary to fully engage with school choice. This makes it more difficult for poorer families to access high-quality education compared to their wealthier counterparts and leads to a reinforcing and widening of educational inequalities between advantaged and disadvantaged children. Indeed, the educational reforms that governments have developed to partially redress disadvantage, such as the creation of new curricula, new subject options, increased use of in-class assessments, allowing greater choice of school catchments, devolving management to schools themselves, have actually delivered 'more flexibility and mobility to better off families and produced more isolation and segregation of poorer families' (Teese and Lamb, 2007: 294).

Teachers' (mis)understandings

The (mis)understanding that the causes of poverty-related educational underachievement lie with pupils or their parents as individuals, rather than within 'institutional structures and practices', are found to be held by teachers and student teachers (Thompson et al, 2016: 2017). Such misunderstanding leads to their falling back on negative stereotypes of children and parents (Thompson et al, 2016: 2017). As poverty is not usually a core subject in initial teacher training, nor in continuing professional development, teachers are often uninitiated in the differences between the causes and consequences of poverty. This leads some teachers to express views linking poverty with 'parental values, choices and financial skills' (Spencer, 2015: 45). This makes them more likely to display attitudes that cause (unintended) exclusion for poor children within schools. When teachers, through their own lack of poverty knowledge, problematise the behaviours of poor children, it can trigger low wellbeing, frustration, disengagement, truancy and exclusion. Yet, teachers and student teachers, unless otherwise taught, cannot be expected to understand the causes and consequences of poverty and its effects on children's education (Ivinson et al, 2016). This suggests that educating the educators on these issues is an essential part of alleviating the effects of poverty on children's education.

The high levels of teachers' shouting reported by children living in poverty has been attributed to the stress teachers face working in highly disadvantaged schools. Schools in such areas are more likely to have children with welfare needs relating to adverse family situations that make the children unhappy, angry or anxious (Lupton, 2005). Teachers report struggling to deal with issues such as hungry children, behavioural problems and angry parents and they feel they take on a caring or social work role for a significant minority of children who live in poverty (Lupton, 2005). Teachers report that battling the effects of poverty puts additional strain on them (Ivinson et al, 2017) and has a very real and damaging impact on the quality of teaching and learning (Lupton, 2005; Horgan, 2009; Lupton and Hempel-Jorgensen, 2012). These additional welfare needs make teaching in the most disadvantaged schools more challenging and stressful, and makes the atmosphere more highly emotionally charged (Lupton, 2005). Such a fraught atmosphere can result in damaging teacher–pupil interactions, such as shouting, which further alienate already struggling children. Additionally, teachers of children facing these adverse circumstances blame parents for many of the problems their children face (Horgan, 2011). In spite of this, although teachers often display misunderstandings towards the causes and consequences of poverty, they do report being keen to reduce stigma for children living in poverty and to do more to ensure they have a successful education (Horgan, 2007). It is vital for the inclusion and success of poor children's education that some teachers' negative assumptions are supportively challenged and their desire to improve children's outcomes encouraged.

To reduce education-related problems for children living in poverty I have been part of work to build an understanding and knowledge of poverty for education professionals in Scotland. I have been part of the City of Edinburgh Council's 1 in 5 project (named after the proportion of children living in poverty in Edinburgh, an otherwise very affluent city). This project takes a multifaceted approach to tackling the effects of child poverty in schools and targets different groups within schools. The project has been successful in: highlighting and reducing stigma; scrutinising the impact of school policies and practices, including school-related costs, on children's attainment and school experiences; providing training on the impacts and causes of child poverty; and developing resources to support schools in their efforts to mitigate poverty at the school level. It does so by working with teaching and non-teaching staff, pupils and parents to learn about the impacts of poverty and how to tackle them locally. As part of this project, we developed a 'school equity framework' to advise schools on assuring equal access and full participation in education for all pupils (City of Edinburgh Council, 2018).

Policy

There are many policies that relate to education and to educational disadvantage. There is insufficient space to consider even a few of them. Instead, this section will focus on the current policy focus across several affluent nations as regards children living in socioeconomic disadvantage: the gap in educational attainment compared to their more advantaged counterparts. This policy aims to raise the attainment of disadvantaged children and to reduce or close the gap in attainment between advantaged and disadvantaged children. The expectation is that this will ensure they achieve a successful transition to a positive destination post-school, for example, into higher education (McKinney, 2014).

The most worrying aspect of the attainment gap between advantaged and disadvantaged pupils is that it does not weaken, but is said to widen, throughout the school years, providing evidence to support the idea that schools reinforce rather than reduce inequalities between social groups (Teese and Lamb, 2007: 302). This widening of the attainment gap is attributed to the less time in their early childhood poorer children spend on activities that stimulate cognitive growth compared to their advantaged peers, that is the family investment model (Teese and Lamb, 2007: 302). This means that poor children in schools are often in permanent catch-up mode while their better-off counterparts are usually in extension mode (Teese and Lamb, 2007: 302).

One of the difficulties with initiatives to close the attainment gap between rich and poor children is that they do not address what happens at the higher end of the socioeconomic spectrum. Wealthier parents use their superior resources to locate themselves close to the best schools, to purchase private education and/or to purchase extensive tutoring for their children. This is in addition to the education they themselves are able to offer their children. Furthermore, more advantaged parents are successful in harnessing educational opportunities for their children that are intended to improve the outcomes of less-advantaged children. So, policies designed to close the educational gap may succeed in raising the attainment of advantaged children more than that of disadvantaged children, thus potentially increasing the gap.

Another difficulty with initiatives to close the attainment gap is the rise of social investment policies aimed at increasing the outcomes of poor children. The market in the form of social investment is now fully active in children's education across high-income countries. Social investment initiatives, which have to balance using investors' money in initiatives with proven success, with their ease and cost of delivery and potential for financial return on investments, will not necessarily lead to the most successful outcomes for children living in poverty. Such policies will mostly succeed in plucking the low-lying fruit – those children living in poverty who are already accessing and engaged in education but who need a bit of support to take full advantage of it. They can thus only enjoy partial success in raising the attainment of poor children.

A further difficulty with initiatives to close the attainment gap lies in its exclusive focus on the educational attainment of children living in poverty and not on other factors that would indirectly support attainment and would also lead to a fuller engagement with and enjoyment of education. In a study of children and adolescents in schools in Scotland, it was found the most important factor to support their participation, influence change, and do well in their education were positive pupil–pupil and pupil–teacher relationships (Mannion et al, 2015). Furthermore, the young people 'felt that relations among pupils, teachers, and their communities needed to involve power sharing and be caring, respectful, trusting, and purposeful to ensure achievement and attainment was supported' (Mannion et al, 2015 2).

This brings us on to an important and often overlooked aspect of inequality, that of *distributive* versus *relational* (in)equality. Distributive inequality is concerned with the 'terms of the distributions of attributes of its individual members that are in some sense ranked: individuals differ – i.e. are unequal – in their incomes, wealth, standards of consumption, the desirability of their occupations, their educational attainments, the extent of their social and cultural participation, etc.' (Goldthorpe, 2010: 732). In the context of this chapter, distributive equality is where children living in poverty have the material resources distributed to them or their families to ensure their full participation in school, for example in relation to the costs of the school day. Relational equality, in contrast, is concerned with 'a deeper level, in terms of social relations in the context of which individuals are in some sense advantaged or disadvantaged ... [relational inequality is] inherent in prevailing forms of social relationships that have in some degree an institutional basis' (Goldthorpe, 2010: 732–3). In the context of this chapter, relational equality forces us to think in greater depth about the nature of the relationships between children, parents and teachers pertaining to ideas such as respect and dignity.

Policy usually focuses on the drive to achieve distributive equality in relation to poverty and education. However, it is not enough merely to absent costs from schools and not to focus on children's feelings of belonging and being valued. Relational equality therefore is equally important. This can begin to be achieved when educational professionals become informed on the causes and consequences of poverty and seek to promote dignity and respect in their schools and classrooms. It is important to educate the educators on the often unintentional yet pernicious nature of stigma, on understanding that for some children living in poverty, especially those facing other adversities, the very fact that they have succeeded in coming to school is to be recognised, and that children living in poverty should be valued and respected for who they are and what they bring to the school environment. Children themselves assert that the most important factor in school for them is positive relationships with peers and teachers (Mannion et al, 2015).

In my work with the City of Edinburgh Council on the 1 in 5 project, there was a focus on not only removing the negatives, such as school costs and stigma, but also to promote dignity and respect to enhance children's wellbeing in education with the understanding that this can help to reduce educational inequalities across the board, not just in future attainment. When attention is predominantly given to distributive equality and policies that focus narrowly on the attainment gap then the more core aspects of the relationship between child poverty and education can be overlooked, that is creating equality in relationships within school. Winter (2018: 349) suggests that we do this by considering the attitudes we communicate in our interactions in schools and work towards communicating empathy, unconditional positive regard and congruence.

Flipping the thinking

This chapter has set out how education has the potential to be a passport out of poverty for low-income children. It sets out how political understandings of the links between education and poverty drive public opinion on who is responsible for poor children's poorer educational outcomes. The deficit model, where children and parents, and schools, are blamed for poor children's low attainment, leads to stigma and shame. It argues how the purpose of education has become a unidimensional focus on future employment to the detriment of the broader education of all children; that education is an increasingly marketised commodity that benefits more advantaged children and parents; that the culture of education is alienating; and that the intrinsic inaccessibility of education precludes full participation for children living in poverty.

Under the deficit model, parents and children are labelled problematic and schools and teachers are labelled ineffectual. When these ideas of deficiency are embraced by mainstream political thinking and the media, they become concrete in the public imagination. Public (mis)understandings of the causes and consequences of poverty, and of poverty's effect on education, form the dominant discourse. The consequence of this for children living in poverty is that they have to endure first the inequity of poverty and education and then the iniquity of stigma and shame.

Educational debates are often focused on issues of social class or group identity (such as ethnicity). One solution to improving children living in poverty's poorer educational attainment lies in realising that these polarities are not mutually exclusive. For example, the focus should not lie in either class or group identities when these two intersect in ways that can multiply and lead to accumulated disadvantage, for example the intersection of gender, ethnicity, migration status, religion and poverty. These groupings do not operate in isolation.

How the relationship between poverty and education is understood is crucial to the policy solutions employed to repair it. Using the deficit model to explain poor children's poorer educational outcomes leads to policy solutions that aim to overcome assumed parental or child personal shortfalls. Any policy solutions that start from a premise of deficiency, though they may be well-intentioned, will be counterproductive. A foundation for action premised on child and family deficiency cannot tackle the drivers associated with poverty and education. By not targeting the structural and wider inequalities that influence the relationship between poverty and education, the opportunity for effective early intervention is lost. Furthermore, the resulting policies and practices will intervene at the point at which educational inequalities are advanced, and entrenched, and may therefore be too late.

As regards the so-called poverty of aspirations, certain knowledge is assumed by politicians and teachers. There is assumed knowledge of the usually middle-class trajectories supported by strong engagement with education and, in, for example, university study, gap year travel, social networks and gaining work experience through internships. It may be that children living in poverty have never heard talk of university, will never have travelled, will have no social networks to facilitate work experience and, even if they did, would not be able to support an unpaid (or low-paid) internship in a location far from home. Children living in poverty usually have limited knowledge and experience of higher-level occupations and education. They often lack the knowledge of what the possibilities are and almost certainly lack the knowledge of how to achieve them. That children living in poverty's (and their parents') aspirations are bounded by their experiences should be more clearly understood by politicians and educational professionals. It is the job of education to expand young people's horizons. That is why a broader curriculum, one rooted in both academic subjects and vocational training, is especially important to children living in poverty. It is also the job of education, once horizons have been expanded, to help children and young people sustain and realise their aspirations.

Education is critical to mitigating the effects of poverty, but it is important to understand that inclusion in the education system is not the same for all children. Rather, it is socially patterned, privileges the middle classes and brings with it costs that are often unseen and poorly understood by educators but keenly felt by children and families living in poverty. For some children, especially those growing up with adverse circumstances in addition to living in poverty, school is very much valued as a place of routine and calm (Hooper, 2007).

As regards inequality in education, there is polarisation between ideas of distributional equality (material equality) or relational equality (recognition and the valuing of group identity). By increasing the importance of relational inequality, by promoting respect and dignity, these will become self-generating and lead to children living in poverty feeling a greater sense of value, acceptance and belonging within school. This, in turn, may increase their desire and ability to become fully active members of the school. In flipping the thinking, it is not enough to reduce stigma; there ought to be an active promotion of dignity and respect. To improve children and young people living in poverty's educational attainment and to close the attainment gap, there needs to be a focus on both relational equality and distributive equality. This would mean devising policies that foster strong school–family–child relationships that would have an associated positive effect on children's schooling. To flip the thinking with teachers, it would be useful for teachers, instead of asking 'what can I do to make poor children value their education?' to ask instead 'what can I do to show the children living in poverty that I value them in my classroom?' The lack of dignity and respect that children living in poverty (and their families) feel from some teachers is a barrier to poor children's education.

In flipping the thinking, it is desirable for those in positions of power in the education system, for example politicians and teachers, to look beyond what they think they are seeing, to move beyond assumptions, and to challenge their own thinking about children and parents living in poverty. For example, children and parents living in poverty go to great lengths to mask their poverty, especially from teachers and other pupils and parents. It is likely then that teachers will not know who is experiencing financial hardship unless there are associated adverse circumstances. In this way, because teachers are most familiar with experiences of poverty that have associated family welfare issues, they conflate poverty with family problems. This is why focusing on teachers' understanding of the causes and consequences of poverty is a good start. Additionally, where poor parents are reluctant to become involved with the school or their child's education, they are criticised for not being interested in their child's success in school. By flipping the thinking, teachers can question what may lie beneath parental reluctance: What were their own experiences of school like? Are they nervous? Do they lack confidence or social skills? Do they have low levels of numeracy or literacy that they are desperate to hide? There are many factors that govern the relationship between poverty and education and, by flipping the thinking and turning assumptions on their head, new understandings can emerge that will facilitate the full inclusion of children living in poverty in education.

6

In and out of work

Full employment means jobs 'at fair wages, of such a kind, and so located that the unemployed can reasonably be expected to take them.' (Beveridge, 1944: 18)

Introduction

This chapter explores the complex relationship between child poverty and families being in and out of work, the role of employment in lifting families out of poverty and how low-quality, low-security employment poses a threat to children and families rather than a route out of poverty. With the dominant status and values attached to employment, and the increase across affluent societies of labour market activation, this chapter highlights the challenges faced by children and families situated at the insecure, fragile end of the labour market. It challenges media and political rhetoric and assumptions about 'skivers' and 'strivers', asking what the impact of these public, corrosive attitudes and perceptions might be for children in their everyday lives. By examining the relationship between employment policies, labour market activation and welfare conditionality it highlights the impact of state policies, regulations and expectations on the everyday lives of children through the governance of their parents.

The chapter shows how children and families who find themselves pressurised into low-income insecure employment can experience considerable stress, financial insecurity and instability. It uses evidence from qualitative longitudinal studies to reveal the importance of time and timing in relation to transitions to work and sustainability within work. It brings children's voices and experiences into the centre of an analysis of employment in relation to child poverty. There are many actions by governments that interplay with employment and unemployment: in particular, this chapter looks at in-work benefits, labour market activation and welfare conditionality.

The dominant status and values attached to employment

Employment has long been presented as *the* route out of poverty. Although employment can produce a route out of poverty for some families, and indeed it remains the best hope of doing so, for many families it remains a hope, as employment without adequate reward and security can produce its own problems and uncertainties for families. The dominant political discourse suggests that, if only those currently not working would find a job then their worries, and their poverty, would be over. The assumption that employment is always advantageous to child poverty goes unquestioned and politicians express a high degree of certitude that this is so. Finding paid work is assumed to have transformative potential and blame for a failure to do so is laid at the door of out-of-work families themselves. This work-first approach to policy-making and to poverty alleviation is also common in the US, where it has led to a reduction in college and university enrolment for people living in poverty, in particular lone parents (Shaw et al, 2009; Kim, 2012). Yet, people living in poverty, in particular lone parents, have lower levels of education than the rest of the population and a post-secondary education results in greater access to jobs and to higher earnings in future, even for the more disadvantaged groups (Kim, 2012). Unfortunately, in the UK, there is particularly poor access to education for those living in poverty.

In the eyes of recent UK government administrations, not being in paid work is viewed as a problem of individual failings. Government policy constructs unemployed people as problematic populations who 'need tough interventions if their behaviour is to be changed such that they become working and productive members of mainstream society' (Patrick, 2012: 5). The Department for Work and Pensions in the UK asserted that 'the failure to find paid work can be explained largely in individual terms due to a "culture of worklessness"' (DWP, 2012: 38 cited in Bailey, 2015: 83) and George Osborne, former UK Chancellor of the Exchequer, said in a speech at the Conservative party conference in 2012: 'Where is the fairness, we ask, for the shift-worker, leaving home in the dark hours of the early morning, who looks up at the closed blinds of their next door neighbour sleeping off a life on benefits?' (NewStatesman, 2012). This disdain for those who are out of paid work matters. If people are repeatedly told that those without paid work are shirkers and skivers, relaxing while the hard-working taxpayers, the strivers, fund their indolence, then this breeds harsh and negative views, which in turn has consequences for the families and children of those not in paid work. In the first instance it legitimises the view of the unemployed, especially those with children, as feckless and lazy. This view of the unemployed filters down into communities, even among those experiencing similar deprivation. It divides people and communities into those who are working (albeit on poverty wages), from those who cannot work for reasons such as disability, and from those who are deemed too lazy to work. In essence, it pits neighbour against neighbour. This has a corrosive effect on communities and a deeply stigmatising and shaming impact on out-of-work families and children. Such is the stigma attached to poverty that those experiencing it refute it and lay the blame at the door of their as-poor neighbours (Shildrick and MacDonald, 2013). This division between the 'strivers' and the 'skivers' is also problematic because it ignores the dynamics of poverty, and of employment, for those on the low-pay, no-pay cycle. There is a high level of movement between the states of working and not working and, furthermore, those who are in work receive benefits just as their unemployed neighbours do (Bailey, 2015).

The income derived from paid work is purported to have a different value to that derived from out-of-work benefits, assigning more than a financial perspective to income and employment (Bailey, 2015). As well as reducing the incidence of poverty, having paid work is believed to confer other wide-ranging benefits associated with having a sense of purpose and a social role (Bailey, 2015). For example, being in employment is said to bring individual and societal-level advantages. It is said to give meaning and value to the person carrying out the paid work and to support their participation and social integration in wider society (Bailey, 2015). Through improving individual material resources and bringing meaning and structure to individual lives, employment is seen as effecting a range of physical and mental health benefits (Bailey, 2015). Yet, while unemployment has been shown to unequivocally impair people's physical and mental health, it is increasingly recognised that poor quality employment may be as, or more, damaging to health than unemployment (Butterworth et al, 2011). Butterworth et al (2011: 806) found that 'moving from unemployment into a high quality job led to improved mental health, however the transition from unemployment to a poor quality job was more detrimental to mental health than remaining unemployed'. This finding has been replicated in other studies, where those 'in employment in the lowest quality quintile reported worse health and wellbeing than the unemployed' (Bailey, 2015: 95). It would seem that, where work is low paid, insecure and of low quality, it is associated with poorer health outcomes than unemployment. Yet, policy has focused on the risk posed by unemployment even though the evidence is clear that poor quality jobs are equally or more detrimental to mental health (Butterworth et al, 2011).

The desire to work

The majority of people living in out-of-work poverty show a clear desire to work. They are subject to the same accounts of the advantages, financial and otherwise, of having paid employment, and are also subject to the same strivers versus skivers discourse played out in public. For these reasons they are keen to find paid employment. A clear finding from Shildrick et al's (2016: 829) research was that 'participants – across generations and genders – expressed conventional attitudes to work and welfare (even though they generally struggled to realize them)'. Similarly, in my longitudinal study of families, all of the families in the study who were not in paid work had the aspiration to gain full-time employment. These conventional attitudes to work, and the desire to find work, and the stigma associated with being out of work, was internalised by families and experienced as shame. Jennifer, a lone parent to three boys, summarises this desire well:

> 'I want to move on. I want … I don't want to be on benefits. I don't want that stigma. I want to work, and I'm not looking for an all-singing, all-dancing job with a massive pay, I just want enough money to provide for myself and my sons without having to rely on anybody, or get handouts … and you're just constantly penalised for that. There's all the barriers, the stigma, everything that goes with that.'

Over the six years of my research with Jennifer, she manages to go to college and does eventually find a job, which she believes confers non-financial benefits, but only marginal financial benefits. She says that the knowledge that she has completed a college course and succeeded in getting a job she loves has had a positive impact on her children, particularly on her eldest son. She says: 'Especially my oldest … he's often said to me, "It's good the way you are now, you're really happy now. Remember when it was like this?" So he feels a positive change. So that's really good'. Although Jennifer and children feel much happier that she has entered work, the benefits are not really financial. She still struggling financially and, furthermore, she's lost entitlement to vital support in the form of free school meals for her three sons (Treanor, 2018a). It could be argued that the benefits of employment, marginal as they are financially, make Jennifer's life better, in ways social and personal, and the fact of her employment is a benefit to her three sons. And at first it seems this way to Jennifer in the excitement of finding a job that she loves after a number of years living on benefits with her boys after her divorce. At the time of finding the job, she says,

> 'I wouldn't say I'm massively better off to be honest, but personally I feel like somebody's just opened up my world. I just love my job. But it just means by the end of the month, once everything's paid, there's a wee bit extra. And it maybe is only about a hundred pounds or something that I would have to play with at the end of the month, but that just means we could go and do something really good.'

As described in Chapter 4, Jennifer ends up having to leave work because of a lack of childcare for her autistic son. She demonstrates a strong motivation to work, even in the most difficult of circumstances, and her experiences highlight the barriers to finding sustainable, secure employment, especially for lone parents, as discussed further in Chapter 4. Other barriers include family care commitments, a lack of training opportunities, and ill-health, often the result of 'poor work' and unemployment (Shildrick et al, 2010). It also demonstrates the role that children play in low-income working households, including those faced by disability. Children are providing childcare, negotiating with services such as education, and providing support, including emotional support, to their families. When parents lose employment this also has detrimental effects on children: 'children feel anxious and stressed when parents endure unemployment or income loss, and they suffer family downturns in subtle and painfully evident ways' (Fanjul, 2014: 2). As Millar and Ridge (2013) found, sustaining employment when it is low paid and insecure takes the whole family and can pose a threat to family cohesion and security rather than provide a route out of poverty.

The role of employment in (not) lifting families out of poverty (in-work poverty)

While employment considerably reduces the risk of poverty, the risk of being in poverty even when working (in-work poverty) is significant across all OECD countries, where the working poor account for between 60 and 80 per cent of all the poor of working age (OECD, 2009). The UK boasts record employment rates, yet the number of people in working families, who live in poverty, rose by over one million in the three years to 2016/17 (JRF, 2018a). More than that, in the UK, two thirds of children living in poverty live in a family where someone works, which equates to almost three million children (JRF, 2018a) and 'one in six people referred to Trussell Trust food banks is working' (Alston, 2019: 8). So employment really is not lifting families out of poverty; for many, work is simply... not working (Treanor, 2018b).

Why is work no longer acting as a lever to winch one's way out of poverty? At the global level the nature of paid labour has changed due to deindustrialisation and advances in technology (OECD, 2011). There has been a global expansion in new forms of employment and a growing risk of job displacement due to automation and digitisation, which has not yet come into full effect (OECD, 2018b). Across many affluent societies, there has been deregulation in labour markets to provide greater flexibility for employers in relation to employment terms, conditions and protection (Bailey, 2015). This has resulted in a decrease in job security, particularly for those in lower paid employment, and an increase in non-standard employment, that is part-time, zero-hours or temporary contracts (Bailey, 2015). This results in people rotating between insecure employment and unemployment in a low-pay, no-pay cycle. Over the course of a year, this leads to lower levels of work intensity, or underemployment, compared to someone in stable, full-time employment.

Across the OECD, underemployment caused by non-standard employment is the major cause of in-work poverty with average work intensity varying greatly between the underemployed and the employed population (OECD, 2009). Across the 21 European countries for which the OECD have data, just over '20% of the working poor work full-time, full year-round and almost 70% of this group work six months or less during the year (in full-time equivalent months)' (OECD, 2009: 167). This compares to more than half of individuals living in a non-poor household who work full-time over the full year (OECD, 2009). In the UK, 38.4 per cent of low-paid workers experience a period of being out of paid work over a four-year period (Thompson, 2015). Furthermore, when these formerly low-paid individuals 'return to employment, it is to a similarly low level of earnings' (Thompson, 2015: 4). As well as making it difficult to avoid low living standards the low-pay, no-pay cycle also makes it difficult to advance in one's job (Thompson, 2015). This is reflected in the data from the Poverty and Social Exclusion UK survey, where one in three adults in paid work is either 'in poverty, or in insecure or poor quality employment' and 'one third of this group have not seen any progression in their labour market situation in the last five years' (Bailey, 2015: 82). Between 2006 and 2016, D'Arcy and Finch (2017) find that only 17 per cent of low-paid employees escaped their low-paid positions. They found that 25 per cent became stuck for the whole period while 48 per cent cycled between low-paid employment and more highly paid employment. For most low-paid workers then, poorly paid positions are not acting as a first rung on the employment ladder, rather it is the only rung and it is sticky (D'Arcy and Finch, 2017). As well as cycling between low pay and no pay, in the UK a large minority of those experiencing in-work poverty do work full-time and/or live in a household with near-full work intensity (Bailey, 2015: 98). These people are arguably 'strivers' in the current political parlance, but as work does not lift them and their families out of poverty, it is 'hard to see how 'more work' can be the solution to their problems' (Bailey, 2015: 98). In my longitudinal study of families, Jamie, a married father of six children, works full-time and describes many of the same difficulties in managing on his income as the families who are out of work in the study. His in-work benefits account for over half of his income each month, and this was at the start of the study before tax credits were squeezed. He describes everyday difficulties in coping financially:

> 'There's definitely an added stress, to try to keep our heads above water kind of thing. That brings stresses and strains. When the kids, like at high school, they need extra money for home economics for cooking and things like that, so they come in and say, because they're twins, they both come in and say, 'I need six pounds for cooking', so suddenly there's £12, which doesn't sound a lot but I mean, that's a couple days' worth of electricity. I think my wife gets more stressed than me. My wife gets stressed out with it. It's tough, it is, it's tough. It's tougher than it has been previously. You're trying to make less money stretch further.'

Even though he works full-time, Jamie's descriptions of how he manages financially, and how he copes with seasonal expenditure such as Christmas, is similar to many of the families who are not in paid work. One of the differences is that Jamie can avoid payday lenders and can ask his bank for a loan. He is also lucky to have close family who help each other out. He explains,

> 'At Christmas, and things like that, it was tough trying to get them what most kids will get. You get there eventually

somehow though. You spend the rest of the year trying to catch up though. ... we have to either put it on a credit card or take a loan, or something. I'm trying to stay away from the credit cards because I got myself in bother with them before. What with high interest and things like that, so, I tend to just, if I have to, just get a loan from the bank, because it's safer, cheaper. And luckily, I've got older brothers and that, that I can borrow money off from time to time, and give them it back at the end of the month sort of thing, rather than go to a payday lender, it's just extortionate.'

What Jamie's experience currently shows, and what Beveridge's quote at the beginning of the chapter highlighted in 1944, is the importance of having decent wages and decent employment. Jamie actually works for a public sector body and so his job would be described as decent; however, the in-work benefit system deems that it only provides half the money he needs, which is why they top it up with benefits. This is clearly showing that there is a disconnect between wages and the cost of living in the UK and across all wealthy societies as per the OECD's figures. While it is important for policy financially to support those with larger families, it remains the case that having decent wages in the first place would prevent poverty upstream, instead of policy measures such as the in-work benefit system having to mitigate it downstream.

Having large numbers of low-paid workers alternating between employment and worklessness in any given country is particularly concerning as: (1) social protection systems, such as the benefits system, are often still designed for the traditional full-time, long-term employee and not for those rotating between insecure employment and unemployment; so for those who have non-standard work contracts there are likely to be gaps in social protection coverage that deepen levels of poverty (OECD, 2018a); (2) social protection for all may be eroded if insufficient income is generated through the tax system (OECD, 2018a); and (3) it places a significant financial burden on the state, which must pay out-of-work benefits to the unemployed as well as providing in-work benefits to individuals in low-paid work (Thompson, 2015: 5). The financial burden of the low-pay, no-pay cycle has been calculated to cost the UK government £1.7 billion each year (Thompson, 2015). Thompson (2015: 5) argues that significant savings could be made if job security for those in low-paid work was strengthened and if the rates of moving between low-paid jobs and no jobs were reduced to match those seen among the non-low-paid.

In an example from my research, having unreliable or uncertain hours adversely affected families over time. One participant, Emma, is married with a three-year-old son. Emma is a receptionist at the local community centre and her husband is self-employed. She has been on a three-monthly temporary contract for years that sets her hours every 12 weeks. Under this contract she does not get paid if she is not at work, for example for holidays or sickness, and she does not know how her hours will change each 12-week period. At Christmas time, the community centre where Emma works was closed for two weeks and so she was not at work and was not paid. The impact of this is that

> 'I was getting three different lots of pay [from the same employer on different temporary contracts] but I had no holiday pay. I got a supplement onto my wages but if I was off sick, or if the centre was closed for holidays, I would get no pay. So what I've done, I was looking for a permanent post within the council, just for a bit more stability really because, for instance at Christmas the centre was closed for two weeks ... so December, January, and even February, I was playing catch up trying to get on top of finances again.'

The difficulty for Emma is the instability of her income, which makes forward planning difficult, means that in-work benefits change frequently, usually resulting in her owing money to the government, and so that she micro-manages her income on an almost daily basis.

Youth employment/unemployment

Children and young people are not just affected by their parent's poverty; young people aged over 16 years old are having to deal with their own poverty through unemployment and underemployment. Those young people who are not in education, employment or training (NEET) are at greatest risk of un- and underemployment, which has long-lasting negative effects on their access to future jobs, their health and their wellbeing. This has been especially pronounced since the Great Recession of 2008. The problem of youth unemployment, while great in the UK, is massive across all affluent societies (see Figure 6.1). In an analysis of OECD countries, unemployment increased to worrying levels in 34 of the 41 countries analysed among those aged 15–24 (Fanjul, 2014). Furthermore 'even when unemployment or inactivity decreases, that does not necessarily mean that young people are finding stable, reasonably paid jobs. The number of 15- to 24-year-olds in

Figure 6.1 Youth unemployment (less than 25 years old) in international context, September 2019 (%)

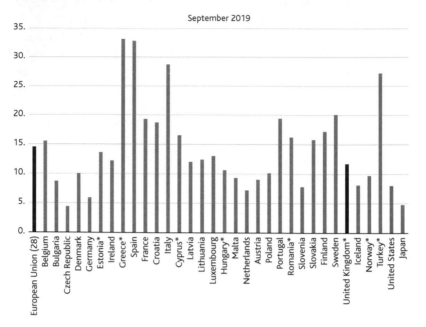

* data from an earlier month in 2019.

Source: Eurostat, Labour Force Survey, ONS, 2019, seasonally adjusted figures. Author's own analysis.

part-time work or who are underemployed has tripled on average in countries more exposed to the recession' (Fanjul, 2014: 3).

Youth unemployment in the UK is high, at 10.2 per cent (see Figure 6.1). Youth unemployment in the UK is higher than the EU and the OECD averages and, although its rate is not the worst of all comparative countries, it is worse than the best-performing countries (Crowley et al, 2013). It does not have to be this way, however. In some countries, youth unemployment is low, for example in Germany and the Netherlands, at 5.3 per cent and 6.2 per cent respectively (see Figure 6.1). In other countries, for example Switzerland, 'the proportion of young people who were out of work remained low and stable throughout the economic crisis' (Crowley et al, 2013: 2). The UK can learn from those countries 'whose youth labour markets are far healthier, and where young people have not been so severely affected by the recession' (Crowley et al, 2013: 10). In other countries, however, 'persistent and high levels of unemployment have been features of the youth labour market for a long time', which the recession only served to exacerbate (Crowley et al, 2013: 2). Figure 6.1 shows the unemployment rates for youths across OECD countries. This clearly then is a problem for many governments, including the UK.

One of the problems with youth unemployment is that it can have long-term effects on wages, employment and health (Crowley et al, 2013). Across all age groups, unemployment carries a scar: scarring is a causal link between unemployment, especially long-term unemployment, and negative experiences and outcomes in future in relation to employment (Gregg and Tominey, 2004: 3). Specifically, the scarring from unemployment damages an individual's future employment prospects and/or earnings, effects that can last for the rest of an individual's working lifetime (Gregg and Tominey, 2005: 488). These effects can be seen up to 20 years later (Gregg and Tominey, 2004).

The negative effects of unemployment when young do not only have repercussions in terms of future employment and wages. Unemployment brings a multitude of negative consequences in relation to physical and mental health, which intensify the longer an individual is unemployed (O'Higgins, 2015). Although unemployment causes unhappiness generally, 'there are enduring effects from spells of unemployment while young, which continues to lower happiness more than two decades later' (Bell and Blanchflower, 2010: 27). Furthermore, those who are currently employed but fear unemployment in a time of job insecurity also experience unhappiness, which is linked to degraded mental and physical health (Bell and Blanchflower, 2010; O'Higgins, 2015). As well as poor mental and physical health, unemployment also leads to helplessness, loss of self-esteem and depression, and increases the probability of outcomes such as heart attacks later in life (ACEVO, 2012). In addition to poor future outcomes, there is also substantial evidence that links youth unemployment to crime (O'Higgins, 2015). High rates of youth unemployment are related to increases in burglaries, thefts and drug offences, an association that is stronger for young unemployed people than older unemployed adults (ACEVO, 2012). This has very real consequences for young people in their youth and will have a lasting impact on the rest of their lives. As O'Higgins (2015: 1) says: 'not only is crime costly for society it is also costly for the individual'.

There are a number of reasons for the high levels of youth unemployment. The first is that there has been a general contraction of the economy and labour market, especially after the Great Recession of 2008 (Hollywood et al, 2012). Secondly, employers can be reluctant to take on new employees, 'especially young people who are perceived as lacking the necessary skills and experience' (Hollywood et al,

2012: no page number). Interestingly, skills and experience are clearly not the same as qualifications, as young people have far higher levels of education than do older people (Hollywood et al, 2012). Thirdly, young people are disproportionately overrepresented in sectors that were badly affected by the Great Recession, such as the construction and retail industries (Hollywood ct al, 2012). Finally, there has been an overall increase in competition for a decreasing number of jobs (Hollywood et al, 2012). In spite of these multifaceted difficulties facing young people in gaining employment, most unemployed young people want to work and are actively trying to find jobs (Tunstall et al, 2012). Tunstall et al (2012: 7) found that young people

> understood employers' requirements, and were, in general, realistic about the types of jobs and wages they could hope to attain. Most followed general good practice in using a variety of job search methods and sources of job search advice and support. All used the internet and for most this was the most important tool. A majority, but not all, had internet access at home. More confident jobseekers also made speculative applications, by email, by post or in person. Some young people engaged in volunteering, others sought to improve their qualifications and some relied on networks of friends to help them find work, with varying degrees of success.

It would seem that the odds are very much stacked against young people finding secure employment, that they very much want to work and that they are doing all the right things to try and find jobs. So, what can governments do to rectify this situation? Ghoshray et al (2016: 442) find that, across the board, labour market reforms are not sufficiently effective to solve the youth unemployment problem. Gregg and Tominey (2005: 506) argue that governments should avoid the long-term scarring associated with youth unemployment by reducing 'the exposure of young adults to substantive periods of unemployment, which would not only positively impact on an individual's life, but would also be a good investment in terms of the returns on the individual's lifetime earnings'. Ghoshray et al (2016) argue that educational policy should come into play to by raising the average qualifications for young people. They also believe that there should be greater interventions in supporting school-to-work transitions (Ghoshray et al, 2016). Young people need different interventions to obtain employment than do older people. Often, governments try to solve the problem of unemployment by focusing on the supply side, that is on the unemployed themselves. They do this by using work activation policies either to increase the 'employability' of the individual or to encourage their participation in the labour market, including by coercive means such as welfare conditionality and sanctions. For young people, however, focus on the supply side of the labour market is not a successful strategy. One strategy that was successful in the UK was called the 'Future Jobs Fund', which was an intervention that focused on the demand-side during a time of economic recession and which led to an improvement in youth unemployment (Patrick, 2012). Unfortunately, this initiative was abolished by the incoming Conservative-led Coalition Government in 2010.

In flipping the thinking on youth unemployment, it is worth considering that young people face far greater disadvantages in the labour market in spite of their higher levels of qualifications than earlier generations. Furthermore, young people have a strong desire to work, try very hard to find jobs, and do all the things that they have been told will lead to employment. That this is not working for them is not a function of their laziness or uselessness as much the function of the inefficacy of government policy, the anaemic nature of the labour market and the unwillingness of employers to take on young people, a final fact that could be addressed with policy.

How policy interacts with employment

In-work poverty is often related to insufficient work participation, for example part-time, temporary or zero-hours employment, and certain groups are more vulnerable to in-work poverty, for example families with children (OECD, 2009). Thus, combating in-work poverty requires a targeted policy response from governments. Well-conceived in-work benefit schemes can be particularly effective for combating in-work poverty and they can be targeted towards the most vulnerable households (OECD, 2009). In-work benefits are means-tested cash transfers targeted at those whose incomes from work is insufficient due to low wages and/or low levels of work intensity. In-work benefits have two basic policy objectives; to reduce in-work poverty and to enhance incentives to work for low-income workers (OECD, 2011; Van der Linden, 2016). This dual motivation is arguably the reason for their political success as they advance the traditional agendas of both the political right, for example promoting work incentives and reducing out-of-work benefit caseloads, and of the political left, for example by combating poverty and promoting redistribution (OECD, 2011). It is for this reason that in-work benefits have become increasingly popular across many affluent countries in recent years. There can be financial disincentives both to finding work and to taking on more hours in a low-paying job because of the interaction between the tax and (in-work) benefit system (OECD, 2011). When an individual increases their hours of paid work they will lose some of their in-work benefits as well as be taxed on their increased income. The balance between the tax and (in-work) benefit system, therefore, has to be carefully considered to incentivise work and not to trap people into poverty. Although in-work benefits have been increasingly implemented in affluent societies there is wide variation in their design, with different weight placed according to the poverty-alleviation or work-incentive goals of each country (OECD, 2011).

Permanent in-work benefits, rather than time-limited ones, have been shown to bring multiple benefits to children and families. Permanent in-work benefits reduce the incidence of in-work poverty and, for lone mothers in particular, increase the transition from out-of-work benefits to employment, which brings an attendant positive effect on their mental health and life satisfaction (Van der Linden, 2016). In the UK, in-work benefits in the form of working tax credits were introduced as a means of topping up low incomes, especially for families with children. These have been incrementally devalued since 2013 and are being gradually phased out to be replaced by universal credit (Grover, 2016). Working tax credits were of great benefit to children's lives and needs as parents whose incomes were boosted spent the additional money on their children, child poverty decreased, material deprivation decreased, and child wellbeing increased. This increased income is key as, Chapter 2 establishes, in market societies, money is necessary and, as every chapter in this book highlights, having sufficient money is the key factor in child development and wellbeing.

In-work benefits do not have universal support, however. They have been argued to reduce wages and offer a subsidy to employers paying low wages (Marsh et al, 2017). This is why it is important they work alongside decent minimum wage policies. Another criticism lies in the rate at which the in-work benefit is withdrawn when an individual increases his or her hours. In such cases this makes it harder to raise one's standard of living by working longer hours or getting promoted (Marsh et al, 2017). A third criticism is that, despite having in-work benefits two thirds of children living in poverty in the UK are in a family in which at least one parent is in employment. Van der Linden (2016) warns that the complexity of the tax and benefit system should not be overlooked, and that in-work benefits should operate alongside other types of support, such as childcare, health care and housing. The policies governing employment and access to in-work benefits fail to recognise that there is vital unpaid work being carried out in society, which is argued to be equally valid to paid work (Levitas et al, 2007; Bailey, 2015). Patrick (2012: 11) notes that the government's exclusive focus on paid work

> simultaneously neglects and devalues other forms of social contribution such as parenting, care work, volunteering and engaging in service user activities. Disabled people, for example, may be over-represented in the out-of-work statistics but are often active as volunteers or service users helping improve service standards for themselves and their peers.

Traditionally, there have been certain groups who were not expected to look for paid work, for example those looking after children, disabled people and the elderly (Patrick, 2012). It was once accepted that looking after children was work, albeit unpaid, and mothers were understood to be performing the vital function of raising the next generation. Until 2008 in the UK, lone parents were expected to look for paid work when their youngest child turned 16 years old. In 2008, this was reduced to 12 years old, then to 10 years in 2009, and further to 7 years old in 2010 and 5 years old in 2012. Now, lone parents are expected to prepare for work when their youngest child turns three. This is a policy that pays little attention to the structure of the current labour market, its insecurity, and to barriers to paid work that people, especially lone parents, face such as access to available and affordable childcare, skills and experience, confidence and self-esteem, and low levels of education. Imposing stringent conditions for receiving benefits and requiring lone parents with school-age children to seek work as a condition of receiving benefits is shown to adversely affect their mental health (Katikireddi et al, 2018: 333). This is discussed further in Chapter 4.

Across all affluent societies there has been a rise in conditions imposed on those seeking employment, especially a much greater emphasis on conduct conditionality (Dwyer and Wright, 2014). Such conditionality requires 'people to behave in a certain way to access welfare goods, such as cash benefits, housing or support services. These behavioural conditions tend to be enforced through penalties or "sanctions" that reduce, suspend or end access to these goods' (Watts et al, 2014: 1). In the UK, there are increasing conditions being imposed on out-of-work and in-work benefits. The penalties for not being adequately successful in being activated for work are severe and are becoming more so as welfare conditionality intensifies after the Welfare Reform Act 2012. This Act 'legislated for a significant extension and intensification of welfare conditionality, including the ultimate sanction of three years without benefits for those who fail three times to comply with various work-related conditions' (Patrick, 2014: 707). In May 2019, the UK Conservative Minister for Work and Pensions called three-year sanctions 'counterproductive', promised to abolish them and to limit the length of penalties to six months. Sanctions of any length are cruel, inhuman and degrading (Adler, 2018).

In my longitudinal study of families living in poverty, at the start of the study, Jennifer, a lone parent of three, has to take her son with her to the Jobcentre Plus, the UK's public job-broking agency with responsibility for out-of-work benefit payments, as he is young and not yet at school. Jennifer is claiming unemployment benefits as her son has turned five years old. This is around six months before she finds a job. She knows that if she cannot make the appointment she will be sanctioned and lose her benefits for a minimum period of four weeks. Here is her experience:

> 'That was a nightmare. Absolute nightmare. For me anyway, for my local job centre, it's like when you go in, it's like you'd think they were giving you the money out their own pocket. It's like you're having to totally justify yourself to get a pittance, just to keep you afloat. And it's an absolute nightmare.
>
> There was one time when I was in a meeting [at the Jobcentre], my youngest would be five at the time, so I'd have to take him with me, and he was needing the toilet, right? And he was saying "Mummy, I need the toilet, I need the toilet, Mummy." And the lady was taking forever, going through this and going through that, questions, questions, questions, and it is the summer holidays when I've got two kids that my mum's minding [looking after] outside.
>
> I said, "Excuse me, is there a toilet in here that he could use?"
>
> "No, we don't, we can't, we can't let him use the toilet".
>
> And I was like, "He's five, honestly he's going to wet himself."
>
> And she said, "Really, there's nothing I can do about that."

I says, "Well, could I just cut it [the meeting] short then because I need to take him to the toilet?"

"Oh, I don't know how that will work out because really you have to stay here for the whole time of the appointment."

And I thought, "Oh my God."

At that time I could understand why people would lose the plot. I could understand why people get ratty [angry], because I'm more interested in my wee boy needing the toilet than you looking at the 21 things I've got to do to find a job ... So I left that meeting thinking "Oh my God, what if I get my money stopped this week?" If I get my money stopped it affects my rent because they automatically send a thing to [the housing benefit] to say to stop the housing benefit ... So I worried myself sick and then three days later I got my money in the bank and it was, like, such a relief.'

Rather than act as a means of incentivising or supporting employment, conditionality and sanctioning has been shown to lead to deeper levels of poverty and destitution (Watts et al, 2014) and 'attributes responsibility for poverty and unemployment to the behaviour of marginalised individuals' (Fletcher and Flint, 2018: 771). Furthermore, as well as having a negative impact on people's financial wellbeing, sanctions have been ineffective at getting people in the UK off out-of-work benefits and into jobs (Taulbut et al, 2018). This is especially the case for lone parents (Whitworth and Griggs, 2013). Internationally, benefit sanctions (especially severe sanctions) were shown to increase exits from benefits but had adverse longer-term outcomes in relation to earnings, job quality and employment retention (Watts et al, 2014). In addition to adverse material and financial effects, sanctions and conditionality have also been associated with 'negative physical and mental health outcomes, increased stress and reduced emotional wellbeing' (Watts et al, 2014: 8), with rising food bank usage (Loopstra et al, 2018), and with reduced 'political and civic participation, political interest and efficacy, and personal efficacy' (Watson, 2014: 645).

In the UK, there is major change underway to the way in which out-of-work and in-work benefits are paid. They are to be replaced by a new benefit called universal credit. This new, single benefit will replace six existing means-tested benefits and tax credits, is based on income, assets and circumstances and will affect around eight million households in the UK (Millar and Bennett, 2017). While there is widespread support for the principle of universal credit, which is to reduce complexity in the benefit system, there are also grave concerns about its implementation and delivery. One of the concerning factors is that universal credit increases the scope and strictness of conditionality and sanctions (Dwyer and Wright, 2014). Individuals seeking to claim universal credit will be expected to look for work as their full-time job; furthermore, those who are already in work but on a low income will also have conditions imposed on them for the first time (Dwyer and Wright, 2014). The implementation and delivery of universal credit has not considered the lives and needs of children living in low-income working and non-working families. There has been months of chaos 'in which long waits for payment and processing errors have left tens of thousands of claimants in debt, rent arrears and reliant on food banks' (Courea, 2018: no page number). Since universal credit was introduced in 2013 it has been cut multiple times, including being capped, making it less generous to children and families, and less able to lift families out of poverty through employment. This is especially the case for lone parents who will suffer most under the new benefit. Furthermore, the UK Government has imposed a two-child limit to universal credit, where parents will no longer be entitled to benefits for third and subsequent children. This is of great detriment to larger families, which is a known risk factor for child poverty, and has been soundly criticised as 'deeply problematic' by the United Nations Special Rapporteur to the UK on extreme poverty and human rights in November 2018.[1] In January 2019, this policy was partially revoked in that it would no longer apply to those who had their children before 2017 but would apply to those whose children were born subsequently. Thus, there is now a two-tiered system in place in the UK for support for third and subsequent children. This will have a particularly detrimental impact on younger families, those with more children, BME families and those who are new to the country; in essence, those with heightened risk of poverty in the first place.

Thus, there are policies that governments can employ to support parental employment, including that of lone parents, and to reduce child poverty; however, often governments work in ways that preclude parental access to employment and aggravate child poverty rates and experiences. As a result of the tax and welfare reforms between 2010 and 2017 in the UK, it is forecast that child poverty will increase by over 10 percentage points, from slightly under 31 per cent to more than 41 per cent, resulting in around 1.5 million extra children being in poverty by 2021/22 (Portes and Reed, 2018). This is nothing short of disastrous for the millions of children who are having their lives degraded by poverty. There are certain groups who are at particular risk of low-quality, low-paid employment and unemployment, for example young people, mothers, the disabled, and BME and migrants for whom dedicated responses are required.

Flipping the thinking

Employment in the UK is at its highest and unemployment is at its lowest for many years. Yet, two thirds of all children living in poverty live in a household where someone is working. This shows that not all work is working as a route out of poverty. Wages are too low and there is an overdependence on in-work benefits, which are being continually contracted by the UK Government, adding to working families' financial worries. Furthermore, the work activation activities are focusing on 'fixing' the supply side, that is the behaviours and characteristics of the unemployed, with little focus on improving the demand side, that is increasing job quality and availability. To flip the thinking on this, it would be useful to look behind the statistics to understand: (1) who is out of work and who is cycling between low pay and no pay, and to work out how this could change; and (2) what type of employment opportunities are being created, for whom and to what effect. To flip our thinking, we should flip our understanding that the problem lies not in those without work, or in low-paid or precarious work, but that the systems governing employment, for example government management of the labour market and the actions of employers, are the real culprits in perpetuating poverty.

The unemployed and the underemployed are held in the lowest esteem today. In the UK in particular there is a very potent and toxic discourse on strivers versus skivers. Even within communities of people living in socioeconomic disadvantage people reserve the harshest judgement for those who are out of paid work, even when their own circumstances may be similar. The stigma we apply to those out of paid work, and the shame they are made to feel, is argued to be a tool used by governments to punish the unemployed or to deter people from being unemployed. One way to flip the thinking on the stigma and shame that is profuse in today's society is to highlight to people the way in which these narratives are manipulated by the government to ostracise the poor and to divide neighbours and communities. Another way this could be achieved, as is currently the case with the Social Security (Scotland) Act 2018, is to ensure that treating all claimants with dignity and respect is written into the charter and into the legislation.

This will change the process and, hopefully, the outcomes of those claiming out-of-work benefits and will filter through society. How a government acts and how a media reports and responds does have an effect on public views.

We know that people go to excruciating levels to avoid the stigma and shame of being unemployed and they try to differentiate themselves from other unemployed people, for example by citing unemployment through caring responsibilities. There is a lack of understanding and appreciation of those who are economically inactive due to caring responsibilities. If we could flip the thinking on this, we would see that carrying out unpaid work in relation to the care of children, the elderly and the disabled is valuable and valid. We would appreciate how much money is saved by people carrying out unpaid work for friends and family and we would wish to support them in these endeavours. If the economic argument was put forward, public attitudes could change.

People, and especially young people, are severely disadvantaged in the labour market, in spite of their superior educations. This disadvantage holds when all other factors are accounted for, leaving the only explanation as conscious and unconscious bias and discrimination. How do we flip the thinking on this? The answer lies in dedicated, targeted policy responses to provide a platform from which to promote a shared understanding, ensure access to the full range of the employment market, and to reduce discrimination against the young.

7

Health

All children have the right to a happy childhood and a standard of living sufficient for their mental health, wellbeing and development. (UNCRC, 1989)

Introduction

This chapter looks at poor health and its impacts on and interactions with poverty. There is the idea that poor health leads to poverty, and it does sounds as though it could or should be the case. However, there is now extremely strong (and growing) evidence that poverty actually leads to poor health. Even short-term falls in income increase the risk of ill health (Smith at al, 2007: 58). This causal relationship is strong and is also seen in people with disabilities: those who become disabled are more likely to have been poor beforehand. This means that factors, such as poverty and inequality, are powerful, pervasive and harmful to health. This sounds counterintuitive: it sounds more logical that ill health prevents you from earning money and so makes you poor. This chapter aims to explain the relationship between poverty and ill health and illuminate the ways in which it has particularly strong consequences for children and young people. This chapter does not focus on disability, as disabled people can have good health even though they are relatively high-frequency users of health services. Disability is, however, discussed in Chapter 8, along with ethnicity, as factors that increase the risk of poverty.

Poverty affects health directly and indirectly through the unequal distribution of health-related factors such as good quality housing, work, education, access to services and social and cultural opportunities. This in turn can lead to the unequal and unfair distribution of good health, ill health, healthy years of life, and life expectancy across affluent (and other) societies. When looking at how health has an impact on child poverty the first aspect to consider is whether the poor health is experienced by the parent or the child – this will have differential effects on child poverty and may affect children's experience of poverty in different ways. Parental health is greatly important for child wellbeing;

having a parent with health issues creates many problems for children, especially in relation to their engagement with school, friends and wider society. The second aspect to consider is whether the poor health is a mental or physical health condition. While poverty has a hugely negative impact on all aspects of physical health, and health behaviours such as smoking and diet, poor mental health brings multiple problems. Stigma can appear invisible to the outside eye and can have a particularly pernicious impact on children and young people. Keeping children at the centre, this chapter illuminates the detrimental consequences on children of living with a parent with a mental health condition. Increasingly, children and young people are experiencing poor mental health themselves. Poverty and poor parental mental health are key factors in the declining mental health and wellbeing of children and young people. This chapter thus focuses on the developing area of child mental health, its relationship with poverty, and its risks for children's current and future wellbeing.

It takes money to achieve positive health. Having a minimum income to support healthy living is shown to have an especially positive impact on those at the lower end of the income distribution (Marmot et al, 2010). Yet, in the UK 40 per cent of households with children cannot afford an acceptable standard of living sufficient to support good health (Donkin and Marmott, 2016). As earlier chapters emphasised, child poverty is increasing, so this is a situation predicted to worsen in the coming years. A corollary of income poverty discussed earlier, material deprivation, is an even stronger predictor of health outcomes than income alone (Donkin and Marmott, 2016). This is because, in addition to income, material deprivation is affected by existing assets, resources, debt, outgoings such as childcare, the number of people in a household, disability and the length of time spent in poverty. The longer a person lives in poverty the higher their levels of material deprivation and the greater its effect on child wellbeing (Treanor, 2014). While both physical and mental health are impacted negatively by poverty, this chapter focuses mainly on mental health, which is a growing problem for parents and children living in poverty.

Health inequalities

Health inequalities result from the political and social decisions that cause unequal distributions of income, power and wealth between groups. Such political and social decisions can lead to the poverty and marginalisation of individuals and groups, due to their, for example, social class, gender, race or other social characteristics. This leads to the unequal distribution of health-related factors such as good quality housing, work, education, access to services and social and cultural opportunities. As well as having an indirect effect on health via the increased probability of living in poverty, being marginalised and having poorer access to health-related factors, the unequal distribution of income, power and wealth between social groups can also have a *directly* negative effect on health. For example, being a member of a non-white ethnic group can lead to poorer health treatment due to widespread and institutional discrimination (Marmot, 2016). Such inequalities are directly related to the unequal distribution of good health, ill health and life expectancy across all societies. These social characteristics interact with the experience of prolonged poverty and material deprivation to adversely affect children's health. Children experiencing poverty linked to their social characteristics 'frequently continue to experience deprivation – and adverse health outcomes – later in life' (Raphael, 2011: 23).

Taking the unequal distribution of good quality housing as an example, where money is insufficient to provide access to good quality housing, there are negative effects on mental health and wellbeing, particularly for children and young people. Children who live in temporary housing can experience insecurity of tenancy, overcrowding, limited access to outdoor space and noise, which negatively affect sleep, mental health and wellbeing (Davie, 2016). Furthermore, over 25 per cent of adolescents living in cold housing are at risk of multiple mental health problems, compared with 5 per cent of adolescents who have always lived in warm housing (Donkin and Marmott, 2016: 52). This was clearly demonstrated in my longitudinal study of poverty with young people, where one 14-year-old boy who lived in overcrowded and damp housing said: 'There's damp, I feel sick all the time. When can I get a new house? I have asthma and at night I can't breathe properly' (Harris et al, 2009: 53).

Health inequalities show a distinctive social gradient. This means that every stepped increase in levels of poverty and deprivation is associated with increasingly worse health outcomes. When people live in poverty and in deprived areas, both life expectancy and disability-free life expectancy (DFLE), that is the number of years spent living in good health, are markedly worse. Furthermore, the gap between the most- and least-deprived areas follows a distinct gradient and people have worse social and health outcomes according to increasing neighbourhood deprivation (Marmot et al, 2010; Marmot, 2016; Marmot, 2017). Additionally, the persistence of poverty in childhood leads to greater adverse health conditions in adulthood (Wilkinson and Marmot, 2003).

Figure 7.1 is taken from Marmot's 2017 paper. It shows that life expectancy and DFLE improved between the periods 1999–2003 and 2009–13. However, the fitted lines show that, although there was improvement overall, the gap between the most deprived and the least deprived lines widened a little, that is the social gradient increased a little. What this graph also shows is that there is a social gradient between each and every level of deprivation, with the gradient being stronger for DFLE than it is for life expectancy. This means that even those who are in the second least deprived group have lower life expectancy and DFLE than those in the least deprived group (Marmot, 2017), that is all of us below the very top have worse health than those at the top (Marmot, 2016). This means that health inequalities affect everyone in society and not just the poor. Marmot's graph shows data for men only. A study that includes women shows that the gap in life expectancy between the poorest and the wealthiest 10 per cent of women in England has increased from 6.1 years in 2001 to 7.9 years by 2016 and the life expectancy of women in the poorest 20 per cent in England actually fell (Bennett et al, 2018; Davis, 2018). This trend is seen more strikingly in data from 2012–2019 in Scotland. The Scottish

Figure 7.1 Social gradient in life expectancy and disability-free life expectancy

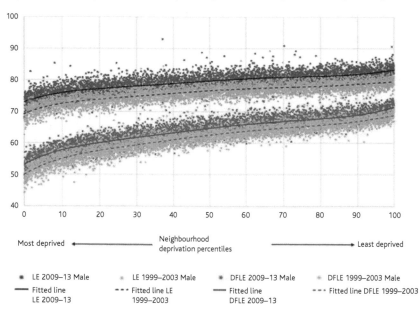

Source: Replicated from Marmot, 2017. Life expectancy and DFLE at birth, males by neighbourhood deprivation, England, 1999–2003 and 2009–13. Data obtained from the Office for National Statistics, which is licensed under the Open Government Licence v3.0.

Public Health Observatory notes that in Scotland, England, Northern Ireland and Wales, as well as in other countries that imposed high levels of austerity after the Great Recession, for example the Netherlands, life expectancy is falling, which they say is unprecedented and requiring of urgent action.[1]

For children, the gradient between their general health and their families' income emerges around the age of two and remains constant between ages 2 to 17 years (Apouey and Geoffard, 2013). In addition to the social gradient in child health, there is also a greater prevalence and severity of chronic conditions among low-income children, which strongly suggests that income is important for child health in the UK (Apouey and Geoffard, 2013). Even before birth, the foundations for children's health are being laid (Wilkinson and Marmot, 2003). The diet, risk behaviours, or stress that a pregnant woman experiences predispose children to either good or poor health regardless of later life circumstances (Raphael, 2011). While the foundations of adult health are laid in childhood and even before, it is equally important to address children's experiences of poorer health, and its associated consequences, in childhood itself.

Inequalities in health are increasing. The health of the wealthiest is improving far more quickly than the health of everyone else; hence, the gap in health due to income and wealth is growing (Marmot, 2016). If you are born into the most advantaged circumstances, you can expect to enjoy almost 20 more years of healthy life than someone born into the least advantaged circumstances. This is stark and it is important. This is not just about the number of years of life, or of healthy life, we can hope to enjoy; rather, 'being at the wrong end of inequality is disempowering, it deprives people of control over their lives. Their health is damaged as a result' (Marmot, 2016: 7).

Child health and poverty

It is not just in chronic health conditions that children living in poverty are disadvantaged; they are disadvantaged across the full spectrum of health and developmental outcomes (Washbrook et al, 2014) and they experience a greater number of adverse health events than children from higher-income families (Noonan et al, 2018). In the UK, health outcomes for children and young people are poorer than they are in other affluent societies. For example, the UK has the highest mortality for children under five years old in Western Europe, twice the rate of Sweden, and the UK's mortality rate for children aged 0–14 years trails behind those in comparable countries in the EU (Taylor-Robinson et al, 2015). These high mortality rates have been linked directly to higher rates of poverty and deprivation in the UK (Taylor-Robinson et al, 2015).

Child poverty is 'the launch pad for a lifetime of health problems' (Raphael, 2011: 24). Child poverty has detrimental impacts on children's health and developmental outcomes across time and place. The timing of poverty is thought to be important, that is whether it occurs in early, middle or late childhood, with early childhood believed to be the most critical time. In addition to the timing of poverty, however, the *duration* of poverty is of primary importance to children's development, with longer spells of living in poverty having a greater adverse effect than shorter spells of poverty (Duncan and BrooksGunn, 1997; McLoyd, 1998; Mayer, 2002; NICHD, 2005). While poverty is an important factor in children's early development, it is persistent poverty that is the most detrimental (Kiernan and Mensah, 2009; Treanor, 2016b). As the negative effects of poverty accumulate over time the longer children live under conditions of social and material deprivation the more likely they are to experience adverse health and developmental outcomes (Raphael, 2011).

Child cognitive development is negatively affected by low income in particular, rather than by material deprivation, and increasing lengths and depths of poverty spells are associated with progressively poorer cognitive development (McLoyd, 1998). Smith et al (1997) found that children living in persistent poverty (poor in each of the four years of the study data) scored lower on the cognitive ability scales than those in transient poverty, who, in turn, scored lower than those who had never been poor. Children's social, emotional and behavioural development is negatively associated with income poverty too (Hanson et al, 1997); but it is also strongly affected by material deprivation (Treanor, 2016b). The persistence of poverty is found to be the primary factor in the probability of a child experiencing behavioural problems at age 11 compared to those who have never experienced poverty (Noonan et al, 2018). Other aspects of family life, strongly influenced by socioeconomic disadvantage, such as parenting and parental wellbeing, also have strong associations with children's social, emotional and behavioural development (Kiernan and Huerta, 2008; Mensah and Kiernan, 2009; Schoon et al, 2010b). The negative effects of income poverty on social, emotional and behavioural developmental outcomes for children appear to be less strong in early childhood but gather strength in middle childhood (Bradley and Corwyn, 2002).

The importance of income to children's health outcomes cannot be underestimated. Children living in income poverty are more likely to suffer from both physical and mental health problems (Fitzsimons et al, 2017). Two reasons given for the effect of income on children's health are: (1) low income creates stress within the household leading to poor health outcomes in children; and (2) income is highly correlated with other factors affecting child health, such as the quality of housing or the relationship/conflict between members of the household (Fitzsimons et al, 2017). It has been shown that when household income increases there is an associated improvement in child and adult health, including mental health (Wickham et al, 2017). It is to mental health that this chapter now turns.

Children's mental health and poverty

Children and young people are usually a very healthy age group, especially when it comes to physical health. Yet across the world, at any given time, approximately one in five children and young people experience a mental health problem, in particular depression or anxiety (WHO, 2012). Across many societies, suicide is among the leading causes of death among young people (WHO, 2012). Mental health problems among children and young people are on the increase around the world, which is a widespread public health concern that is thus far inadequately addressed. As we shall see, the public health consequences of poor mental health in childhood are complex and far-reaching (Wickham et al, 2017).

Poverty, across all societies, is strongly related to children's mental health problems. Children and young people living in poverty across the world are two to three times more likely to develop mental health problems than their wealthier counterparts (Wickham et al, 2017). In the UK, child mental health is poor and getting worse. At any one time one in five children and young people experience mental health problems and those in the poorest households are up to three times more likely to develop mental health problems than those in higher socioeconomic circumstances in the UK (Donkin and Marmott, 2016).

The mental health problems that affect children and young people include depression, anxiety, and drug and alcohol abuse (Fitzsimons et al, 2017). There are severe consequences in adulthood of childhood mental health problems; for instance, it is associated with poorer future socioeconomic success (Fitzsimons et al, 2017). However, it is also crucial to note that the effects of poor mental health in childhood itself is an urgent cause for concern. In childhood, poor mental health is associated with absence from school, poor educational attainment, impaired cognitive development, social isolation, low self-esteem, discrimination, bullying, and a lower life expectancy (Wickham et al, 2017: 141). In the UK, children and young people growing up in poverty say they feel like a failure, useless and more hopeless about their future than their more affluent peers (Ayre, 2016).

The timing of poverty is important to children and young people's mental health. Early childhood is thought to be a sensitive period in determining adolescent mental health (Mazza et al, 2017; Green et al, 2018). It is proposed that poverty and deprivation during early life, when children's physical, social, emotional and cognitive capacities are developing rapidly, can have lasting impacts and these impacts may lead to poorer health and behaviours in adolescence (Green et al, 2018: 137). As well as the sensitive period model, there is believed to be an accumulation of risk caused by the duration of poverty (Mazza et al, 2017), with higher rates of mental health problems for those living in persistent poverty (Wickham et al, 2017). Where a child is chronically exposed to poverty, they have a higher incidence of experiencing mental health problems early in childhood and these problems strengthen over time (Comeau and Boyle, 2018). This accumulation of risk model suggests that the initially small differences in social, emotional and behavioural development between poor and non-poor children, which increase over time for children in persistent poverty, will lead to a mental health gap that widens throughout childhood (Mazza et al, 2017).

Change in exposure to poverty also has strong associations with childhood mental health problems with persistent and transient poverty being associated with poorer mental health (Fitzsimons et al, 2017). Compared to children who have never experienced poverty, those who experience change in poverty have distinct mental health trajectories (Comeau and Boyle, 2018). There is a distinct gradient to the patterns of child mental health problems and child poverty. Those who live in persistent poverty face greater problems than those who experience recurrent or transient poverty and they, in turn, have poorer mental health than those children who have never been poor (Comeau and Boyle, 2018). Additionally, when children first experience poverty, that is where there is a negative change in family income, there is an associated increase in children's mental health problems (Reiss, 2013). Despite the strong evidence that poverty has a causal relationship with poor mental health in children and young people, government policy and mental health services in the UK often do not recognise children in poverty as a vulnerable group nor as a priority group for access to mental health services (Ayre, 2016). Worldwide, over 90 per cent of countries have no mental health policy that includes children and young people (WHO, 2001). The World Health Organization (2001) emphasise that children should be highlighted as a vulnerable group with special mental health needs in national health policies.

In addition to poverty and the persistence of poverty, other risk factors associated with poor child mental health include social exclusion, violence, peer rejection, isolation and lack of family support (WHO, 2012). Living in poverty increases the probability of experiencing these risk factors. Furthermore, the more risk factors children experience, the higher the probability of poor mental health (WHO, 2012). Children living in poverty are at greater risk of being bullied and stigmatised by their peer group. This was demonstrated in my longitudinal study of poverty, where a 12-year-old boy who had just gone up to high school was displaying deteriorating social, emotional and behavioural wellbeing at home and was disengaging from school. His mother discovered the following:

'I had to go and pick him up from the school one day because he had been sick. Just before lunchtime. He never had any dinner money left. And I said to him, "What's happening? What's going on?" And he said, "I'm getting bullied because I'm poor and I've not got any money for a bacon roll."'

Being bullied by peers in childhood is shown to have a greater influence on later mental health than maltreatment by parents (Davie, 2016) and children living in poverty say that being bullied for being poor is a key source of unhappiness (Hooper, 2007).

Protective factors for child mental health and poverty

As well as risk factors for poor mental health in childhood and adolescence, there are also factors that can protect young people. My research showed the direct and indirect relationship pathways between poverty, maternal emotional distress and child mental wellbeing, the results of which suggest that increasing income and dedicated support to mothers suffering from emotional distress would be beneficial to children's mental health (Treanor, 2016a). An increase to permanent family income has since been shown to have a protective effect on children's mental health, findings that have led the authors to posit that psychosocial and financial supports for families affected by parental mental health issues should be a priority (Noonan et al, 2018).

Peer relationships and inclusion in the peer group is also shown to be an important protective factor for child wellbeing, with time spent with friends consistently emerging as beneficial for social, emotional and behaviour outcomes (Noonan et al, 2018). There are also protective factors from being connected to and supported at the community level, through access to adolescent-friendly social services, including health services, and through policies that increase income and facilitate community cohesion and integration (WHO, 2012). On an individual child level, both verbal cognitive ability and self-regulation independently are protective factors for children living consistently in poverty (Flouri et al, 2014: 1050). This relationship is robust even after controlling for factors related to both self-regulation and adjustment in children, such as verbal cognitive ability and the home lives of their families (Flouri et al, 2014: 1050–3). However, although they are protective factors, neither factor fully attenuated the effect of socioeconomic disadvantage (Flouri et al, 2014: 1047). While focusing on these individual psychological protective factors may seem worthwhile, it is worth considering what effect the material circumstances of the children have on their ability to self-regulate and to develop a strong verbal cognitive ability.

We learned in Chapter 2 that poverty is dynamic. It is also the case that mental health is not a static category or experience (Elliott, 2016). This means that an individual's, household's, family's or community's needs in terms of protective, preventative action on mental health and socioeconomic deprivation will change over time, particularly at transition points and pressure points (Elliott, 2016: 15). For individuals, because the impacts on mental health of advantage and disadvantage are cumulative, the World Health Organization emphasises the need for early intervention (Elliott, 2016: 15).

Parental mental health and poverty

The relationship between mental health and poverty is particularly important: worldwide the poor and the deprived have a higher prevalence of mental health disorders (WHO, 2001). Even an initial entry into poverty causes maternal psychological distress and socioemotional behavioural problems in children (Wickham et al, 2017). Given how dynamic poverty is, with people unremittingly cycling into and out of poverty, such transitions into poverty are constantly being made to detrimental effect on mothers and children. Although the concern thus far has been with persistence of poverty, it is shown that even a single transition to income poverty affects children's life chances. It is argued that 'actions that directly reduce income poverty of children are likely to improve child and maternal mental health' (Wickham et al, 2017: 141). Furthermore, it is not only family or household income that causes poor mental health; the income inequality of an area is also shown to be negatively correlated with mental health. This suggests 'that income distribution may have a significant influence upon mental health over and above the effect of poverty. The findings imply that mental health can be improved not only by influencing individuals' health knowledge and behaviour but also by implementing a more equitable economic policy' (Hanandita and Tampubolon, 2014). In addition to low income, other socioeconomic and social factors that correlate with maternal mental health are low educational attainment, unemployment, ethnicity and lone parenthood (Liu et al, 2016), all of which increase the likelihood of living in poverty and experiencing health inequalities.

In my longitudinal study of families, mental health problems among parents are the singular biggest issue they faced. All of the families, whether they are working, studying or currently not in paid work, experience anxiety due to the financial struggles that they face. Jamie is a father of six who works full-time. He describes the difficulties he and his wife face trying to manage on a low income: "There's definitely an added stress, to try to keep our head above water kind of thing. That brings stresses and strains. I think my wife gets more stressed than me ... I just let most things slide and deal with it ... My wife gets stressed out with it.' Jamie also says that it is his wife who takes responsibility for managing their low income, a finding that is common across several studies of poverty. This is in contrast to families who have a higher income where men are shown to be more likely to control family finances. It is the stress that families face that they believe leads to negative health consequences. Sarah is the mother of one teenage boy:

'I was waking up at 4 o'clock in the morning, bolt upright, heart pounding, worrying about something, and going, "What is it I'm actually worrying about here?" And I would have to talk myself down to go back to sleep. And it was things that are out of my control ... And it always comes down to money. It's always about money. That's always the root of it ... I've been really ill, I've had really bad depression and anxiety and stuff over the last two years.'

Mary is the mother of one son who has developed mental health difficulties. She too has mental health difficulties. She experiences acute and chronic levels of anxiety:

> 'It [her anxiety] has just gone overboard now. I was actually at the doctor's today about it. But again, that's money worries. My anxiety is making me really, really ill. My anxiety has gone through the roof. The minute I wake up, all I'm thinking about is money, money, money. What have I to pay tomorrow? How am I going to get the electricity to do another two days? It's quite scary ... Sometimes I just get really down and think I'm absolutely hopeless and I'm no good to anybody, because I've no money.'

Thus, the impact of poverty on maternal mental health is large, greater than it is found to be for child mental health (Wickham et al, 2017). However, the mental distress experienced by mothers due to income poverty is shown to have a massively detrimental impact on children (Treanor, 2016a).

A final consideration, but a very important point, is that people with mental health problems are highly unlikely to claim benefits. Reasons put forward for this low take-up of entitlements include 'the complexity of the system, the lack of knowledge among claimants, and that the social security system is not well adapted to the episodic and fluctuating characteristics of some mental health problems' (Elliott, 2016: 60).

The consequences on children of living with a parent with a mental health condition

Children are especially vulnerable to their parents' poor mental health. This is because, compared to adults, children have more limited coping skills, are more dependent on other people, and have fewer psychological defence mechanisms (Leahy, 2015: 100). There are many factors relating to parental mental health that interact with and negatively affect children, such as 'genes, the direct effects of behaviour associated with maternal illness, intrauterine environment, impaired parent–infant interaction and parenting styles, parental conflict, socio-economic disadvantage, and temperamental factors in the child' (Manning and Gregoire, 2009). How these factors operate and the pathways involved in their mediation are complex and interrelated (Manning and Gregoire, 2009). Thus, there is no easy solution to mitigating the adverse effects of parental mental health and children.

Poor parental mental health significantly affects all aspects of family life and, in particular, children's wellbeing (Leahy, 2015). Poor parental mental health has been shown to affect attachment formation (Manning and Gregoire, 2009) and the child living with parental mental health problems are more at risk of developing social, emotional and behavioural problems (Leahy, 2015). Furthermore, they are 'also at increased risk of developing psychiatric disorder in childhood, adolescence, and later adult life' (Manning and Gregoire, 2009). Children with parents who experience mental illness are 2.5 times more likely than the children of parents unaffected by mental illness to experience some level of psychiatric disorder in their lifetimes (Liu et al, 2016). Maternal mental health in particular is shown to be an important determinant of child physical and mental health outcomes (Wickham et al, 2017). Other factors that are important to the impact of a parent's poor mental health are 'the severity and the duration of the illness, the child's age and resilience, and the influence of the healthy parent', where there is one (Leahy, 2015: 100).

The following list of negative effects of living with a parent with a mental illness, compiled in collaboration with children, is taken from Cooklin (2009: 19):

- the loss of close intimate contact with a parent;
- neglect and/or violence, including verbal, physical, and/or sexual violence;
- ambiguous expectations/demands, for example one parent making demands that contradict those of the other parent, or contradictory demands from the same parent at different times;
- invasion of the child's thinking and feelings by exposure to the parent's delusions and hallucinations;
- fears for the parent's safety;
- fears for the parents' future as a couple (if there are two parents), for the future of the family, and who will look after him or her;
- contradictory expectations, that is that the child be 'grown up' and 'a carer' at home, and a child at school;
- rejection, harassment, and/or bullying by other children at school or in the neighbourhood;
- self-isolation, through stigma and fear of rejection;
- isolation of the family through stigma;
- lower standard of living and financial hardship;
- experiencing different and potentially confusing care patterns if looked after by others;

- experiencing separation from other family members, for example siblings, if children cannot be cared for together;
- disruption of education;
- underachievement in education and reduced life chances as a consequence.

When children with parents experiencing mental ill health have to live with other family members, for example grandparents, it can have both positive and negative impacts on children. It is positive that support from extended family is available and this is shown to be essential to children's wellbeing and ability to cope (Leahy, 2015). However, the negative effects are that children report feeling 'a deep sense of loss and sadness when their mentally ill parent was either in the hospital or emotionally absent', and that the children in the family leave the home, and those who remain behind, describe a feeling of grief (Leahy, 2015). At times, siblings can be separated from each other with great distress and personal loss.

There are also concerns for the mental wellbeing of the family member who becomes the guardian to the children of mentally ill parents. Guardians have extremely high rates of self-reported mental health problems (Liu et al, 2016). Oftentimes, the guardian is a single grandmother parenting on their own and the task they undertake can lead to mental health difficulties, impacting on their caretaking abilities (Liu et al, 2016). It is important that the mental wellbeing of guardians is also taken into consideration and necessary supports to care for their charge put in place (Liu et al, 2016).

Stigma

In the UK, there is a great deal of stigma towards those who are living in poverty and seen as 'scrounging' of the state in a re-emergent public discourse on the 'deserving' and 'undeserving' poor. It used to be the case that those who were ill or disabled were not included in the 'undeserving poor' (Garthwaite, 2011). However, the vitriol has increasingly turned towards those who cannot work through reasons of ill health and disability, and there are now increasing levels of vicious attitudes among the general public. As Shildrick and MacDonald (2013: 296) found, there is 'an increase in resentment, abuse and record levels of "hate crime" against people with disabilities ... it is difficult not to see this current "scroungerphobia" as chiming with a more general public intolerance towards those "at the bottom"'. Stigma now, therefore, extends beyond poverty to those in poor physical health. It was always the case, however, that poor mental health was, and remains, highly stigmatised.

The impact of this increasing stigma is that, as with the masking of child poverty for fear of stigma and unwanted service intervention, mental ill health is also frequently masked for fear of the same. Although mental ill health is a leading cause of disease and disability worldwide, approximately half of people with a mental illness do not seek help due to stigma and discrimination, even in affluent societies with high quality mental health care (WHO, 2001). For those with a mental illness in low- and middle-income countries, between 76 and 85 per cent of people do not seek help for the same reasons (WHO, 2013). The proportion of people who do not seek help is much larger among poorer groups and in poorer countries (WHO, 2001). Other reasons for parents in particular not seeking help for mental health problems is the fear that their children will be removed from their care (Liu et al, 2016). Due to such a high proportion of the mentally ill population not seeking help, their needs are not being addressed. Furthermore, the needs of their children are even more overlooked and neglected, making the children of mentally ill parents a hidden population (Leahy, 2015). What this means for children is that those who encounter them on a daily basis, for example teachers, may not be aware that there is a parent with poor mental health in a family, or that the child may either be bearing inappropriate responsibility for a parent or siblings, or may be residing at times with other family members (Leahy, 2015). Children themselves may also mask mental health issues in their family for fear of being bullied by their peers (Leahy, 2015).

Stigma for children and young people living in poverty and who are affected by ill health in the family, especially poor mental health, is especially high. Children's feelings of stigma 'leads to loneliness, depression and loss of confidence' and can adversely affect young people's view of the world and their place in it (Ayre, 2016: 11). This prevents children being able to participate fully at school, in their communities and within their peer groups (Griggs and Walker, 2008). You may think that even if one lays the blame for poverty at the door of the adult experiencing it, that this blame would not also extend to the children (Reutter et al, 2009) but this is too often not the case. Marmot (2016: 113) emphasised this most eloquently in his book:

> You might blame adults for their absent-mindedness in being poor, let alone what you see as their disgraceful behaviour in risking their health by eating cheap food and being too ground down and poor to join a gym or Pilates

class. Fecklessness, it has been called, or being one of the undeserving poor – but don't blame the children! They do not choose their parents; they do not choose to be born in poverty.

We know that children do not choose to be born into poverty and do not choose their parents and yet public attitudes and, often, public policy fails to recognise this.

Protective factors for the children of parents with poor mental health

While the children of parents with mental health problems are at greater risk of problems with their wellbeing in childhood, and their outcomes in future, there are factors that can be protective. One key factor is for public services to exist and for children and young people to be able to access them. Another key factor is the presence of one or more alternative caring adults, one described as 'warm, concerned, but relatively uninvolved' (Cooklin, 2009: 18). Another factor pertains to information. If children can make sense of their parents' behaviours through age-appropriate knowledge and information about their parents' mental illness then this provides a certain level of protection (Grove et al, 2017). It helps children to understand that they are not the cause of, and are not responsible for, their parents' mental ill health and its associated behaviours. Additionally, the social environment of a child, including their family, peer, school, and neighbourhood contexts, also exerts a protective influence (Wlodarczyk et al, 2017). If the necessary support were to be provided it would help mitigate the negative effects.

Flipping the thinking

This chapter explains how child mental health is strongly associated with the timing and duration of poverty. This suggests that children's mental health is highly sensitive to socioeconomic status, income and material deprivation and that child mental health is not a fixed trait but can respond to intervention (Treanor, 2016a). It leads one to believe that were the financial conditions of their families to improve, child mental health might too. It has been suggested that if a meaningful income increase could reduce the gaps in mental health between poor and non-poor children it could constitute a socially important change (Comeau and Boyle, 2018).

The circumstances in which children grow and develop have a profound effect on their health and mental health in childhood and in adulthood. The ideal is to empower children, that is to help them develop the capacities to enable them to enjoy the basic freedoms to lead a life meaningful to them now and in the future (Marmot, 2016). Early child development is influenced both by the quality of the caregiving children receive and by the circumstances in which the caregiving takes place (Marmot, 2016). These are not mutually exclusive as the ability to look after children and to support them to reach their full potential is also influenced by the circumstances in which one lives. Social and economic characteristics such as living in poverty and/or being a member of a marginalised group can lead, separately and in combination to: poorer (mental) health, more stressed parenting, and disempowerment in adults and children. The stigma associated with having or experiencing these social and economic characteristics causes parents and children to mask poverty and mental health problems. This makes the children who are most in need, and at greatest risk, a hidden population. Additionally, the shame that results from experiencing stigma is a disincentive in itself to seeking support. To flip the thinking, we need to reduce the stigma and shame associated with mental health problems that involve children and young people, either their own or their parents. Given that at any one time 20 per cent of children and young people experience mental health problems, and this figure will be around three times higher for those from at-risk groups relating to their social and economic characteristics, it makes most sense to boost awareness and provide (access to) services where children and young people most frequent. This is likely to be their school or educational establishment. Providing specialised information and services within an educational setting would have the attendant consequence of raising the awareness and understanding of teachers too, which, as Chapter 5 affirms, would also improve children's engagement with and success in their education.

Problem behaviours in childhood, but especially in adolescence, are strongly related to parental mental health problems. To flip the thinking, instead of thinking of children and young people's behaviour as proactive, think of it as *reactive*, as a response to their parent(s) mental wellbeing. Child social, emotional and behavioural wellbeing is 'malleable and that children are emotional barometers responding to and corresponding with their mothers' wellbeing' (Treanor, 2016a: 691). This indicates that were parental mental health conditions to improve, child mental health might too. The first solution would be to treat a mother's mental health as it is likely to be a beneficial way to improve child mental health (Noonan et al, 2018). The second would be to provide respite and support to the children and young people affected by parental mental ill health. This could happen via screening for the presence of children where the parent is engaged with services, especially mental health services. It could also happen for children directly in the school setting, which would be easier if the services mentioned earlier in this chapter were in place.

There has been a huge focus in relation to child poverty and child development on the early years and early intervention, in response to the work of the Nobel Prize winning economist, James Heckman. Heckman's work emphasises that, for disadvantaged children, the pivotal time for intervention is between 0 and 5 years old as this is when children are developing most. He argues that even beginning to invest at ages 3 or 4 is too late if we want to disrupt the cumulative effects of poverty on children's health and development. It should be noted that Heckman did not say *only* invest in young children and ignore the needs of older children, although this is what tends to have happened in practice. While early investment and intervention is undeniably important, it has in practice taken investment and attention away from young people, which has been to their detriment, as adolescence is arguably another period of great developmental change, ripe for intervention at a time when young people can understand and take ownership. To flip the thinking, we also need to direct funding and attention to the key transition times in adolescence, to intervene at the stage of potential disengagement from school and risky health behaviours. We need to flip our thinking of adolescents as badly behaved under-developed adults to fast-growing children in need of support and care.

As a final point I would like to emphasise that, in writing about the negative effects of parental mental and physical health, and health behaviours, on children and young people I am in no way blaming the families for the stress and stressful conditions that they find themselves living in. It is common and too easy to blame families living in poverty and poor health for their situations and for the negative effects this has on their children. However, many of these negative effects could be prevented and mitigated by an increase in income and a reduction in material deprivation of families living in poverty and for the accessible provision of mental health support services for children and young people. To flip the thinking, families do not want to struggle, and parents do not want their children to experience the negative effects of the poverty and poor mental and physical health. Rather, they want what all parents want, which is the best for their children, but they do not have sufficient resources to create the conditions for healthy living. Thus, if we want to understand more about mental health and poverty, then mental health must be addressed within poverty research and poverty must be a component in mental health research: furthermore, 'a mental health and poverty research agenda should be co-produced with individuals, families and communities with lived experience of these issues' (Elliott, 2016: 4).

8

Ethnicity and disability

It's because of my physical appearance and because I'm Asian that I am bullied. Sometimes people make fun of me and ruin my belongings but I don't tell my parents. (Ditch the Label, 2018: 15)

Introduction

This chapter turns to those children at increased risk of poverty either through their belonging to a non-white ethnic minority or through their own or a family member's disability. As well as having an increased risk of living in poverty, these are circumstances that, when combined with poverty, have an interactive effect.

Ethnicity

While the focus here is on ethnicity, it is recognised that ethnicity operates as a proxy to other characteristics, such as skin colour and culture (religion), which have been shown to be the predominant 'mechanisms that operate to reinforce disadvantage among some groups or to facilitate social mobility amongst others' (Khattab, 2009: 319). The relationship between ethnicity, skin colour and religion is complex and there is much to learn about how these factors operate in relation to each other to produce and reproduce inequalities (Khattab, 2009: 319). With this understanding in mind, this discussion uses the term 'ethnicity' to encompass those factors relating to race, culture and religion that creates and recreates disadvantage in our society for children. Here we look at the impacts on children and young people, and their parents, of society's responses to their ethnicity in relation to poverty, education, bullying and wellbeing, and employment, under-employment and unemployment.

Ethnicity and education

The three characteristics that affect educational experiences and attainment most are ethnicity, socioeconomic status and gender (Tackey et al, 2011). If a child has more than one of these higher-risk characteristics, the effects are that much greater. However, the relationship between ethnicity, socioeconomic status, gender and education is not consistent, it depends upon the age of the child and their stage of education (Barnard, 2014). Chapter 5 details the gaps in experience and attainment faced by children living in poverty. There is also a gap in experience and attainment of children based on their ethnicity. These gaps are smaller in early childhood and gather strength as children grow towards adolescence.

In the educational stage known as key stage 1 in England and Wales, black pupils and white pupils from economically disadvantaged backgrounds with high attainment at age four did not progress as might have been expected between the ages of four and seven (Strand, 1999). This raises the question at what age do the gaps associated with ethnicity appear in children? In Strand's (1999) study it was clear at this early age that more able black Caribbean pupils made especially poor progress compared to their white peers. Furthermore, children of Chinese and Indian origin made more progress than their white peers, even if they were from a low socioeconomic background (Strand, 1999). This emphasises that the relationship between ethnicity and education is complex and inconsistent. What is also shown is that the large gap in attainment at age five between children from the poorest and richest backgrounds continues to expand during the primary school years and beyond (Goodman and Gregg, 2010).

Moving from primary to secondary school, at this stage poverty is found to be the largest driver of differential performance with an effect size that is three times greater than the difference between ethnic minority groups who are equally disadvantaged (Tackey et al, 2011: 5). At this stage there are also notable gender discrepancies in attainment 'with boys (especially black Caribbean boys and white boys from deprived households) doing worse' (Tackey et al, 2011: 5). In fact white working-class boys in the UK make almost the least progress over the course of secondary school, even after all socioeconomic factors are taken into account (Tackey et al, 2011). Black African students, together with Bangladeshis and Pakistanis, achieve higher GCSE scores than equivalent white students (Tackey et al, 2011: 7). The children with the highest level of achievement with regard to non-white ethnicities are Chinese and Indian pupils (Tackey et al, 2011). For students of

Indian ethnicity, of those who were in the bottom 10 per cent of achievement in their early years, almost nine out of ten climb out of it (Tackey et al, 2011). However, the ethnic group across each of the four nations of the UK who do most badly in educational attainment are the Gypsy/white Traveller group also known as the Gypsy/Roma/Traveller group (Tackey et al, 2011).

Children from Gypsy/white Traveller ethnic backgrounds have lower educational attainment than all other ethnicities. In early childhood they are only a third to a half as likely to achieve 'a good level of development' in their early years foundation stage profile compared to 'other white' children in England (EHRC, 2016). Moving forward to secondary school, children from Gypsy/white Traveller ethnic backgrounds are only a third to a quarter as likely to achieve at least five A* GCSEs compared with 'other white' children in England (EHRC, 2016). In Scotland, the number of Gypsy/Traveller pupils is small; however, they are still the lowest attaining of all other children based on ethnic background (EHRC, 2016).

This ethnic patterning within education extends to the rates of exclusion too. Children in England of black Caribbean and mixed white/black Caribbean ethnicities are around three times more likely to face permanent exclusion compared to the exclusion rate for all pupils (EHRC, 2016). The highest rates of both permanent and fixed-period exclusion, however, is for children from Gypsy/white Traveller ethnic backgrounds (EHRC, 2016). Despite an overall decrease in the total number and rate of permanent exclusions in England, pupils from ethnic minority backgrounds experience disproportionate rates of exclusions (EHRC, 2016). However, higher rates of absence and fixed-period exclusions were found among white pupils from disadvantaged backgrounds (EHRC, 2016). In Scotland, ethnic minority pupils are *less* likely to be excluded than white pupils; however, once again, the exclusion rates for children from Gypsy/white Traveller ethnic backgrounds in Scotland are the highest of all ethnic minorities (EHRC, 2016).

The potential explanations put forward for the gaps in education among ethnic minority children, especially black Caribbean pupils, are that pupils from different ethnic groups attend lower quality schools, that teachers have lower expectations of black pupils, and that, among ethnic minority communities, there is a perception of low returns to educational qualifications due to a prejudiced labour market (Tackey et al, 2011: 7).

There is evidence to support the proposition that teachers in the UK have lower expectations of black pupils. Strand's (2012: 75) research suggests that there is a 'white British–black Caribbean achievement gap at age 14 which cannot be accounted for by socioeconomic variables or a wide range of contextual factors'. In an analysis of different patterns of entry to the different tiers of national mathematics and science tests at age 14 across different ethnic groups, Strand (2012: 75) shows that 'that black Caribbean students are systematically under-represented in entry to the higher tiers relative to their white British peers'. It should be noted that being put forward for these different tiers is based on teachers' judgements. This difference between black and white students 'persists after controls for prior attainment, socio-economic variables and a wide range of pupil, family, school and neighbourhood factors' (Strand, 2012: 75). What is also of note here is that black Caribbean students were the most likely to have been excluded from school during the year prior to the age 14 tests, to have the highest level of identified special educational needs, and were the most likely to have truanted at some time during the first three years of secondary school compared to other ethnic groups (Strand, 2011). Among teachers it is found that their perceptions of students' behaviour constitutes a large component of the academic judgements they make on pupils (Strand, 2012). As such, Strand (2012: 89) concludes that 'black Caribbean students may be disproportionately allocated to lower test tiers, not as a result of direct or conscious discrimination, but because teachers' judgements of their academic potential are distorted by perceptions of their behaviour. If the behaviour of black Caribbean students is more challenging, or even if it is simply that teachers perceive their behaviour as more problematic, there may be a tendency to underestimate their academic ability'.

Another factor that is shown to impede access to and participation in education and, therefore, lead to lower educational attainment of ethnic minority children is peer-bullying. Children who are bullied in primary school are less engaged compared to those with positive friendships (Gutman and Vorhaus, 2012). Furthermore, as children move towards adolescence and into secondary school, their emotional and behavioural wellbeing are shown to be more important than demographic and other characteristics in explaining school engagement (Gutman and Vorhaus, 2012). When children are bullied, they experience low wellbeing and the effects have long-term adverse impacts on young adults' mental health (Lereya et al, 2015). As discussed in 7 seven on health, peer relationships and inclusion in the peer group is an important protective factor for child wellbeing, with time spent with friends consistently emerging as beneficial for social, emotional and behaviour outcomes (Noonan et al, 2018).

Children and young people are frequently bullied in the UK because of their ethnicity, culture or religion (Ditch the Label, 2018). In Scotland, one in four pupils said they were aware of peers in their school experiencing prejudice-based bullying based on race, disability, sexual orientation or socioeconomic status (Dennell and Logan, 2015). Furthermore, in this study, approximately 40 per cent of teachers were aware of bullying based on ethnicity or sexual orientation (Dennell and Logan, 2015). These teachers said they had responded to prejudice-based bullying, but that they were not always satisfied with how their reports of prejudice-based bullying were handled (Dennell and Logan, 2015). Bullying results in a range of negative consequences for children and young people, in their present lives and future outcomes. Of those saying they were bullied in the past 12 months, 50 per cent say they felt depressed, 45 per cent felt anxious, 34 per cent had suicidal thoughts, 28 per cent self-harmed and 21 per cent truanted from school as a consequence (Ditch the Label, 2018). Peer bullying in childhood is of great concern to future mental health and is argued to be a public health concern that ought to be widely addressed (Lereya et al, 2015).

Ethnicity and poverty

The incidence and prevalence of child poverty vary greatly across different ethnic groups in the UK. For this chapter I conduct analysis using the UK government's latest Households Below Average Income data (2019) in collaboration with the Joseph Rowntree Foundation. The rates are calculated using three-year averages due to the small number of people in each ethnicity and are shown in Figure 8.1. In this figure we can see that white and Indian children are least likely to be in poverty with average rates of 26 and 27 per cent respectively in the period 2014/15 to 2016/17. As well as being less likely to be in poverty in the first place, Indian and white children are more likely to exit poverty (Nandi and Platt, 2010). Figure 8.1 shows that the gap between Indian and white children used to be much higher in the 1990s, with a gap of over ten percentage points, which has since been successfully reduced.

As Figure 8.1 shows, the situation for other ethnic groups is more discouraging. Historically, children of Pakistani and Bangladeshi origin are most likely to experience poverty. Their rates have decreased from over 70 and 80 per cent respectively in the mid-1990s to 54 and 60 per cent in the period 2014/15 to 2016/17. These rates are alarmingly high and suggest that children of Pakistani and Bangladeshi ethnicity are among the most disadvantaged in the UK today. As well as a higher

Figure 8.1 Child poverty risk (after housing cost) by ethnicity (3-year averages), 1994/95 to 2016/17

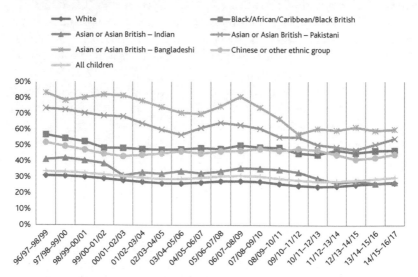

Source: Households Below Average Income (2019). Author's analysis in collaboration with the Joseph Rowntree Foundation.

incidence and prevalence, Bangladeshi and Pakistani also children have a very high risk of being persistently in poverty (Nandi and Platt, 2010), which as we have learned in earlier chapters, leads to poorer current development and wellbeing and future outcomes.

The Black/African/Caribbean/Black British and Chinese/Other ethnic groups lie somewhere between the two extremes. Their rates are still quite high at 47 and 44 per cent respectively. Black Caribbean and black African children also have a lower risk of persistent poverty than Pakistani and Bangladeshi children although it remains higher than that of Indian and white children (Nandi and Platt, 2010). The effect of having a non-white ethnicity is to have a rate of child poverty that is two to four times that of white children. Although those from non-white ethnicities are at calculated to be at greater risk of being in poverty, due to the far smaller numbers of non-white children, the overwhelming majority of children living in poverty are still white.

Ethnicity and employment

In addition to having higher rates of poverty, BME groups are also more likely to be members of groups at particular risk of poverty: lone-parent families, large families, families with a disability and/or workless families. It is important to note, however, that the higher poverty risks for BME families are not simply the result of membership of these higher risk categories (Platt, 2009). Even after membership of high-risk categories is taken into consideration, there are ethnic poverty penalties associated with being non-white in the UK (Platt, 2009). While poverty is higher among BME groups compared to the white British population, all BME groups are not the same; there is variation within and between ethnic groups in poverty profiles. For example, men and women with the same ethnicity are likely to have different experiences of poverty (Barnard, 2014). In fact, the risk of poverty can be multiplied due being a member of a BME group and the interaction it has with other factors such as gender, class, education, disability, migrant status and geography (Barnard, 2014).

There are a number of reasons for the BME population having a higher poverty rate than the white population. For example, some ethnic minority groups, such as white Gypsy/Traveller groups, African groups and mixed white and Caribbean, have higher unemployment rates and others have higher rates of economic inactivity linked to unpaid caring responsibilities in the home, for example women from Pakistani and Bangladeshi backgrounds (Weekes-Bernard, 2017). For those in employment, ethnic minority groups are overwhelmingly concentrated in low-paying sectors with little prospect of progression (Weekes-Bernard, 2017). BME groups are overrepresented in low-paid, insecure employment in spite of their higher levels of educational attainment compared to white British groups (Weekes-Bernard, 2017). Forty per cent of African and 39 per cent of Bangladeshi graduates are overqualified for their roles (Weekes-Bernard, 2017). The differing experiences of access to good quality, secure employment between ethnic groups and their experiences when in work raises questions about equality of opportunity (Catney and Sabater, 2015). It leads us to the main reason for the BME population having a higher poverty rate than the white population, poorer access to decent employment, and difficulties in progressing in work, namely the experience of racism and discrimination (Barnard, 2014; Weekes-Bernard, 2017).

Rates of employment

Using data from June–September 2018 from the ONS my analysis of the employment data shows that 75.7 per cent of the working age population in the UK (people aged 16 to 64) were employed (ONS, 2018). The employment rate has increased annually since 2004 in all ethnic groups (ONS, 2018a). Between ethnic groups, 77 per cent of white people of working age were employed compared to 67 per cent of people from all the other ethnic groups combined, the highest rates for both groups since 2004 (ONS, 2018a). Within the white ethnic groups, 76 per cent white British are employed compared to 81 per cent of other white ethnic groups (ONS, 2018a). The black African/ Caribbean rate was just above the combined ethnic minority average at 67.7 per cent and the employment rate for Bangladeshi, Pakistani and Chinese ethnicities was lowest at 57.3 per cent, 54.2 per cent and 60.3 per cent respectively (ONS, 2018a).

Between genders across all ethnicities 80 per cent men and 71 per cent of women were employed in 2017 (ONS, 2018a). 81.1 per cent of white men and 75.8 per cent of men from all other ethnicities combined are employed. The rates between ethnic groups for men, disaggregated as far as possible using ONS (2018) data, are: 70.3 per cent for men of mixed backgrounds, 84.5 per cent for Indian men, 74.1 per cent for Pakistani men, 71.1 per cent for Bangladeshi men, 65.9 per cent for Chinese men and 73.4 per cent for black African/Caribbean men. As well as lower rates of employment for men of a non-white ethnicity, there are also higher rates of part-time employment among some BME men, which is particularly important because the hourly pay for men in part-time work is only 58 per cent of that for full-time work (Barnard, 2014).

For women across all ethnicities, 73.3 per cent of white ethnicity and 58.5 per cent of all other ethnicities combined are employed. Between ethnic groups for women, 64.6 per cent of women of mixed backgrounds, 70.8 per cent of Indian women, 40.5 per cent of Pakistani women, 32.8 per cent of Bangladeshi women, 56.6 per cent of Chinese women and 62.6 per cent of black African/Caribbean women are employed (ONS, 2018a). Bangladeshi women are less than half as likely to be employed compared to all women combined (EHRC, 2016). The ONS data do not disaggregate by the white Gypsy or Traveller group; however, this group is also particularly disadvantaged in rates of employment, which were 67 per cent for men and 41 per cent for women in 2013 (Nazroo and Kapadia, 2013).

Rates of unemployment

The economically active population in the UK includes all people who are available for work, whether they are employed or unemployed (and it excludes people who are retired, caring for family, or in full-time education and not in paid work) (ONS, 2018b). Using data from June–September 2018 from the ONS my analysis of the unemployment data shows that the total unemployment rate in the UK was 4.3 per cent. Broken down by ethnicity, the unemployment rate for the white ethnicity was 3.9 per cent, down from 6.3 per cent in 2013 (EHRC, 2016), and 7 per cent for all other ethnic minority groups combined (ONS, 2018b), down from 12.9 per cent in 2013 (EHRC, 2016). It should be noted that there is a significant decrease in unemployment across all ethnic groups, including white, although differences between ethnicities remain.

Between BME groups, the lowest unemployment rate is among Indians at 4.5 per cent and Chinese at 3.6 per cent, and the highest is among Pakistani and Bangladeshi ethnic groups at 7.5 per cent and 9.7 per cent respectively, a decrease from 17.3 per cent in 2013 but still the largest group of unemployed by ethnicity in the UK (EHRC, 2016; ONS, 2018b). African/Caribbean black groups have an unemployment rate of 9.5 per cent, down from 15.5 per cent in 2013 (EHRC, 2016; ONS, 2018b). The gender differences in unemployment within and between BME groups are also important. For men, 4.0 per cent of white compared to 6.4 per cent of all other ethnicities are unemployed. Between ethnic groups, 11.2 per cent of mixed, 4.2 per cent of Indian, 5.2 per cent of Pakistani, 7.7 per cent of Bangladeshi and 8.9 per cent of African/Caribbean black men are unemployed. There are no data for Chinese men as the numbers are too small to be robust. For women, 3.7 per cent of white compared to 7.7 per cent of all other ethnicities are unemployed. Between ethnic groups, 5.8 per cent of mixed, 4.8 per cent of Indian, 11.5 per cent of Pakistani, 14.8 per cent of Bangladeshi and 10.2 per cent of African/Caribbean black women are unemployed. There are no data for Chinese women as the numbers are too small to be robust. While the ethnicity data are not broken down sufficiently for the white Gypsy or Traveller group in the Office for National Statistics data, this group is known to be particularly disadvantaged in rates of unemployment at 16 per cent for men and 19 per cent for women in 2013 (Nazroo and Kapadia, 2013).

Profile of employment

Despite the improving and optimistic statistics for employment and unemployment in the UK, its labour market is replete with low-paid, low-skilled jobs, which leads to greater insecurity and fewer opportunities for progression (Barnard, 2014; Weekes-Bernard, 2017). These low-quality, insecure jobs affect people from ethnic minority groups particularly strongly as they tend to gain employment in lower level jobs with lower pay (Platt, 2009; Barnard, 2014). This concentration of BME workers in low-paid work is a main driver for the disproportionately high poverty rates among some ethnic groups (Catney and Sabater, 2015). As well as being financially disadvantaged, people who are low paid are also less likely to receive training or to have access to opportunities to move into more sustainable and better paid work (Barnard, 2014). This effectively traps workers, particularly ethnic minority workers, into low wages (Barnard, 2014) and it is this lack of movement out of low-paid work that increases the risk of poverty among these groups (EHRC, 2016). Black and Asian workers are twice as likely as white workers to be in involuntary temporary employment and twice as likely to be in agency work (EHRC, 2016). Furthermore, black and Asian workers are moving into more insecure forms of employment at higher rates than white workers (EHRC, 2016). Black workers with degrees earn 23.1 per cent less on average than white workers with degrees and black people who leave school with GCSEs typically get paid 11.4 per cent less than their white peers (EHRC, 2016). This is in spite of a higher level of education among the ethnic minority community, demonstrating that 'these differences in employment and earnings are not explained by differences in education or other individual characteristics' (Barnard, 2014: 3).

Ethnicity and discrimination

The higher poverty risks and lack of access to higher-quality, higher-skilled jobs faced by those from minority ethnic groups suggest other barriers are in operation, including in the form of employer discrimination (Platt, 2009). More explicitly, 'the ways in which ethnicity is perceived by others affects the opportunities and treatment experienced by those assumed to be part of some minority groups. The strongest part of this is the racism and discrimination faced in many areas of life by people from visible ethnic and religious groups' (Barnard, 2014: 5). Racism is not always openly hostile, although sometimes it is; it can also lurk 'in institutional cultures and practices', limiting 'the opportunities and life choices individuals make' (Gilchrist and Kyprianou, 2011: 7). For these reasons, people from ethnic minorities may choose to reside in a neighbourhood where they can ensure access to familiar cultural goods and supportive social networks (Gilchrist and Kyprianou, 2011). This can have positive and negative effects. On the one hand, it can lead to employment and job security. However, on the other hand, it can lead to jobs with little prospects of promotion, can preclude opportunities for new employment elsewhere and, for young people, 'ethnic networks can be beneficial in terms of employment, but also limiting in the longer term, restricting their choices and aspirations for education and careers' (Gilchrist and Kyprianou, 2011: 8).

Young BME and (un/under)employment

Although there have been some improvements in recent years, ethnic minority young people remain disadvantaged in the UK labour market, despite their increase in educational success (Morris, 2015). The challenges ethnic minority young people face are both unemployment, for school leavers with lower levels of education, and underemployment, for young employees with higher levels of education (Morris, 2015). There has been sustained improvement in educational attainment among ethnic minority groups, particularly black African and Bangladeshi students, which is not being translated into labour market success (Morris, 2015).

There are signs that young ethnic minorities in the UK may be experiencing worse long-term employment outcomes than white young people (EHRC, 2016). There was a 49 per cent rise in 16–24-year-olds from ethnic minority communities who were long-term unemployed from 2010 to 2015 (Runnymede Trust, 2015). This compares to a contemporaneous fall of 1 per cent in overall long-term youth unemployment and a 2 per cent fall in unemployment among young white people (Runnymede Trust, 2015). The current youth unemployment rates for young people from black and Pakistani and Bangladeshi backgrounds are more than twice that for white young people, at 26 per cent and 23 per cent respectively compared with 11 per cent (McGuinness, 2018b). For Indian young people the rate is 13 per cent and for the 'other' ethnic category it is 16 per cent (McGuinness, 2018b).

The political response to un- and underemployment has been centred on how best to activate the economically inactive and the steps it believes unemployed people should take to make themselves more employable (Patrick, 2012). It has not focused on the problems associated with structure, such as the state of the labour market and the prejudices towards the young and those from a BME background. Instead, a 'work-first approach predominates that utilises tough conditions and sanctions to activate those not engaged in paid employment' (Patrick, 2012: 8).

Disability

> States parties are obliged to protect children from all kinds of discrimination irrespective of the child's or his or her parent's or legal guardian's race, colour, sex, language, religion, political or other opinion, national, ethnic or social origin, property, disability, birth or other status. States parties, at all administrative levels, should serve to prevent discrimination and shall not directly or indirectly discriminate against children in budget-related legislation, policies or programmes, in their content or implementation. (UN, 1989)

Disability and poverty rates

Where children live in a house where there is disability, whether it be their own or a family member's, they have an increased chance of being in poverty. Disability is an important risk factor for poverty: 31 per cent, 4.3 million people, in a family with a disabled member, live in poverty in the UK, compared to 19 per cent of those who do not have a disabled family member (JRF, 2018b). Furthermore, 30 per cent (6.6 million) of those living in poverty have a disabled adult or child in their household (JRF, 2018b).

Across the age range of disabled adults, 39 per cent of those in working-age families are in poverty compared to 18 per cent of those who are not disabled (JRF, 2018b). This rate is 4 percentage points higher than 20 years ago and fluctuates depending on whether the disabled adult lives in a working or non-working household (JRF, 2018b). For disabled adults in working families, the poverty rate rose from 18 per cent to 21 per cent between 2011/12 and 2016/17 and the poverty rate for disabled adults in non-working families is 67 per cent (JRF, 2018b).

Profile of childhood disability

Boys are reported as having higher rates of disability than girls, disabled children are more likely to live with a lone parent and are also more likely to live with other disabled adults and children in the household (Blackburn et al, 2010). Even after accounting for socioeconomic disadvantage, childhood disability is still significantly associated with lone parenthood and parental disability (Blackburn et al, 2010). In fact, almost 50 per cent of disabled children, compared to 20 per cent of non-disabled children, live with a parent(s) with a disability and approximately 25 per cent of disabled children live with one or more siblings who also has a disability (Blackburn et al, 2010). For disabled children, the odds of living with a parent with a disability is over three times greater than for non-disabled children controlling for other factors (Blackburn et al, 2010). Thus, there is clear evidence of a clustering of child and adult disability (Blackburn et al, 2010). Why this should be the case is currently unclear. As regards the relationship with lone parenthood, it is hypothesised that there are higher divorce rates among parents of disabled children, lower rates of repartnering and perhaps a higher prevalence of births of disabled children to lone mothers (Blackburn et al, 2010). Given that, as demonstrated in Chapter 4, lone mothers are already the poorest, most materially deprived, the most overladen with childcare and the most overworked, this relationship with caring for disabled children, alone, is a cause of additional concern and requires a dedicated response from policy and practice.

Disabled children in the UK experience higher levels of poverty, personal and social disadvantage and are more likely to experience deprivation, debt and poor housing than non-disabled children (Blackburn et al, 2010). Debt is more prevalent in families with disability: those with both disabled children and disabled adults in the household report the highest level of debts (Blackburn et al, 2010). Being behind with payments for council tax, water rates and telephone bills are the most commonly reported sources of debt (Blackburn et al, 2010). In my study of families living in poverty, there are several families living with disability and debt featured highly. One lone mother, Mary, who has a disabled son, Jason, and who is facing increasing levels of physical incapacity herself but who has not been formally diagnosed with a disability, is in debt to council tax, TV licensing and a catalogue company. Over the five years of my study, Mary's indebtedness increases as she is being fined for non-payment of the television licence, which only increases what she owes but does not take into consideration her abject inability to find the funds to pay it. In year four of the study, Mary says,

> 'And I got a fine for my TV licence, an £80 fine. Plus, they wanted me to pay it at £10 a week. So I've to pay £10 a week fine, £10 a week for my TV licence, but I couldn't pay both, so I was paying a fine obviously because I didn't want to end up in jail or go to court or something, and I couldn't pay [the licence itself], so again, I fell into arrears.

> I tried to explain to them I can't pay both … But they were having none of it. They were saying that I could go to jail for it. So I fell behind again. The boy was at my door … I actually said to him, "I can't give you what I've not got." I can't do it.'

When next we meet in year five of the study, Mary is still struggling with the television licensing authorities who are continuing to fine her, which means she is not paying her actual licence fee as she cannot pay both at the same time. This time she says,

> 'I've not paid it in months. Not paid it in months. They had offered me to pay it … quarterly? Through direct debit, but because I was behind in it, I've still got to pay it. But I can't seem to find that £6 a week. And they were like, "We can't reduce it anymore, and you're going to end up getting another fine." I said, "Well, if you give me another fine, it's going to put me down even more."… But they're just not listening. Even when you go to Citizen's Advice or that, they'll tell you there's nothing we can do to help you with a TV licence, it must be paid. But I'm honest with them when they phone or come to the door. I'm like, "I can't pay you." '

As a woman and as a lone mother, Mary is not unique in her ongoing struggle to pay her television licence. The television licence is a particular problem as you can be prosecuted, fined and even go to prison for non-payment. In England and Wales, prosecutions for non-payment of the TV licence currently account for around 10 per cent of all criminal cases in the magistrates' courts (Evans, 2017). It is also a highly gendered debt with women being particularly disadvantaged. In 2017, females accounted for 72 per cent of *all* prosecutions for television license evasion (Ministry of Justice, 2018). Furthermore, and even more worryingly, television licence evasion remains the most common offence for which females are prosecuted, at 30 per cent of *all* prosecutions for women in 2017 in England and Wales. (Ministry of Justice, 2018). The fact that almost a third of all female prosecutions are for non-payment of the television licence is criminalising poverty and women in poverty in particular. The BBC and the TV Licensing Authority recognise that there is a gender disparity in prosecutions for failing to pay the television licence. A review into this gender disparity, undertaken by the BBC itself, found that there is 'no evidence to suggest that enforcement activity is unfairly and intentionally targeted at women' and that 'there is no evidence of any discriminatory enforcement practices on the part of TV licensing' (BBC, 2017). One of the reasons the BBC gave for the gender disparity was that a female was more likely to engage positively with a TV Licensing enquiry officer; this suggests that TV Licensing enquiry officers may be targeting female-headed households as a soft target for television licence enforcement. Contrary to BBC assertions, this is a clear source of bias: (1) if TV Licensing enquiry officers target women because they are more likely to engage, often through fear of prosecution and fear that such prosecution might result in losing their children, then this is a clear source of bias and discrimination, and the intention is irrelevant. Unintended bias is still bias; and (2) women are at greater risk of non-payment because they are more likely to be on low incomes, whether in or out of work. This interaction with poverty compounds their likelihood of being targeted by TV Licensing enquiry officers. This is a multiple source of bias.

The ability to live in a law-abiding fashion is a basic human functioning that is threatened by poverty (Wolff and De-Shalit, 2007). If meeting the needs of a family coerces an individual into acts that break the law, often at great stress and anxiety to that individual, then this is a demonstrative disadvantage caused by the society we live in, its policies and laws. That we then cast aspersions on that individual, and deem all poor people to be of a particularly criminal class, further compounds their disadvantages. By not being able to afford a TV licence, or to meet the fines for failing to pay the TV licence, we criminalise those living in poverty. As Wolff and De Shalit (2007: 47) note: 'a society that is constructed in a way that in effect forces some people to break the law in order to lead a materially decent life is especially incompetent or unjust'.

Disabled children's views

When asked their views, disabled children say that, like all children, the important things in their lives are their relationships with family, friends and at school. In a study of disabled children from Scotland on quality of life, children reported highest satisfaction in being at school (Sylvester et al, 2014). The majority of children were also positive about relationships with parents and their physical health; however, one in three children reported often feeling sad and depressed, which was associated with feeling excluded from social and sporting opportunities (Sylvester et al, 2014). When compared to findings from a larger European study using the same questionnaire with mostly non-disabled children, the Scottish sample scored lower in every area suggesting that disabled children in Scotland report a comparatively lower quality of life than do non-disabled children (Sylvester et al, 2014: 763). The areas the children showed most dissatisfaction with was the friendship indicators of the study, highlighting that friendships and a social life are extremely important to disabled young people, as with all young people, but also that they experience difficulties in making and maintaining friendships (Sylvester et al, 2014). When 'asked whether there was anything that other children could do at school that the respondent could not do but would like to, most expressed a desire to have friends, or more friends, and to be better included in social and sporting activities' (Sylvester et al, 2014: 770)

The presence or absence of friendships is very important to disabled children generally. In an Australian study, around one third of children said they had very happy and positive relationships with 'best friends' (McMaugh, 2011: 857) What disabled children report as being valuable to them in their friendships are: having friends with similar interests, having a shared sense of humour and shared academic goals (McMaugh, 2011). As with the Scottish study, however, most of the disabled children also reported being bullied for their disability; however, they also reported that 'friends provided a defence and buffer against disability-related peer harassment' (McMaugh, 2011: 857).

Disabled children often report higher quality of life and life satisfaction than their parents do when asked about their children. It may well be that parents are more aware of what they feel a child may be missing out on or lacking. Or it may be that parents see the constraints and barriers rather than the possibilities. In my study of families, Mary has a son with learning disabilities and mental health problems. She describes the consequences of her son's disabilities:

> 'It's heart-breaking for me and I feel that I'm at a standstill because I can't do anything for him. I can only give him emotional support and love and, like I do, and be there for him and support him, but he's a very difficult child sometimes… That makes me sad. Like I said to you, he's not had a kid's life. Everything's been a struggle for him in life. And it's a shame because he gets so excited, he's like, "Mum, I want to do this and I want to do that." But then all these mental health problems slip in and it's a barrier for him and it's a shame. I just get on with it. It does make me sad sometimes. But I think I can only imagine how

he's feeling. He's got all these disabilities and things going around in his head. How does he feel?'

Changes for disabled people in the UK

As a result of austerity in the UK, one of the groups most affected financially are disabled people. By 2018 disabled people had lost £28.3 billion worth of financial support from the government, which affected a total of up to 3.7 million disabled people (Cross, 2013). It is not only in financial retrenchment that disabled people have suffered under the UK's austerity measures; they have also had to face the indignity of repeated amateur assessments of their condition, the iniquity of having their disability benefits withdrawn, the stress of having to appeal wrongful official decisions, and a wait until monies have been reinstated. For some, this was happening on a six-monthly rotation. The UK Government instituted a benefit cap, which disproportionately affects families with disabilities. They also introduced the 'spare room subsidy', colloquially known in the UK as the 'bedroom tax', which penalises anyone receiving housing benefit who has what the government considers a 'spare' bedroom (Cross, 2013). What the government failed to realise was that for many

> a room has been specially created and/or adapted for a disabled person, or is needed to store equipment such as hoists or wheelchairs, nor for any other reason previously regarded as unarguable. People either have to find ways of dealing with the further loss of significant amounts of money, or look for smaller properties. (Cross, 2013: 721)

This is very much the case for one participant in my study, Janice.

Janice's story

Janice is a married mother of one, with a physical health condition, who has been in receipt of disability benefits, which, under the UK's austerity measures, are being revoked and reinstated on a regular basis over the six years of the study. She faces a constant struggle to prove her disablement and the ongoing requirement to justify it causes her great personal stress and a deterioration of her mental health: "I was at my doctor and I said, 'I'm having a nervous breakdown here. I can't cope'... I've been so ill, and the stress, which doesn't help, it makes it worse. And I'm on antidepressants as well again because I couldn't cope... I just couldn't cope." Janice's partner receives carer's allowance to look after her. He gave up his job in order to look after their daughter due to Janice's disabilities. Janice has a local authority tenancy and, since the introduction of the 'bedroom tax', she was having to pay £10 per week from her benefits, even though the room in her house was not spare but was used to help with her disability. The Scottish Government later mitigated this tax on its disabled community and Janice managed to have it reduced on appeal to £6.40 per week. At our interview in February, Janice explained that, to enable her to pay this tax, "For two days every month I wasn't eating food because I needed that money to pay my bedroom tax ... it doesn't help my condition because when I get stressed it makes me worse. I've been in hospital five times since November". During the period of living on a reduced income between November and February due to the bedroom tax and the withdrawal of her disability benefits she lost two stones (approximately 13 kilograms) in weight and was really quite ill as her disability is gastroenterological. Janet explains that every time she has to go through the process of having her disability living allowance (DLA) or her employment support allowance (ESA) reassessed she becomes extremely stressed, which exacerbates her illness. She explains that she is on ESA until the end of this year and then she will have to go through this stressful process again. "You know it's there. It's going to come. You try not to think about it but ... I'm always ill anyway, but then I'm worse with the worry."

Janice suffers from a physical disability as well as having suffered from depression over the years. This year, she has a new condition in relation to her eyes, which is not yet fully diagnosed. At one hospital appointment she was told there was a possibility that she may go blind and she received immediate laser eye surgery. When we met, she was still waiting to find out if the laser surgery had been successful or whether she might yet lose her sight. She made the point, aghast at her own thinking, that at least they would no longer mess about with her disability benefits if she went visibly blind:

> 'I have to think positive: well, at least I'll get more money
> from my disability so I won't be worrying. I'll get more help
> then. And you think – God, it's a horrible thing to thing to
> say – but at least, you know, see, if you go blind? You are
> not going to have to worry so much [about money]. It's a
> terrible thing – that you're going to have to get like that
> [go blind] so you can survive. There's something wrong
> somewhere.'

It is a searing indictment on the situation for disabled people that the prospect of worsening health conditions can almost be a type of relief if it convinces the authorities that a person is genuinely disabled and prevents their disability benefits being withdrawn.

Impacts on disabled adults

As a result of the cuts to benefits in the UK, the impacts on those with disabilities has been severe. In England, those with a higher number of disabilities, across all household members, resulted in the greatest loss of income (over £2,900 per year) than those with fewer disabilities, largely because of social care cuts (Portes and Reed, 2018). In Wales, the losses are lower, while in Scotland households with more disabilities fare slightly better than non-disabled households, due to increased spending on social care, health and social housing (Portes and Reed, 2018). However, in all three countries, households with more disabilities have larger losses as a percentage of final income, with England suffering the greatest impact, where households with the most disabilities face losses of 10.5 per cent of their final income, compared to 4.5 per cent in Scotland and 5 per cent in Wales (Portes and Reed, 2018).

The cuts to disability benefits notwithstanding, the benefits system itself is found to be unpredictable and difficult to understand for disabled people, a situation that many find distressing (Saffer et al, 2018). Many disabled people report feeling judged and unfairly treated because they claim benefits, a situation that is leading to their poorer mental and physical health and, in some cases, increasing social isolation (Saffer et al, 2018). It is an unfortunate fact that their feelings are accurate; there is increasing stigma and an increase of negative views towards disabled people who claim benefits. As described in Chapter 3, this relates to the age-old distinctions between the 'deserving' and 'undeserving' poor, an idea prevalent in Victorian society. At one time, being in poor health or having a disability would have made you very definitely one of the 'deserving' poor, even though the idea of 'desert' is not one I encourage. But even this contract in society has broken down due to the increasingly vitriolic rhetoric emanating from government and the media.

There has been a visible shift in the media's reporting on disability in relation to the quantity of articles on disability and in the tone of the descriptions of disabled people. There are fewer articles that report on disability sympathetically; instead, the focus is more on benefit fraud and questioning disabled people's entitlement to benefits (Briant et al,

2013). As a consequence of this shift in the public and media discourse on disability, those receiving benefits for sickness and disability are often called dependent, workshy, and unwilling to work (Garthwaite, 2011) and words such as cheat, scrounger or fraud are used much more commonly than previously (Briant et al, 2013). For those living with a disability, the knowledge of this stigma and living in a judgemental society, in addition to the difficulty in applying for disability benefits, has led to them having difficulties with finances and health (Saffer et al, 2018). People, including disabled people, internalise this negativity and it is common for sick and disabled people not to want to rely on benefits and to be unwilling to claim them.

In my study, Mary, who has a disabled son and increasingly poor health over the six years of the study, explains that she had been preparing to become self-employed with a cleaning business when she started having lower limb problems, which resulted in her needing surgery on her back. This incapacitated her a great deal, which increased her struggle financially. It was suggested that she try to obtain disability-related benefits and she was exceedingly unwilling, saying:

> 'No, I don't how I feel about that. I was thinking about it last night because my mum said, "You know there's bound to be help you can get financially [for disability]", and I says, "That would be the final nail in the coffin for me", if I had to go and do that.'

Mary's increasingly poor health, her acute awareness of claiming disability benefits and her unwillingness to do so begins to take a toll on her mental health too:

> 'I'm struggling. I was actually at the doctor's on Monday, and I said, "I'm struggling mentally with it." It's easy for some folk, they just say, "Oh, but just keep your chin up." But it's not as easy as that. I'm sitting here at 38 years of age and I feel like I've got nothing. I've not achieved anything. I didn't expect I'd be sitting here with chronic pain, and I'm trying to look after my mum as well just now. She's not good at all. So what do you do?'

Rather worryingly, this reluctance to apply for disability-related benefits also occurs when it is a child who has the disability. In my study of families, Jennifer is a lone parent to three boys. At the start of the five-year research, her middle son is on the autistic spectrum and receives additional support at school, although he has not been formally diagnosed at this point. She does not claim any disability-related benefits for him as she is keenly sensitive to the stigma of receiving benefits and, as such, is reluctant to claim her full entitlement for her son. She explains,

'I don't want to push for my son to get diagnosed just to get more money. As long as he's getting the support at school that he's needing, and if he gets a bit better understanding, that's all I'm asking. It's not really that important for me, getting extra money just because my son's got a disability.'

After a few years in the study, Jennifer's son gets a formal diagnosis with autism, which was necessary to have the support put in place at the transition to secondary school. At this point Jennifer accesses a service for carers in her local area that the new school has put her in contact with. This service helps her to realise that her eldest son is a young carer for his younger brother, discussed further in Chapter 9, and they also encourage her to apply for disability payments for her son, which she has always been reluctant to do:

'I didn't want to apply for any benefits or money or that to help with my son. He's my son and I should be providing because I work and I should be looking after all that and I didn't want to apply for anything to help financially, but from meeting with them [carers' organisation] they've pushed me [to apply for disability benefits]. So I've applied for it and have qualified for it and also, through [the carers' organisation], they've put me in touch with the family fund and somebody came out to the house to speak to me about that. And again, I actually feel embarrassed them coming out to the house for me to apply for money, because I just feel like, I feel, I don't know, I just feel embarrassed I'm having to ask for money to benefit my son. He's my son. I could have had it a long time ago but that was the first of me applying for it. Because I just didn't, I hated the thought of applying for anything.'

In flipping the thinking, it would appear, therefore, that rather than be unwilling to work and to desire to take it easy on disability benefits, people experiencing disabilities, their own and their children's, are painfully affected by living in a judgemental society and are unwilling to apply for the benefits to which they are entitled. This leads to difficulties with finances and difficulties with health, including mental health and wellbeing. Almost all research participants in the disability studies researched for this chapter, including my own research, say that they do not want to rely on benefits.

Flipping the thinking

It takes a strong mind to challenge the onslaught of media attention fixated on a set position, that is that people in receipt of disability benefits are either lazy, workshy or downright fraudulent. However, it is this type of thinking that we need to challenge. Instead of believing that people's disability is exaggerated or fictional, what we learn in this chapter is that no-one wishes themselves or their child to live with disabilities, they are reluctant to claim the benefits they are entitled to and they find the benefits system overwhelming and impenetrable. Furthermore, when they do engage with the benefits system they are not always treated well and can experience a deterioration in mental health as a consequence. Garthwaite (2011: 371) expresses hope that the horror stories of terminally ill people being deemed 'fit for work' may shock the public into thinking twice before making the assumption that the majority of sickness benefit recipients are simply 'unwilling'. It would be flipping the thinking if, instead of unwilling, those in receipt of disability benefits were seen as 'unable'. The could begin to be achieved, 'by listening to the narratives of people who are labelled in this way, perhaps then the vilifying discourse surrounding them can be erased or at least challenged by giving a voice to people who are not 'other' but could be any of us' (Garthwaite, 2011: 372). This change in narrative would need to start with government and feed into the media. A change in direction in narrative could also accompany a change to the benefit system to make it less stressful for claimants experiencing ill health and disability. There ought to be more support for disabled people who claim benefits to help them claim benefits. We should also encourage those who are entitled to, but who do not claim, to take up their full economic entitlement.

9

Adversity and poverty

I got hungry because I was smelling the other food. I had to take my eyes away from it. The most unfair thing is the government knows families are going through hard times but they decide not to do anything about it. (John Adebola-Samuel, 12, whose family could not get school meals in Dumfries, Scotland, because of their immigration status. (Booth and Butler, 2018))

Introduction

Thus far, this book has centred on children living within, arguably, ordinary family environments. However, some children live in families that are not functioning well and others do not live in a family setting at all. There are some children, who, in addition to facing particular adversities, are also exposed to the highest poverty risk; for example: young carers; refugee and asylum-seeking children; children in the criminal justice system; teenage parents; children facing 'adverse childhood experiences' (ACEs); and children who are looked after by the state. There is insufficient space in this chapter to explore the experiences of all these children; however, often their vulnerabilities are multiple and intertwined. For example, a young person dealing with ACEs is more likely to experience the criminal justice system or be looked after by the state. The following sections address the circumstances of young carers, looked-after children, refugee and asylum-seeking children, and those facing ACEs.

At present, across the US and the UK, there is a particular focus on children facing ACEs. These adversities are based on family situations such as domestic abuse, physical and sexual abuse, imprisonment, mental health problems, among other factors. I am giving particular attention to ACEs because they are a good example of the ways in which certain issues get codified and then not much examined. They are examples of something being labelled, which

159

then influences the way we see the issues; we then get drawn into a particular policy public narrative, practice or direction. Every now and again we categorise an issue as it seems a way of understanding it, but the thinking can become fossilised. This is not to deny that some children do face extremely high levels of adversity, or trauma and, when they do, they require a sensitive and dedicated service provision. However, this chapter will discuss how the current focus on ACEs ignores the social and structural factors, such as poverty, inequality, unemployment and poor quality housing, bullying, racism and discrimination, which adversely affect children's lives and increase the risk of them facing ACEs.

In exploring ACEs, this chapter sets out how children living in poverty may be at greater risk, but that it is still the minority of poor children who experience them. It explores how ACEs are often, wrongly, mistaken for poverty per se, and examines the outcomes for children who experience such familial adversity. It also addresses children cared for by the state – the often overlooked children and yet among some of the poorest and most vulnerable. It reveals some of the risks that young people face on entering care and the impact of a period spent in care on children's health, wellbeing and education. Traumatic experiences, including care experience, bring greater vulnerability to future poverty and disadvantage for young people. They become particularly vulnerable to experiencing teenage pregnancy, mental health problems, substance misuse, homelessness and involvement with the criminal justice system.

Young carers

Young carers are defined as children and young people under 18 years old who provide regular and ongoing care and emotional support to a family member who is physically or mentally ill, disabled or misuses substances (The Children's Society, 2012). In one study, almost one-in-eight pupils said they provided care for someone in the household and almost one third of them said that no one knew about it (Robison et al, 2017). In this way young carers are a hidden population whose numbers are thought to be underestimated. It is likely that there are up to 700,000 young carers in the UK (Carers Trust, 2016) far higher than the figure of 175,000 taken from the census data (Aldridge, 2006). Being a young carer is linked to poverty, with factors such as deprivation and lone parenthood being identified as increasing the risk (Robison et al, 2017). There is a higher proportion of girls who are young carers than boys, which highlights its gendered nature. In one study, around 60 per cent of young carers were female (Robison et al, 2017). However, there are more boys undertaking caring responsibilities that we might expect. In a recent analysis of Scottish data 55 per cent of young carers were girls and 45 per cent were boys (Scottish Government, 2017).

Poverty and young carers

Poverty relates to the circumstances of young carers in three ways. Firstly, young carers and their families are more likely to live in poverty than their non-caring peers (Watt et al, 2017). This is likely to be in part due to the relationship between poverty, ill health and disability, and the relationship between lone parenthood and poverty. If a family has other healthy adult members or sufficient financial resources, there would be no need for the young person in the family to be the carer in the first place. Secondly, there is a relationship between the extent of caring and area deprivation: young carers in the most deprived areas compared to carers in the least deprived areas are more likely to have substantial caring roles (Scottish Government, 2015; Carers Trust Scotland, 2017). Thirdly, the costs of providing care are high and can be a catalyst for families to fall into poverty, as was discussed in Chapter 8 on disability. As Carers Trust Scotland (2017: 1) summarise: 'the links between young people's caring responsibilities and living in poverty can be complex, but are primarily connected to the household's limited capacity for paid work alongside caring roles and the extra costs associated with living in a household where someone has an illness or disability'.

The effects of caring on young carers

The effects of caring on young carers can be good and bad with the extent of caring and the type of condition faced by the parent being critical factors. Young carers can have poorer physical and mental health, lower levels of happiness, lower satisfaction with their lives, are more likely to be bullied at school and have poorer educational aspirations and outcomes than their non-caring peers (Lloyd, 2013: 67). They can feel isolated because having caring responsibilities negatively affects their social or leisure activities (Hamilton and Adamson, 2013). It can also cause tiredness, worry, stress and affect their ability to access services (Carers Trust, 2016). Furthermore, young carers are twice as likely to say they have a limiting illness or disability themselves compared to non-carer peers, with poorer physical and mental health outcomes among those caring for someone with mental health or addictions issues (Robison et al, 2017).

The situation for young carers who are caring due to parental mental health problems is more complex and potentially detrimental to young carers own mental health and wellbeing. Children who care for parents with serious mental health problems do many of the same tasks and roles that young carers do whose parents have physical health problems or disabilities. However, they also do a lot more, especially as regards emotional caregiving, crisis management and support, monitoring and assessing parents' emotional health and wellbeing, and even overseeing the safe and regular administration of prescription drugs (Aldridge, 2006: 81). Where a young carer has a parent with mental health problems, they, or their parents, may reject the label of 'young carer' due to a lack of awareness of quite the levels of responsibility a young person takes on. They may, conversely, be glad to have a label that describes their role. Cooklin (2009: 17) explains,

> Defining children as 'young carers' is problematic, even though the term may describe the reality of the role they play. This is because most children and young people who have a parent with mental illness do not think of themselves as carers. They may think of themselves as surviving, as lonely and isolated, and as suffering all the common experiences listed below. Many parents with mental illness do not acknowledge that their child has become their carer, rather than the converse. Many children and young people may be left vulnerable to sometimes extremely damaging and distressing situations, but without a role that recognizes their contribution – or even commands appropriate respect. Thus there is a danger that simply defining these children and young people as young carers may provide a cloak of acceptability that allows quite intolerable demands to be made on them. On the other hand, some children welcome almost any title that recognizes their plight, particularly if their parent's mental disorder is difficult to define. In this situation, the designation of 'young carer' may be of some use until a better descriptive term can be created.

Poorer mental health outcomes for young carers is also associated with the extent of caring a young person does. One study created a measure of the extent of caring and found a significant relationship between the level of caring responsibility and negative attitudes towards caring

(Watt et al, 2017). Those with higher levels of caring responsibilities are more likely to feel stressed or lonely, have lower life satisfaction and lower levels of happiness (Watt et al, 2017). While young carers in general have poorer mental health than their non-caring peers, girls in particular can have especially low levels of mental health and wellbeing (Cree, 2003). In one study of young carers, twice as many girls as boys had contemplated suicide (over 50 per cent vs 26 per cent), twice as many girls as boys had self-harmed (50 per cent vs 20 per cent), and almost three times as many girls as boys worried about not having friends (58 per cent vs 20 per cent) (Cree, 2003). Not only is the gendered aspect of these problems noteworthy; the sheer magnitude of the severe mental health issues, contemplating suicide and self-harming, is staggering.

Other negative impacts of being a young carer include finding things very difficult at school – young carers report a lack of understanding and interest from teachers to their situation (Fleming, 2016) and also being bullied for being a carer (Barry, 2011; Lloyd, 2013; Fleming, 2016). One child explained: 'I have not noticed any changes, I get bullied all the time at school because of my mum and nothing happens about it. I have been put down a year at school because of how much I have missed. There is no recognition from school I am a carer' (Fleming, 2016: 8).

It is not a completely negative story for young carers, however. Some young carers are positive about their caring role and feel that it brings benefits (Scottish Government, 2017). Young carers are often willing to provide care to their parent and are motivated by love for their family (Aldridge, 2006). Positive effects of caring include the children learning empathy, responsibility and feeling mature (Sahoo and Suar, 2009). Factors important to young carers feeling more positive about their responsibilities include having dedicated support and participating in young carer support projects (Scottish Government, 2017). Such young carers report feeling recognised, supported and valued (Scottish Government, 2017).

Young carers as a hidden population

As the underestimation of the extent of young carers in the official statistics show, young carers remain a hidden population and their circumstances are still relatively unknown (Barry, 2011). The reasons that many young carers are hidden or not known about are: many young people who care for others do not identify themselves as being a 'young carer'; they may not think that their role is exceptional or unusual;

and they may see their caring as part of routine family responsibilities (Scottish Government, 2017). As well as being hidden, young carers may actively seek to hide their caring role, as a means to conceal a stigmatised identity. Stigma is a fear for young carers, especially when they are caring as a result of substance misuse or parental mental health problems (ACMD, 2011). Young carers are concerned that they may face greater levels of peer-bullying if they are 'found out'. They are also fearful of unwanted intervention and being separated from their parents (Scottish Government, 2017). And this is not an unwarranted fear as parental ill health is a common reason for being taken into care, with 5 per cent of young carers in 2008 being admitted to state care because of parental ill health or disability (Barry, 2011).

Policy and service support for young carers

In spite of the difficulties inherent in the definition and acknowledgement of being a young carer, and in their being a hidden population with unmet needs, it is incontrovertible that they need dedicated and targeted support (Hamilton and Adamson, 2013). Although young carers live in a family setting, its non-standard setup makes their passage through childhood and entry into young adulthood particularly difficult. To flip the thinking on young carers, they should be treated in policy and practice the same way as other disadvantaged and highly vulnerable young people, such as those who are looked after or whose schools receive the pupil premium due to their socioeconomic disadvantage. Reasons given for why the pupil premium should be extended to young carers include: it would encourage schools to prioritise young carers; and, if the pupil premium helps disadvantaged pupils of all abilities perform better, and helps close the gap in attainment between them and their more advantaged peers, then young carers are a prime group to be considered (Mesie, 2018).

There are now several policy and practice initiatives in the UK that are working with young carers in schools and other settings to positive effect. For example, there is a 'Young Carers in Schools Programme' that helps schools to support young carers. They help to identify and support young carers in schools across England so that they get the help they need to enjoy and achieve in their education (Mesie, 2018). Since working with this programme, schools reported that they were more able to identify young carers, 73 per cent of schools reported that classroom engagement had improved, 72 per cent thought that young carers' motivation to learn had improved, and 63 per cent reported improvement in the achievement of young carers (Mesie, 2018: 19).

There was also a reduction in absence rates reported due to the schools involvement in the young carers programme (Mesie, 2018). This type of initiative could be rolled out to prevent the potentially damaging effects of being a young carer on all aspects of their lives from mental health to engagement in education. In Scotland, a new young carer's grant is available to young carers aged 16–18 from autumn 2019. As part of a package of measures, young carers aged 16–18 will also be entitled to free bus travel from 2020/21. This is a welcome focus on this group but, again, it raises the question: why does the rest of the UK not follow suit? This chapter now turns from young carers to children who are looked after and accommodated by the state.

Looked-after children

Children and young people looked after by the state can be known by different labels such as 'in-care' or 'looked-after'. This chapter uses 'looked-after' in the absence of a better term, but acknowledges that 'when used as an adjective, "looked-after" labels the child rather than the situation; being known to be a "looked-after child" is potentially as stigmatising as being known to be a child "in care"' (Welch, 2018: 202). It may be time for a less stigmatising term for being in care that describes the situation and not the child.

Looked-after children and poverty

There is a very strong relationship between poverty and children being looked after by the state. Neighbourhood deprivation, acting as a proxy for a family's socioeconomic position, is a strong predictor of children's chances of state intervention. Bywaters et al (2018: 18) find that 'these inequalities are very large: children in the most deprived 10% of neighbourhoods in the UK are over 10 times more likely to be subject to an intervention than children in the least deprived 10%'.

Looked-after children's outcomes

The outcomes for looked-after children are universally poor. They are more likely to experience adverse 'socio-economic, educational, legal and health outcomes in excess of that associated with coexisting childhood or adult disadvantage' (Jones et al, 2011: 614) in later life. However, this chapter is more concerned with the adversity of their experiences in childhood. Looked-after children are more likely to experience educational, behavioural, physical and psychological problems in childhood and the risk of becoming looked-after is 'strongly associated with poverty and deprivation including low income, parental unemployment and relationship breakdown, and over 60% of children are in care because of abuse or neglect' (Jones et al, 2011: 614). The third most prevalent reason children being in care is having a physically or mentally ill parent who can no longer look after the child properly, which in part explains why young people who may be caring for an ill parent wishes to mask their situation (Aldridge, 2006).

Looked-after children and young people are reported to blame themselves for their family's situation, believing their (distressed) behaviours to be the reason for the family's separation and minimising any role played by abusive or dysfunctional parents (Baker et al, 2016). This is because maltreated children form and maintain attachment relationships with their abusive caregivers, although the quality of the attachment is disorganised compared to a non-abused child. (Baker et al, 2016). Through this disorganised attachment, looked-after children attempt to understand the actions of abusive parents and, in order to continue loving them, blame themselves for the abuse (Baker et al, 2016). Thus, when children are removed from an abusive home, they can experience internal conflict due to relief at being removed and yet feeling yearning for the birth parent (Baker et al, 2016). This makes working with abused and traumatised children extremely difficult and sensitive and 'children may need help understanding that it is normal and understandable to have mixed feelings about parents whom they both love and fear, and yearn for and are relieved to be away from' (Baker et al, 2016: 181).

When looked after, children often face 'great uncertainty due to an extended period in temporary arrangements often with multiple placement moves' (Welch, 2018: 203). This can make the experience of being looked after 'distressing, disruptive, and potentially damaging' to children even if the alternative care is judged to be better than remaining in their family situation (Welch, 2018: 203). Some birth mothers in research with looked-after children mentioned that they had been in local authority care themselves when young (Welch, 2018), which suggests that they needed more support than they received to successfully negotiate the transition to adulthood and parenthood, and have experienced a lifetime of having professionals intervene in their lives.

Looked-after children report being aware of the 'complex, severe, and enduring' troubles their families face; troubles that often 'could not have been predicted or easily prevented, and most often resulted from the actions (or inaction) of others' (Welch, 2018: 211). Furthermore, some children, although they were aware of their family's troubles, and acknowledged that they were still their biological family, were clear to emphasise that they did not share their family's negative characteristics and did not want to be labelled by their family's actions (Welch, 2018). This rejection of a stigmatised identity occurred in young people who distanced themselves from their family's behaviours and expressed a desire to have a different life, for example to go to university (Welch, 2018: 206). Young people in care are keen to emphasise that they are more than the sum of adverse circumstances ascribed to them.

Refugee and asylum-seeking children

Other children who are often, but not always, living outwith a family setting are refugee and asylum-seeking children and young people. Even those who live with their families, however, are not able to live the types of life they may value due to the restricted existences and the restrictive conditions imposed upon them. Refugee and asylum-seeking children are among the poorest and most vulnerable children in any society. To discuss some of the implications of being a refugee or asylum seeker, it is important to explain what the different terms mean to avoid confusion. An asylum seeker is a person who is seeking protection from persecution in another country, but who does not have any defined status in the country in which they are seeking asylum (Hands et al, 2016). A refugee is someone whose asylum claim has been determined and who has been granted refugee status in that country (Hands et al, 2016). A migrant is someone who voluntarily moves to another country, often for economic reasons (Hands et al, 2016). This chapter focuses on the needs of children and young people who are refugees and asylum seekers.

Refugee and asylum-seeking children and poverty

The most poor and the most vulnerable status is the asylum seeker as, even as adults, they are not allowed to work and only receive a small stipend on which to live (Hands et al, 2016). In the UK, this stipend amounts to half the value of a single person's jobseeker's allowance, which is already considered by public consensus to be too low to live on. Thus, asylum seekers are the most impoverished group of people and among the most vulnerable. For children of asylum seekers, life is particularly difficult financially. Such financial difficulty can adversely affect children; parental worries about money have a particularly damaging effect on the mental health of refugee children (Fazel et al, 2012: 273). Furthermore, in one study, refugee parents with poor mental health directed feelings of anger towards their children (Fazel et al, 2012: 273). If a family's claim to asylum is rejected 'the child or family may be asked to leave the country, or be detained and forcibly removed' (Hands et al, 2016: 37).

Refugee and asylum-seeking children and outcomes

Children who escape persecution and resettle in high-income countries have often endured great trauma in their home countries, immense physical and mental challenges during displacement, and then suffer additional hardships in their new countries (Fazel et al, 2012: 266). The conditions that prompted children to flee their countries, including exposure to violence, trauma and bereavement, can lead to post-traumatic stress disorder, as well as other mental health difficulties such as anxiety, poor social adjustment, and low self-worth (Fazel et al, 2012). Furthermore, once they flee, there begins a long period of 'turbulence and uncertainty' where children might 'travel for weeks or months in dangerous circumstances to seek asylum in a high-income country, and are sometimes temporarily or permanently separated from family' (Fazel et al, 2012: 266). Even when they arrive at their country of safety there begins a complex legal process in order to obtain refugee status as well as the problems associated with being an asylum seeker or refugee in a high-income country.

Where an asylum seeker or refugee child is ethnically different from the dominant group in their new country, 'they can experience varying degrees of prejudice, racism, rejection, or indifference' (Bourgonje, 2010: 24). Furthermore, prejudice, racism and bullying is often 'exacerbated by policies to accommodate asylum seekers in already impoverished and disadvantaged areas' (Fazel et al, 2012: 266). In the UK, 57 per cent of refugees and asylum seekers are housed in the most disadvantaged areas compared to 10 per cent in the least disadvantaged areas (Lyons and Duncan, 2017). This is problematic as local authorities do not receive central government funding for refugees and asylum seekers, which means that already disadvantaged areas are taking the strain of providing housing and services to this vulnerable group, and wealthier areas are not (Lyons and Duncan, 2017). This pressure on services and housing in deprived areas can mean that refugees and asylum seekers experience increased racial harassment, which mirrors the 'war and political conflict in the countries individuals had fled'

(Netto, 2011a: 140). To alleviate these problems, Netto (2011b: 300) suggests that policy should incorporate the needs of refugees and asylum seekers into anti-poverty initiatives that target the socially disadvantaged neighbourhoods where refugees and asylum seekers are housed. These increased tensions and racial harassment, exacerbated by thoughtless government policy that seeks to keep refugees and asylum seekers out of the wealthiest areas, cause greater distress to refugee and asylum-seeking children, who have no choice but to make use of local services such as education.

Education, however, has been shown to be crucial to refugee and asylum-seeking children. Children who feel safe at school have lower risks of post-traumatic stress disorder and those who have a sense of belonging in school are protected against depression and anxiety (Fazel et al, 2012). Furthermore, having acceptance and social recognition by their peers in school promotes positive wellbeing in refugee and asylum-seeking children (Fazel, 2015). A further important protective factor is good parental mental health, particularly in mothers (Fazel et al, 2012: 273).

Refugee and asylum-seeking children may arrive with their family, may come to stay with friends or family, or may arrive alone, as an unaccompanied minor. In the latter case, the refugee and asylum-seeking child will fall under the same legislation as looked-after children, but will also have separate needs and vulnerabilities related to their experiences and current status. A major problem for the unaccompanied minor is the difficulty in accessing mainstream education due to the lack of a parental advocate (Bourgonje, 2010). This is especially detrimental given the positive part schooling can play in the life of the asylum-seeking or refugee child.

Refugee and asylum-seeking children and protective factors

Research with refugee children shows that the most important empowering experience they had was not the granting of refugee status but the social recognition of their peers (Fazel, 2015). This 'gave them the motivation to change, the confidence to seek psychological help, to study harder and make more friends' (Fazel, 2015: 259). Refugee and asylum-seeking children themselves suggest that their school peers 'could be prepared in advance of the arrival of a refugee, for example by educating the students about current global conflicts or the potential experiences of refugees. This might help those arriving be better understood by their peers and help them in building friendships, something they highly valued' (Fazel, 2015: 258). As is often the case, when children and young people with experience of a certain circumstance or situation are asked for their views on how to improve things, they come up with the most salient and practical solutions. Thus, school-based interventions hold promise to support peer relationships and a sense of belonging for refugee children (Fazel and Betancourt, 2018).

Adverse childhood experiences

ACEs are defined as stressful events that occur in childhood that are believed to have lifelong impacts on health, wellbeing and health-related behaviours. ACEs is a particularly catastrophic concept, being linked to suicide, depression, heart disease, cancer, chronic lung disease, liver disease and other conditions leading to premature mortality, and also to drug and alcohol misuse, smoking, promiscuity, and problems with finances and employment (Marryat and Frank, 2019: 2). It is also a particularly deterministic concept: the effects of having ACEs is thought not only to lead to a degraded life and early death, but also to defective parenting, which will certainly lead to ACEs in the next generation. The original study, which is being replicated uncritically, defines ACEs in relation to: domestic violence; parental separation/divorce; having a parent with a mental health condition; being the victim of abuse (physical, sexual and/or emotional), being the victim of neglect (physical or emotional); having a member of the household in prison; and/or growing up in a household in which there are adults experiencing alcohol and drugs misuse (Felitti et al, 1998).

The ACEs approach has been widely adopted across service sectors in the US (McEwen and Gregerson, 2019) and is gaining traction in the UK, particularly in the devolved nations of Wales and Scotland (Edwards et al, 2019). Across the UK, ACEs are being used as a tool by policy makers and professionals in public services such as health, social work, education and policing, to construct a 'score', a simple summation of adversities experienced, to make decisions about resource allocation and interventions, not retrospectively for adults who may have suffered traumatic experiences in childhood, but for children and young people prospectively (Edwards et al, 2019: 411). There are multiple problems with ACEs, in relation to their conceptualisation, methodology and operationalisation, including the indicators selected to represent childhood adversity or trauma, as I will come on to explain.

The problem with the original ACE study

The original study suffers from not being a population-based study, rather it comprises a sample of predominantly white, middle-class, adult, private health insurance (Kaiser Permanente) patients (Felitti et al, 1998; McEwen and Gregerson, 2019). This makes it a very biased sample, one that, for example, excludes the study of socioeconomic disadvantage (privately insured) and ethnicity (predominantly white). This means that disadvantages such as barriers to housing, nice neighbourhoods, education and employment, associated with structural inequalities pertaining to poverty, ethnicity, gender and religion as discussed in earlier chapters of this book, are automatically excluded. This is a grave limitation in that these are the conditions under which we, and our families, grow, work and live.

Another grave limitation is that the study only identifies a limited number of potential adversities to be an ACE, all of which are situated in the home (Felitti et al, 1998). ACEs are centred on the quality of parental caregiving, particularly mothers', making the family the cause of, and the solution to, adversities experienced (Macvarish and Lee, 2019). As with other policy approaches that put the family at the centre of a child's adverse experiences, for example the troubled family agenda outlined in Chapter 4, ACEs are based on a deficit model of the family, of parents, and of mothers especially. It does not include assets, or protective factors, or family and community support, or other resources (McEwen and Gregerson, 2019). Furthermore, parenting and family is culturally specific. Hartas (2019) finds that there is a very low prevalence of ACEs reported in Asian families compared to white, Hispanic and other groups, suggesting that there are cultural and ethnic influences on perceptions of parenting and childhood experiences. This insensitivity to culture is thrown into sharp relief in New Zealand, where the ACEs checklist is described as a deceptively 'common sense' tool that privileges Western and white-centric models of family and ways of parenting, which does not consider that 'colonisation, poverty and racism might be deployed and used against populations that have a long history of having such tools used against them' (Joy and Beddoe, 2019: 495). Even within the UK context, 'what could have been described as 'good enough' parenting three to four decades ago, in an era of intensive parenting may be seen as parental negligence' (Hartas, 2019: 3). As with other family-deficit models that seek to explain inequalities in childhood, the parenting of those from a lower social class and/or non-white ethnicity, particularly mothers, is being held up against upper-middle class white standards and found lacking.

The ACEs study also lacks nuance. Each of the ten adversities listed are summed to give a total ACEs score, with no distinction between types of ACEs, which include everyday occurrences such as parental separation and, rarer, criminal acts such as sexual abuse. Each ACE is weighted equally in the final score. This 'risks blurring the boundaries between normal and abnormal experiences, pathologising a very large proportion of the population and undermining the possibility of meeting the specific needs of people with serious problems' (Macvarish and Lee, 2019: 469). In some situations, for example in the US and in Scotland, children are being 'screened' in certain contexts for the presence of ACEs and assigned a score. According to Finkelhor (2018), to screen children for ACEs, several important questions ought to be answered. These are: what effective interventions and responses need to be in place once ACEs have been identified; what are the potential negative outcomes to screening; and what exactly should we be screening for (Finkelhor, 2018: 173). He cites the cautionary tale of when domestic violence screening began. He explains that, 'given the widespread occurrence of domestic violence, many health care settings hastened to develop and adopt such screening. But reviews and assessments have concluded such screening did not reduce incidence in the screened population compared to controls or result in long term health benefit' (Finkelhor, 2018: 174). This is because no additional support or services were put in place once the incidence of domestic abuse was identified. In a time of sustained austerity and cuts to services for children and families, this is a very important caveat to the ACEs vanguard: if you identify children with ACEs, what next?

As well as being limited in context and nuance, another problem with ACEs is that, instead of shedding light on an emerging social problem, old problems are repackaged and the thinking becomes ossified. The idea of ACEs is simple, simplistic and intuitive, which is why it has caught the political and public imagination. It offers a simple solution to complex problems. However, it very much lacks scrutiny through a critical lens and has been adopted without question. This leads to further problems. For one, there is no distinction made between the age at which an ACE occurs, the length of time it lasts, its severity, nor who is the perpetrator. Research focusing on the chronicity, severity, children's attributions of causality, and other contextual information in the study of childhood adversity, can provide guidance on the protective factors related to resilience and their differential impact on outcomes depending on a child's level of exposure to adversity (Ungar, 2015). This offers a more nuanced and non-deficit-based approach to childhood adversity and is absent in the ACEs approach. Another issue arises because ACE advocates advance that the first three years of a child's life is critical to the rest of its life and that untold damage can be done in this period. A problem with this is that such ideas would deem older children to be irreversibly damaged. This takes away attention, funding and potential interventions for one of the most important stages of childhood, one with immense periods of growth and developmental malleability, at a time when they can exercise agency and take ownership of interventions, that is adolescence. The ACEs approach writes children off at critical stages of transition: one of the core themes of this book is that we must focus attention on adolescents too. It also does not acknowledge that adversity can cause damage at any age, not just in childhood and, importantly, damage is not an inevitable consequence of having adverse experiences in childhood. There are a variety of factors that can influence how different people experience the same event in different ways (Barrett, 2018). Such factors include: age, gender, previous history of traumatic events, health factors, individual resilience and social support systems (Barrett, 2018).

The statistical analysis in the original ACEs study is also flawed because it uses conceptually distinct statistical terms such as 'causality' and 'association' interchangeably. As such, rather than drawing *associations* between childhood adversity and adult ill health, which could take confounding factors such as poverty into account, the study states that adult ill health is *caused* by childhood adversity, rather than them both being caused by poverty and inequality. This and other methodological flaws are expertly delineated in Hartas's (2019) analytical deconstruction of Felitti's approach. One note of support for Felitti and his study is that it was never meant to be used in the ways it has. The study authors understood they were measuring downstream effects, for example the consequences of structural problems such as poverty, and noted the importance of upstream preventative actions, which they recognised could only come from social changes that would provide support to improve family environments (McEwen and Gregerson, 2019: 792). Thus, their study was never meant to try and identify individuals at risk but to draw attention to wider societal influences on child development. Structural and social adversities known to be highly detrimental to children's wellbeing and outcomes – for example: peer-bullying; racism; discrimination due to social class, gender or sexuality; bereavement; homelessness or other housing problems; weak social ties and support; neighbourhood violence; food insecurity or hunger; natural disasters; political conflict; being in state care and being a refugee or asylum seeker – are not considered to be ACEs. In fact, the whole ACEs approach shows a studied indifference to poverty and inequality, both as causes and consequences of adversity in families. This is problematic for several reasons.

ACEs and poverty

On the whole, children are more likely to experience adversity in childhood when they also experience poverty and inequality. As outlined in earlier chapters, poverty has hugely detrimental effects on all aspects of a child's life, including education, family life, mental and physical health, and future (un)employment. This means that poverty and inequality have detrimental effects on the areas of life that are being attributed to ACEs, usually without any analysis of poverty or inequality per se (Steptoe et al, 2019). In a systematic review of ACEs and the socioeconomic position of the family, Walsh et al (under review) screened 2,825 papers on ACEs; only six included family socioeconomic position. They widened their screening to include 'child maltreatment' and, of 4,562 papers, only 35 (including the aforementioned six) mentioned family socioeconomic position as a potential explanatory variable (Walsh et al, under review). In one study that does consider socioeconomic disadvantage, the authors find that ACEs are over ten times more likely to occur in the poorest 20 per cent of the population compared to the richest 20 per cent (Marryat and Frank, 2019). A second study shows that a main factor in the relationship between ACEs and poorer health in middle-age is wealth accumulation in adulthood (Kelly-Irving and Delpierre, 2019). Despite the strong evidence on the effects of poverty on children's lives, ACE advocates posit that poverty is caused by the presence of adversity in childhood and not the other way around. A recent study of ACEs in Wales argues that 'those with 4+ ACEs were more likely to live in deprived areas, be unemployed/on long-term sickness and have no qualifications' (Bellis et al, 2013: 89). Once again, association is being mistaken for causation and cause and consequence are being conflated. By assuming that ACEs lead to poverty, rather than be a consequence or manifestation of it, policy focuses firmly on 'family intervention to support parents to "nurture" their children as a means of countering the toxic effects of rising inequality' (Hartas, 2019: 6). That is, parents are being encouraged to better nurture their children to alleviate the negative impacts of systemic inequalities, such as poverty, rather than society tacking the systemic inequalities in the first place (Hartas, 2019). This risks promoting policies that do not increase and, in fact, may decrease income to families facing poverty and inequality, such as we have seen in this past decade of austerity.

Poverty in childhood is sometimes described as another ACE (NHS Health Scotland, 2017). This is flawed conceptually as poverty is a structural issue governed mainly by political and economic factors and ACEs are behaviours and characteristics held within the family. By holding that poverty is another ACE we further demonise families living in poverty and, once again, blame them for the socioeconomic conditions in which they find themselves. Although people living in poverty may be at greater risk of experiencing certain ACEs, they do occur across the socioeconomic spectrum. It is that better-off families often have sufficient material resources and greater social, emotional or practical support to counter the negative effects of ACEs. As a result, wealthier families do not usually seek assistance from publicly funded services and so do not come to the attention of statutory bodies. In this way ACEs in wealthier families are more hidden than they are in impoverished families, who are almost always subject to greater public intervention.

This is not to say that poverty is not a damaging experience; the whole of this book describes why it is. Rather, poverty has its origins in political processes and is far more pervasive than ACEs. In the US, where the ACEs approach is more embedded, Metzler et al (2017) ask that the narrative be shifted in relation to ACEs. In particular, they emphasise that attention would best be focused on

> policies that have the potential for changing conditions for children and families include policies that reduce poverty, especially concentrated poverty; policies that assure stable and affordable housing, access to high-quality and affordable child care and early education; and policies that assure access to health care, particularly mental health care for both children and parents. (Metzler et al, 2017: 147)

That is, the best way to alleviate ACEs is to provide financial and other support, such as housing and income, to families with children. This is demonstrated in a study in the US, where changes in state and federal minimum wages were opportunistically used to explore the impact of increases in incomes of individuals and families in low-paying jobs on the incidence of child abuse and neglect (Raissian and Bullinger, 2017). The results show that increases in the minimum wage reduce the risk of families having involvement with child welfare services, especially in relation to neglect and especially for young and school-aged children (Raissian and Bullinger, 2017). A $1 increase in the minimum wage led to a 9.6 per cent decline in neglect reports (Raissian and Bullinger,

2017). They conclude that increasing family incomes would lead to a reduction in cases of child abuse and neglect. It is important to note that while child abuse and neglect has a strong relationship with family socioeconomic circumstances, rates of child abuse and neglect do not divide neatly between families who live in poverty and those who do not (Bywaters, 2016). Child abuse and neglect has a graded relationship with poverty and inequality and many children who do not experience poverty will experience it and the overwhelming majority of children living in poverty will not (Bywaters, 2016). This is overlooked by the ACEs approach, which is why it is described as 'a chaotic concept, one that prioritises risk and obscures the material and social conditions of the lives of its objects' (White et al, 2019: 1).

By overlooking poverty and inequality as drivers of adversity in families, the ACEs approach focuses instead on individual family behaviours and characteristics as the solution to the problem. The ACEs movement has gained traction across the health sector and is increasingly gaining a hold in the legal system and in schools. This is problematic as it then places responsibility on teachers to identify and propose solutions to ACEs on a child-by-child basis. As was discussed in Chapter 5, teachers often have insufficient understanding of the structural issues of poverty and inequality and do not understand how their own social class position impacts on children and families from lower socioeconomic backgrounds. To place on teachers the task of identifying or monitoring children who may or may not have ACEs is to try to identify deficiency in children and their families and further stigmatise them. Although the aim of the ACEs approach is to show understanding and kindness towards children who are believed to have ACEs, the result is that, rather than looking at families as having strengths and assets, it instead sees them as deficient.

Severe multiple deprivations in adulthood

Poverty can increase the likelihood of poorer children facing complex needs, or severe multiple deprivations, such as homelessness, mental health problems or imprisonment, later in life (Bramley et al, 2015). Research with young adults revealed that they attributed their severe multiple deprivations to a combination of poverty and family stress (Bramley et al, 2015). Other factors identified as being associated with severe multiple deprivations in adulthood are: 'violence between parents, parental substance misuse or mental health problems, serious problems at school, being underfed as a child and, especially, childhood homelessness' (Fitzpatrick et al, 2012: 162). In research with families with complex needs, it was found that, unlike families who could be resilient when faced with one or two problems, the volume of problems families faced, and their complex interactions, resulted in their feeling swamped with troubles (Shildrick et al, 2016: 827). Families with multiple and complex needs found their lives destabilised, their wellbeing drained, and their social capital exhausted' (Shildrick et al, 2016: 827). Yet, the children of the families in Shildrick et al's (2016) study showed incredible resilience and drive. They emphasised that they did not wish to have the same type of troubled and impoverished lives that their parent(s) had, but had conventional aspirations and wished to live a 'normal' or 'ordinary' life (Shildrick et al, 2016: 829–30).

This brings me to my final point regarding ACEs. There is a risk that the ACEs approach reduces young people to the sum of their traumatic experiences. There is concern that children are being encouraged to count their ACEs and consider themselves to be a ' two ACE' or 'three ACE' person for example. This risks fossilising both the thinking and practice of ACEs and making them overly deterministic. As Ginwright (2018) argues in his critique of the 'trauma-informed' approach, the term slips into a deficit-based, rather than an asset-driven, approach to support young people who have been harmed. As one young African-American working with Ginwright (2018) emphasised: 'I am more than what happened to me, I'm not just my trauma.'

Flipping the thinking on ACEs

To flip the thinking on ACEs, the structural processes that underlie families' vulnerability to adversity has to be recognised. Furthermore, we need to move away from a deficit model to an asset-based approach. It is important that children and young people are not written off in adolescence due to the severity, chronicity and timing of any traumatic experiences they may have experienced. It is also important that they are not defined by what happened to them but that dedicated services are put in place that will support them to understand their experiences and to recover from them. There is reason to believe that children and young people experiencing adversity can overcome the potential damage and lead full and healthy adult lives.

In the UK, dedicated services have been decimated due to the past eight years of austerity and there are now gaps in provision. This means that where there used to be community-based family support and youth workers who worked with children's adversities in context, within the settings of their families and community structures, there is now very little. The consequence of this is that the problems associated with adversity in childhood are being picked up in acute ways through primary health care services. This has led to the further problem of ACEs being pathologised and medicalised, which leads to a further lack of understanding on the socioeconomic and structural factors facing families. Rather than having a trauma-informed, or an ACE-aware, approach, there needs to be financial and other resources targeted at families and services based in the community to support children and young people. This way we can move from a deficit model towards a model that is rights based, positive, respectful, with a wider appreciation of adversity and trauma, family and child strengths, and poverty and inequality.

10

Conclusions

It may be worth reflecting, if indeed a little sadly, that possibly the ultimate test of the quality of a free, democratic and prosperous society is to be found in the standards of freedom, democracy and prosperity enjoyed by its weakest members. (Townsend, 1964)

Introduction

The principal reason for writing this book is to invite the reader to 'flip their thinking' on child poverty; to set aside what they believe they understand and to consider a fresh perspective, one rooted in children's experiences and in the data collected about them and their families. The reason for using this book to try change people's minds is simply to improve the lives of children living in poverty in the UK and beyond. Townsend's quote at the start of this chapter was written more than half a century ago and was the final sentence of his book *The Last Refuge* on the circumstances of the elderly living in nursing homes. However, it just as easily applies to children. How we treat our children in society is a strong marker of the type of society we are. This book is an entreaty to create a better society for children. If we can get that right then many good results for everyone in society will ensue for many years to come.

There is much misunderstanding about the risks, causes and consequences of child poverty. The key sources we all rely on to inform our understanding of the social world, usually the media and what politicians say in the media, provides us with what we believe to be accurate knowledge. This poverty knowledge, or received wisdom, advances an often biased, and a certainly superficial perspective on children and families living in poverty. It focuses on salacious stories about individuals and families, rather than telling the truth about why families and children experience poverty. The most damaging element of such misunderstandings about poverty is that professionals, who work with children affected by poverty, such as health visitors, teachers and social workers, also rely on these sources for information and, in the absence of dedicated poverty teaching and learning of the type I have been involved with in Scotland, will misunderstand the problems children face and waste time and energy on false solutions. When these false solutions cannot solve a problem misunderstood, then the problem gets diagnosed intractable and the people affected as 'difficult' and 'hard-to-reach'. One of the actual solutions, to reinforce O'Connor's (2001) point, is not to understand poverty by focusing on the poor and how they choose to live their lives, but by studying poverty itself, how it is created by the political economy and the actions of politicians. Then tangible, viable solutions will emerge.

So far, this book has set out quantitative and qualitative evidence on the lives of children living in poverty. This evidence has, where possible, come from my studies of the same children and parents across time to allow us to explore patterns and change. As far as space permits, it has laid bare some of the faults in the systems and processes governing child poverty. It has done this by focusing on the following substantive areas: the family, education, employment, health and mental health, and the context of poverty. Throughout these substantive areas, and in dedicated sections, this book has also addressed the experiences of children at increased risk of poverty due to their group identity, for example having a lone parent, being of a non-white ethnicity or having disability in the family. It has also tackled the issues faced by children who, as well as being at an increased risk of poverty, do not fit into the expected norms of society, for example children who are looked after outwith a family setting, refugee and asylum-seeking children, and those who experience extreme adversity, such as neglect and parental substance misuse. While it is absolutely the case that children who face extreme adversities are at greater risk of having poor experiences in childhood, and especially poor outcomes in adulthood, and that they require additional resources and dedicated service provision to recover from traumatic experiences, it is also crucial to understand that these experiences do not define poverty itself. There remains a miscomprehension that adverse circumstances *are* poverty, rather than the result of, or exacerbated by, poverty. This is a misapprehension that is relatively common among professionals who work with families, who may identify families with extreme problems, see their poverty, and conflate the two. For this reason, it is vital that professionals receive the teaching and learning that means they will not confuse adverse circumstances with poverty itself and will not risk writing off young people with multiple adverse circumstances as having intractable problems.

There are, of course, important areas that this book did not have space to cover, such as housing and the effects of neighbourhoods on children. This is not to suggest that these areas do not equally affect children living in poverty, for they most certainly do; it is that decisions had to be made on what issues to focus on in this book and what to leave for another time. In the remainder of this final chapter I reiterate what we have learned from the preceding chapters before focusing on the implications I believe to be the most pertinent and pressing from that learning. The implications I believe to be the most apposite are: the importance of money, the importance of relationships, received wisdoms and unconscious bias, addressing the living conditions of those looking after children, and making successful transitions.

The learning from each chapter

Chapter 2

In Chapter 2 on the context of poverty, I emphasised that children benefit society and, so, it is in the interests of us all to ensure that children have as secure and stable a childhood, and that they achieve as successful a transition to adulthood, as possible. We learned that there are many reasons why it is in everyone's interest to make an investment in children and to prevent poverty or, where poverty already exists, to mitigate the negative consequences of growing up poor. The principal reasons are that child poverty is a fundamental source of inequality, a social injustice, a breach of a child's rights and a source of national shame in a wealthy society. To those for whom such injustice is an insufficient reason on its own to justify us all contributing to the upbringing of other people's children, Chapter 2 also emphasised that: (1) it is today's children who will pay for the health care and pensions of tomorrow's older generation; and (2) as children are necessary for all of our futures, and bring additional costs to those who have them, we should all contribute to ensure their needs are met. Chapter 2 also emphasised that ignoring child poverty brings great economic and social costs to society and that the social costs will continue to bear economic costs in future. The cost of child poverty to the economy in 2013 was estimated at £29 billion, with the caveat that were child poverty rates to increase by their predicted amount by 2020, the cost to UK society would rise to £35 billion (Hirsch, 2013).

Chapter 2 also described the dynamic aspect of poverty; that it is not the same group of people who live in poverty year after year, but that people regularly enter into and out of poverty. This is especially the case in the UK, whose particularly high entry and exit rates of poverty shows us that the poor do not neatly divide into a 'them and us' population, but that many of us cycle into and out of poverty, signifying that vulnerability to poverty is higher than the cross-sectional poverty rates would suggest. Chapter 2 also established that the actions governments choose to take increases or decreases child poverty and that they have the tools available to make a difference. This was best demonstrated in the actions of governments and the fluctuations in child poverty rates across wealthy societies after the Great Recession of 2008. While tax cuts and increases to minimum wages have the capacity to improve child poverty rates, or the conditions of children living in poverty, this capacity is limited when there are concurrent countervailing policies, such as reductions to in-work and out-of-work benefits. It is not enough to give with one hand and then to take away with another. All of this highlights the importance of money: in a market society money is essential and, at its core, poverty is a lack of money.

Chapter 3

Chapter 3 focused on the family and we learned that the family can be the very seat of inequality for some children. We also learned that families living in poverty are vilified, with parents who are 'poor' being perceived as 'poor parents'. However, while the political focus has been on the term 'parenting', the intensity of that focus has mainly been on women, emphasising the strongly gendered nature of the family and parenting practices. When we talk about parenting in poverty, it is working-class mothering practices that are considered to be the antithesis of good parenting. Very little is mentioned about fathers, except in relation to lone mothers' apparent inability to provide one for their children, as is discussed in the summary of the next chapter.

There is extreme social pressure to attain society's idea of the 'ideal' family and, when families living in poverty fail to attain this ideal, for they surely will, then there is judgement on parents and negative consequences for children and young people. The ideal family, that is the middle-class family who provide their children with everything they could need and more, and who treat childhood as a special phase of life protected from any troubles whatsoever, is virtually unattainable, but it is the benchmark against which all families are compared. Whether or not this is an optimum style of parenting or of 'being a family' is not as important as the pressure to conform. Against a benchmark attainable only by high levels of wealth and education, disadvantaged families are destined to fail. In light of this family ideal, in Chapter 3 we learned that it is, therefore, *advantaged* parents who reinforce and perpetuate the disadvantage of poor children and families by employing their superior resources to confer further advantage onto their own children. Thus, in order to understand poverty and inequality it is as important to study what is happening at the advantaged end of the socioeconomic spectrum as it is the disadvantaged.

In Chapter 3 we also learned that there is great stigma for poor children and their families; they are viewed as scroungers or skivers compared to the working non-poor who are seen as strivers. Stigma is pervasive, strongly felt and leads to feelings of shame. It is such feelings of shame that drive children (and their parents) to attempt to mask their poverty to counterproductive effect. Derogatory descriptions of families living in poverty flourish in the media and in the public rhetoric of politicians. In spite of the historical and contemporary evidence that families' poverty is a function of prevailing social and economic conditions, and that individual characteristics and behaviour, while not irrelevant, are not its dominant cause, low-income families continue to be portrayed in a disparaging fashion. Despite evidence to the contrary these negative beliefs and attitudes towards poor people have been around for a long time and continue to predominate. It is important for studies of poverty to explore why these ideas capture the public and political imagination and why they continue to prevail.

Chapter 4

In Chapter 4 on lone parents, we learned that there is little that excites the public and political imagination more than the notion of family 'breakdown'. Lone parenthood is routinely believed to have negative impacts on children's wellbeing; however, using annually repeated data of the same families over time, my research shows that it is not the state of lone motherhood, nor separations, nor parents meeting a new partner, that are deleterious to child wellbeing but the impoverished and materially deprived conditions that lone mothers often find themselves living in (Treanor, 2016b). This is because family separation and divorce is the point at which a lot of children experience poverty. As a consequence, lone parents often sacrifice their own basic needs, such as eating, to ensure their children are adequately provided for, making lone parents an even more deprived group of people than their children. The implications of this, as will be discussed later, is that lone parents, usually mothers, need to be considered in policy and practice terms when trying to prevent or mitigate child poverty. It is not possible to remedy child poverty in a vacuum; children are situated in families and communities, which requires a holistic approach to their financial security and wellbeing.

As with discussing 'the poor' it is important to understand that lone parents are not a homogenous group. Lone parenthood is not a fixed state but another stage in family life, which is usually temporary, lasting on average around five years in the UK. Ninety per cent of lone parents in the UK are female, which emphasises its gendered nature: when we talk about lone parents, we are really talking about lone mothers. Furthermore, some groups are at an increased risk of lone parenthood, for example mothers of black Caribbean origin. In such cases, there is an interacting effect between gender, ethnicity and lone parenthood that makes the incidence of poverty, and the barriers to escape poverty, all the greater. Lone mothers are disproportionately poor in most (but not all) countries, which demonstrates that, as with poverty, the policies that governments choose to implement make a difference to the rates of lone-parent poverty. In the UK, lone-parent poverty is high and children living in lone-parent families are twice as likely to be in poverty and are three times as likely to experience material deprivation as those in two-parent families.

The final learning I would like to draw out of Chapter 4 pertains to the role of non-resident fathers in the lives of their children. Where a non-resident father pays child maintenance, they are more likely to remain actively involved in their children's lives, which is shown to be important to children's social and emotional wellbeing, academic achievement and behaviour. Children also benefit from the increase in income from the child maintenance itself, emphasising once again the importance of money to children at risk of poverty. Unfortunately, however, compliance with paying child maintenance is low in many countries, especially in the UK. One solution to the problem of non-compliance would be for the state to pay child maintenance to the resident parent and then to recoup the cost from the non-resident one. Where child maintenance is guaranteed in this way, for example in Sweden, Denmark, Finland, Norway and Germany, not only do children benefit in the ways mentioned earlier, child poverty rates are also improved. One of the recommendations of this book would be for the state to guarantee child maintenance.

Chapter 5

In Chapter 5 we learned that education is compulsory and forms a large part of childhood, and that it has the potential to be an equaliser of opportunities and a leveller of outcomes. However, among children of equal academic ability, poorer children are less likely to gain higher level qualifications than wealthier children. Assumptions about why this is the case often fall back to the individual explanations, that is the personal attributes and behaviours of the child and their family. These assumptions lay the blame for educational failure at the door of poor children and their families, suggesting that they lack the characteristics of success and so are in some way deficient. What these explanations ignore, are the structural inequalities that have been discussed throughout this book, and the alienating nature of education. Poor children often experience difficulties in assimilating to the school environment, finding it intrinsically alienating due to its inherently middle-class culture. The everyday lives of children living in poverty often differ from those of middle-class children and these differences emerge in school settings. It is a culture that can lead to insufferable pressure on children living in poverty and, in spite of this, they continue to strive to belong in school.

Although education is notionally free in most countries there are associated costs to school. Children living in poverty are frequently disciplined for not having the right equipment and teachers often do not understand the huge efforts poor children make just to come to school at all. Children living in poverty are acutely aware of the costs associated with school and worry about how their parents are going to afford school items and about being bullied by their peers for being poor. Children are ashamed and stigmatised for not having what is required of them in the school setting, which leads them to conceal their poverty and to self-exclude.

Another explanation proposed for poor children's less successful progress in education is their and/or their parents' low aspirations, known as the 'poverty of aspiration'. Raising aspirations has become a key educational policy driver across affluent societies; yet, parents are repeatedly shown to have high hopes and aspirations for their children. In every study of families living in poverty I have ever undertaken I have never met a parent who did not want more for their child than they themselves had. Teachers also report children and their parents as lacking aspirations. Furthermore, we learned that teachers and student teachers also think that the causes of poverty-related educational underachievement lie with pupils or their parents as individuals, rather than within institutional structures and practices. Such misunderstanding leads to their falling back on negative stereotypes of children and parents. In spite of this, though, teachers do report being keen to reduce stigma for children living in poverty and to do more to ensure they have a successful education. We should capitalise on teachers' desire to help poorer children by providing training to teachers to build their understanding and knowledge of poverty. It is also important to promote dignity and respect in schools and classrooms. It is important to educate the educators on the often unintentional yet pernicious nature of stigma, on understanding that for some children living in poverty, especially those facing other adversities, the very fact that they have succeeded in coming to school is to be appreciated; and that children living in poverty should be valued and respected for who they are and what they bring to the school environment. Children living in poverty say that the most important factor in school for them is positive relationships with peers and teachers.

Chapter 6

From Chapter 6 on being in and out of work, we learned of the complex relationship between child poverty and employment, the role of employment in lifting families out of poverty and how low-quality, low-security employment poses a threat to children and families rather than a route out of poverty. We also learned that society attaches particular status to paid employment and does not consider unpaid work, such as caring, in equal regard. The majority of people living in out-of-work poverty show a clear desire to find paid work. While employment has long been seen as *the* route out of poverty, for many families it remains a hope, as employment without adequate reward and security can produce its own problems and uncertainties for families. We learned that in-work poverty is high across all of the OECD area where the working poor account for between 60–80 per cent of all the poor of working age. In the UK, two thirds of children living in poverty live in a family where someone works, which equates to almost three million children. In-work poverty is often related to underemployment, for example part-time, temporary or zero-hours employment, and certain groups, such as families with children, are more vulnerable to this.

Children and young people are not just affected by their parents' poverty; young people aged over 16 years old are having to deal with their own poverty through unemployment and underemployment. The negative effects of unemployment when young do not only have repercussions in terms of future employment and wages but have negative consequences in relation to physical and mental health, which intensify the longer an individual is unemployed. Although unemployment causes unhappiness generally, 'there are enduring effects from spells of unemployment while young, which continues to lower happiness more than two decades later' (Bell and Blanchflower, 2010: 27). Given the extent of youth un- and underemployment across wealthy societies, action needs to be taken to ensure an entire generation of young people are not abandoned and left socially and economically bereft.

Chapter 7

In Chapter 7 on health we learned about how poverty leads to poor health and about the health inequalities experienced by the marginalisation of individuals due to their belonging to a minority group, based on, for example, ethnicity. We learned that, unequivocally, it takes money to achieve positive health and that those at the lower end of income distribution especially benefit from having a minimum income to support healthy living. We also learned that, in the UK, 40 per cent of households with children cannot afford an acceptable standard of living sufficient to support good health.

We learned that children living in poverty are disadvantaged across the full spectrum of physical and mental health and developmental outcomes. For example, the UK has the highest mortality for children under five years old in Western Europe, which has been directly linked to higher rates of poverty and deprivation. In all low-, middle- and high-income countries, poverty is also strongly related to children's mental health problems. We discovered that children and young people living in poverty across the world are also two to three times more likely to develop mental health problems than their wealthier counterparts. In the UK, children and young people in the poorest households are up to three times more likely to develop mental health problems than those in better socioeconomic circumstances. For children, we learned that the relationship between parental mental health and poverty is also important. Even an initial entry into poverty causes maternal psychological distress and social, emotional and behavioural problems in children. Given how dynamic poverty is, with people cycling into and out of poverty, such transitions are having relentlessly detrimental effects on mothers and children. The effects of parental poor mental health are long-lasting. Children with parents who experience mental illness are 2.5 times more likely than the children of parents unaffected by mental illness to experience some level of psychiatric disorder in their lifetimes. This is especially the case when the poor mental health is experienced by the mother.

There has always been, and there remains, a high level of stigma attached to poor mental health, across all societies. Approximately half of people with a mental illness in affluent societies do not seek help due to stigma and discrimination and between 76 and 85 per cent of people do not seek help in low- and middle-income countries. The proportion of people not seeking help is much larger among poorer groups and in poorer countries. Parents and guardians in particular can be reluctant to seek help for mental health problems for fear that their children be removed from their care. Stigma for children and young people living in poverty who are affected by ill health in the family, especially poor mental health, is especially high. Children's feelings of stigma 'leads to loneliness, depression and loss of confidence' and can adversely affect young people's view of the world and their place in it.

As well as the mental health crisis we also learned in Chapter 7 of the factors that can be protective and provide the support necessary to mitigate the effects of poor parental health on children. One key factor is for children and young people to be able to access appropriate public services. Another key factor is the presence of one or more alternative caring adults, one described as 'warm, concerned, but relatively uninvolved'. Another factor pertains to information. If children can make sense of their parents' behaviours through age-appropriate knowledge and information about their parents' mental illness, this provides a certain level of protection. It helps children to understand that they are not the cause of, and are not responsible for, their parents' mental ill health and its associated behaviours. Additionally, the social environment of a child, including their family, peer, school and neighbourhood contexts also exerts a protective influence. Once again, for children living in poverty, and those experiencing additional issues such as poor mental health, the quality of their relationships and support available to them is key to their growing up without poor outcomes.

Chapter 8

In Chapter 8 we learned of the effects on increased risk of poverty for children caused by belonging to a non-white ethnic minority or through their own or a family member's disability. We also learned that there is an interaction between belonging to more than one group that creates the conditions for the highest risk of poverty, for example being a disabled child, from a non-white ethnicity, in a lone-parent family. On ethnicity, we learned that there is much conscious and unconscious racism and discrimination faced in many areas of life by people from visible ethnic and religious groups. It is not easy for a white person to spot racism as it is not always openly hostile, but is often an integral and, therefore, hidden factor in institutional cultures and practices. One way for us to try to redress this is to be mindful of the assumptions we make about children from a non-white ethnicity and ask ourselves 'would I have had this thought if this child were white?' Disabled children or those with a disability in the family are likely to experience higher levels of poverty, personal and social disadvantage, deprivation, debt and poor housing than non-disabled children. Furthermore, they are living in a time when there is decreased sympathy and empathy towards those who receive disability benefits. Disabled people internalise this negativity and it is common for sick and disabled people not to want to rely on benefits and to be unwilling to claim them. For the children, they face first the discrimination of having a disability and then the vitriol of the public attitudes towards their families.

Chapter 9

In Chapter 9 on children who are in situations that are particularly adverse, and which interact with poverty, we learned about young carers. Young carers are children and young people under 18 years old who provide regular and ongoing care and emotional support to a family member who is physically or mentally ill, disabled or misuses substances. Almost one-in-eight pupils say they provide care for someone at home and almost one third of them say that no one knows about it. In this way young carers are a hidden population and so the number of young carers is thought to be underestimated. In Chapter 9, it was recommended to flip the thinking on young carers, to think of them as needing the same additional resources as other groups who receive increased funds, for example the pupil premium in schools.

In Chapter 9 we also learned about children looked after by the state. The outcomes for looked-after children are universally poor. They are more likely to experience educational, behavioural, physical and psychological problems in childhood and the risk of becoming looked after is strongly associated with poverty and deprivation. Being looked after interacts with other groups and experiences too; for example, the third most prevalent reason for children being in care is having a physically or mentally ill parent who can no longer look after the child properly.

Other children who are especially vulnerable to poverty and who have likely experienced great trauma are refugee and asylum-seeking children. For these children, life is particularly difficult financially and the parental strain of money worries has a particularly damaging effect on their mental health. Children who escape persecution and resettle in high-income countries have often endured great trauma in their home countries and immense physical and mental challenges during displacement. When in their new country, an asylum seeker or refugee child, who may be ethnically different from the dominant group in their new country, can experience prejudice, racism, rejection or indifference. This is often exacerbated by policies to accommodate asylum seekers in already impoverished and disadvantaged areas, leading to stressed community relations. There are factors that can be critical to the integration and support of refugee and asylum-seeking children. One such factor is education: children who have a sense of belonging in school are protected against depression and anxiety. Once again, the importance of relationships is emphasised, as having acceptance and social recognition by their peers in school promotes positive wellbeing in refugee and asylum-seeking children.

The final learning from this chapter is on the increasingly prevalent idea of ACEs. While there are children who undeniably experience great adversity in childhood and who require dedicated support and service provision, the problem with ACEs as it is currently constructed is that, instead of shedding light on an emerging social problem, old problems are repackaged and the thinking becomes ossified. The ACEs approach ignores poverty and inequality as drivers of adversity in families, focusing instead on individual family behaviours and characteristics, much the same as all the other individualised approaches set out in Chapter 3 on the family. Also, only a limited number of possible adversities make up the 'ACEs list' with important adversities such as peer bullying and racism being omitted. In this way the thinking on ACEs is both limited and limiting.

Having summarised the learning from the topical chapters of the book, this chapter now turns to the implications of this learning, including the policy and practice changes required to improve the lives of children living in poverty. The implications addressed in this chapter are: the importance of money, the importance of relationships, received wisdoms and unconscious bias, addressing the living conditions of those looking after children, and making successful transitions. The chapter finishes with an entreaty to flip our thinking so that we might improve the lives of children experiencing poverty.

Implications of the learning from the previous chapters

The importance of money

There is some debate over the income thresholds at which poverty is set and, while these thresholds are arbitrary, they serve an important purpose in that they enable us to identify those with low income, to compare across societies and to monitor change over time. Income is key to living in poverty and a lack of money is a critical factor that permeates all the topics addressed in this book. Putting aside exact poverty thresholds, those close to the poverty line will have very similar experiences and living conditions as those below it, although they will not make the official definition of poor. This indicates that there are many more families struggling financially than official poverty statistics would suggest, which could have consequences that make these families' struggles equal in magnitude to those living in official poverty; for example, not being entitled to some of the benefits and passported benefits, such as free school meals, as those who are in official poverty. This means that the effects of poverty on children will be more prevalent and more widespread than we currently understand. It also means that many children living in poverty will be a hidden population, either through their and their parents' masking of their poverty out of fear or shame, or because their public services, such as school, will not understand that they might be in poverty. This is especially the case with parents who are in employment: in-work versus out-of-work poverty is especially pertinent given the rates of children in poverty residing in a household where someone works.

In-work poverty is increasing in the UK in spite of the increase in the national minimum wage. Although the increase in the national minimum wage was a welcome positive policy change that put the onus on employers to step up to improve people's work and living conditions; it was, unfortunately, offset by other government changes, such as the reductions to child tax credits. The national minimum wage was increased by a Conservative government, which may seem surprising except when you think that it had the consequent effect of reducing the in-work benefit bill for government. There are other employment and employer-related areas that could be changed to increase families' incomes and to improve the lives of children living in poverty. As set out in Chapter 5, working conditions have been eroded for many at the lower end of the income scale over the past two decades: there has been a fragmentation of the labour market, an increase in zero-hours contracts, seven-day shift patterns, and not having fixed shifts or hours on a week-by-week basis, all of which makes it incredibly difficult for families with children to manage logistically and financially. When families need to use childcare, they must pay for fixed days and hours that remain the same each week. Where employment does not allow this, there are unintended consequences – such as parents, usually mothers, not being able to access employment due to issues with childcare. This is especially the case for lone parents whose older children often have to take on childcare and domestic duties to facilitate their lone mother's employment. What is important here is that people need decent wages as per Beveridge's own definition of full employment. An increase in wages and, therefore, income, as well as improving the lives of children, would also have strong value in preventing their poverty in the first place.

For those who are out of work, an increase in the rates of benefits back in line with earlier indices, and to account for inflation, would reverse some of the damage inflicted during these years of austerity in the UK. As would the cessation of negative policies such as the two-child policy of child tax credits, conditionality for lone parents, sanctions for those with children, and the reduced benefit entitlement for refugee and asylum-seeking families, all of which are arguably against the tenets of the UNCRC. There are particular groups of people who have suffered enormously under the austerity policies of the UK. As shown in Chapter 8 on disability, even for those otherwise in good health, disability brings additional costs that puts financial pressures on families. The removal of disability premiums for families with a disabled child under child tax credits is a practice that should be ended and other reduced monies for disability reinstated. In a 2018 visit to the UK, the United Nations Special Rapporteur on extreme poverty and human rights, Professor Philip Alston (2018: 2), summarised the impacts of these years of austerity in the UK thus:

> Key elements of the post-war Beveridge social contract are being overturned. In the process, some good outcomes have certainly been achieved, but great misery has also been inflicted unnecessarily, especially on the working poor, on single mothers struggling against mighty odds, on people with disabilities who are already marginalized, and on millions of children who are being locked into a cycle of poverty from which most will have great difficulty escaping.

The changes to government policies that have reduced income to families with children, and the government's refusal to change direction, are having grave consequences on millions of children's wellbeing, development, health and outcomes. The positive and protective factors in children lives, of those living in poverty and those experiencing increased risk and other adversities, are relationships.

The importance of relationships

In Chapter 5, on education, distributive equality was discussed in comparison to relational equality. Relational equality was identified as the less common, less considered equality. Yet, relational equality, with its focus on social relations, especially within institutions and particularly when the relationships contain a power imbalance, for example in relation to age or socioeconomic disadvantage, such as poor children in schools, has the power to make a difference to the lives of children living in poverty. Relational equality forces us to think in greater depth about the nature of the relationships between children, peers, parents and professionals and to think about how to promote equality, respect and dignity in those relationships.

Promoting positive and equal relationships for children living in poverty is a protective factor for many of the injustices they experience that inflict stigma, shame and emotional distress. If policies to foster strong school–family–child relationships were implemented, that would have an associated positive effect on children's schooling. They would feel more connected, valued and would have the sense of belonging that is critical to full participation and engagement. Children living in poverty say that the most important factor in school for them is positive relationships with peers and teachers. This could be facilitated by having family/school liaison officers to promote the wellbeing of families and to boost home/school relationships. In my work with the City of Edinburgh Council on the 1 in 5 project, there was a focus on not only removing the negatives, such as school costs and stigma, but also to promote dignity and respect to enhance children's wellbeing in education with the understanding that this can help to reduce educational inequalities across the board, not just in future attainment.

It is not only in the school environment, or to children living in poverty, that the quality of relationships matters. The importance of relationships is emphasised for refugee and asylum-seeking children, as having acceptance and social recognition by their peers in school promotes their inclusion and positive wellbeing. Similarly, for children experiencing additional problems, such as their poor mental health or that of a close family member, or who are young carers, or looked after by the state, the quality of the relationships and support available to them is key to their growing up without poor outcomes. Among the barriers to relational equality and relationships based on dignity and respect, however, are the received wisdoms and unconscious biases surrounding poverty that permeate our society and public life.

Received wisdoms and unconscious bias

The received wisdoms and unconscious bias of poverty derive from the derogatory political and media discourses, which have a disparaging focus on perceived parental shortcomings. When governments do not fully understand or accept the causes of child poverty, they turn to blaming parents for their children's poverty. This is especially the case for parents from groups with an increased risk of poverty to begin with, for example lone parents, ethnic minority parents, disabled parents and parents who are underemployed or unemployed. This blame successfully shifts the focus, and the responsibility for poverty, from the actions of government to the behaviours of individual families.

The fact that poverty is a dynamic phenomenon is important to unconscious bias and received wisdoms. When people assume that the same fifth or so of people are in poverty each year it lends credence to the political and media portrayals of poor people as a fixed 'underclass' of 'skivers', 'shirkers' and 'scroungers'. If people understood that half of the people who are living in poverty this year will not be living in poverty next year and that new people will be in poverty next year who are not in poverty now, then they would understand that there is a large swathe of the population at risk of at least a temporary experience of poverty and, hopefully, flip their thinking. When the poor are believed to be a fixed rather than a dynamic group, a misunderstanding that cross-sectional statistics do nothing to dispel, then this leads to the 'othering' of people living in poverty. To 'other' someone living in poverty is to treat them as different from the rest of society; as two tribes, the poor and the non-poor, 'us' and 'them'. In this way, the marginalised position of people living in poverty is used against them, to stigmatise them and to exclude them.

Even among communities with high levels of poverty, there are increasing instances of poor people othering those in similar circumstances to themselves in their community. Poor people deny being poor and lay the blame at the door of their equally (or more) poor neighbours. That such negative portrayals have been absorbed into the narratives of the poor themselves is testament to the pervasiveness of political and media discourses. The result of this othering is that it engenders a lack of sympathy towards those living in poverty and a lack of respect for the efforts they do make to bring their children up in straitened circumstances. This then permits undignified treatment and public shaming to prevail. And the people who suffer most from these negative beliefs and attitudes, and the attendant treatment, are the children living in poverty. With the roots of child poverty being fiercely debated, the outcomes of these debates are likely to lead to (further) negative changes to how child poverty is understood and tackled by national governments and, by extension, on programmes and initiatives to prevent or eradicate it. At present, the social, political and economic landscape is in flux and low-income children's lives and wellbeing are particularly vulnerable to marginalisation and misrepresentation. This is driven by the conflation of the risks, causes and consequences of poverty.

Risks causes and consequences of poverty

The risks, causes and consequences of child poverty are frequently conflated in the UK and internationally. Yet, how a government understands the causes of child poverty is key to the steps it would be willing to take to mitigate and prevent it. It is important not to conflate the risks, causes and consequences of poverty. Many professionals working with families living in poverty do not appreciate this nuance of its risks, causes and consequences. This is especially the case with those professionals who work at the sharp end of family and community life and who come into contact with high levels of adversity. Their understandings of poverty can be skewed to the experiences of particular families, which can make individualised and behavioural accounts of poverty seem most reasonable.

The risks of being in poverty are exacerbated by belonging to one or more minority, or less powerful, group; for example women, ethnic minorities, refugees/asylum seekers, the sick and disabled, the young, the unemployed, those with larger families, and those with lower levels of education and lower social class positions. Child poverty is not caused by being a member of one of these groups; however, they are at greater risk of experiencing poverty due to the imbalance in power structures and relations. When a child (or adult) is a member of multiple groups then the risks of poverty, and the barriers to avoid poverty, are greater. This may be exemplified in the discrimination faced by being female and non-white, or disabled and non-white, or all three or more.

The causes of child poverty are a complex blend of structural issues relating to macro-economic, political, social and individual factors. Macro-economic factors, such as the structure of the labour market, the housing market, low pay, irregular hours and insecure employment cause child poverty. Political factors, such as the level of social security payments, availability of affordable housing and regulation of employment are also causes. More weakly, as these factors often reflect underlying social and economic processes, individual factors in relation to capacities and choices play a part too.

The consequences of child poverty start before birth and accumulate across the life course. Poverty has negative impacts on all aspects of children's lives, now and in the future, which is why it is so important to do something about it. The way child poverty is being tackled now results from a misunderstanding of the risks, causes and consequences. The main treatise of this book is to flip the thinking on child poverty so that new solutions to old problems can be proposed and the lives of children living in poverty can be improved.

Addressing living conditions of those looking after children

Previous governments managed to get child poverty on the policy agenda and subsequent governments have managed to keep it there. Child poverty is seen as a more palatable area for policy intervention than, say, the increased risk of poverty of lone parents, the disabled or those from an ethnic minority background. This is because children have traditionally been viewed as blameless, as innocent bystanders of their parents and, as such, deserving of society's care and protection from poverty. However, children do not usually live isolated from family or community. One of the central tenets of this book is the importance of money for all aspects of children's lives and wellbeing: we cannot address child poverty and improve children's lives without also raising the incomes and improving the lives of their families. It is just not possible. What we need to do, therefore, is flip our thinking and understand a few things differently.

For example, we need to appreciate that many parents, especially lone parents, sacrifice their own basic needs to ensure provision for their children. This means that these parents, especially lone parents, are as, or more, deprived than their children. To appreciate this, we need to look at the needs of the whole family and not just the child in isolation, for example we need to boost family income, wellbeing and relationships with school, rather than trying to boost children's aspirations or attainment at school. We also need to look at whether there are interacting factors facing children and their families, for example in relation to health, mental health and disability, among others, so that children's whole needs are attended to and not just one in isolation. We have to remember that children living in poverty can be a hidden population as they and their parents may be masking their poverty to hide a stigmatised identity. This means you cannot always know who is living in poverty: it may not be obvious. This is especially the case with in-work poverty as families do their best to hide financial struggles. This may be because they wish to avoid negative attention or because they may fear unwanted service intervention, for example, if they need to use a food bank to help feed their children. Remember too that there are other hidden populations of children at high risk of poverty and other issues, such as young carers and those with mental health problems or where there is substance misuse in the family.

Finally, as well as improving the lives of those surrounding children living in poverty we also have to address their needs on multiple levels at the same time. There is no point in focussing on a child's education if they are living in damp, overcrowded accommodation far from school. In this way, we need to focus, simultaneously, on families' needs in relation to income, housing, community and neighbourhoods, education, health, employment, childcare and the myriad other factors that prevent poverty in the first place or that permit or preclude an exit from poverty.

Making successful transitions

Children negotiate many transitions in their lives: (1) of the age and stage variety; for example, from pre-school to primary school, primary to secondary school, post-school onto education and/or employment, and from adolescence to young adulthood; and (2) sometimes of the personal and social variety; for example, parental separation, moving homes, parental repartnering, siblings being born, family members dying, and having to move home or even country. Some transitions are more difficult to negotiate than others and living in poverty can make certain transitions more arduous. For example, the transition to secondary school is one of the most difficult and stressful periods for a young person. It occurs at the point of adolescence and is a massive change in the life of a young person. The transition to secondary school is shown to exacerbate inequality and be particularly difficult for young people living in poverty, and a negative transition at this stage can have adverse impacts on outcomes in adolescence and also beyond into adulthood. The next transition, onto young adulthood and education/employment, is especially difficult when there are few sources of capital to draw on for children living in poverty and wealthier parents use their advantage to great effect for their young people. As well as poverty, there are also young people who face additional challenges in the transition to adulthood, for example those looked after by the state and those who have asylum or refugee status, among others. In my studies of poverty, it was clear that many parents living in poverty had had difficult transitions to adulthood themselves, which made escaping or evading poverty in adulthood all the more difficult.

Transitions are the time when there should be intervention and investment in children and young people. The policy focus of the past two decades in the UK and the US has been on the early years as this is the age/stage believed to provide the greatest return on investment. It is a stage when there are increased costs, and developmental leaps are being made, which is why it is positive that the Scottish Government is introducing payments to families at three points between the ages of 0–5 years old. However, while this is a progressive move it is equally important that investment and intervention in the early years does not come at the expense of adolescents, who are often overlooked by policy and practice and can effectively be 'written off'. Some adolescents are dismissed in the school system through exclusions, are failed by mental health services and, if they are identified as having a high number of ACEs, it is thought that the damage is insuperable. This can leave adolescents with no remedial or restorative routes. What would help in these instances would be to identify young people at risk of poor adolescent transitions, for example those who have been excluded from school, and to intervene at this stage to support them. The key to this, once again, lies in the quality of relationships and the level of support offered to the young person.

Flipping the thinking

The final section of this book draws together ways in which we can flip our thinking on child poverty drawn from the learning from the substantive chapters and the implications from the chapters discussed earlier. In essence, the entreaty to flip our thinking is to urge us to think about things in a different way so that we might see new solutions to old problems. Its ultimate aim is to encourage change so that we can improve the lives of children living in poverty.

How we understand poverty is crucial to the policy solutions employed to prevent or mitigate it. Using the deficit model to explain poor children and their families' socioeconomic position leads to policy solutions that aim to overcome assumed parental or child personal shortfalls. We need to target the structural and wider inequalities that influence the relationship between poverty and all the components of children's lives, for example family, friends, school, health, etc. We need to study, understand and teach about poverty, about the political decisions and processes that cause and affect it, and not focus on studying the poor and making judgements on how they live their lives. This would have the associated effect of being able to prevent poverty in the first place.

We need to flip our thinking by studying the wealthy and the advantaged too. The very resources and actions available to the advantaged exacerbates the disadvantage of others. For example, in the poverty of aspirations, it is assumed that we all have access to the same knowledge and experiences. Such assumptions lead to a deficit understanding of what poor families offer their children. Instead of focusing on what poor children lack in their family settings, we should endeavour to understand what our advantaged children gain and work out ways to best replicate it for children living in poverty. For example, instead of boosting aspirations, education should expand young people's horizons and, once horizons have been expanded, help children and young people sustain and realise their aspirations.

Continuing with education, there are several more ways we can encourage educators to flip their thinking. The first would be with teachers. It would be useful for teachers, instead of asking 'what can I do to make poor children value their education?' to ask instead 'what can I do to show the children living in poverty that I value them in my classroom?' The lack of dignity and respect that children living in poverty (and their families) feel from some teachers is a barrier to poor children's education. The next way we could encourage educators to flip their thinking is in relation to identifying families living in poverty. It is important to remember that children and parents living in poverty go to great lengths to mask their poverty, especially from teachers and other pupils and parents. It is likely then that teachers will not know who is experiencing financial hardship unless there are associated adverse circumstances. In this way, because teachers are most familiar with experiences of poverty that have associated family welfare issues, they conflate poverty with social problems. This is why focusing on teachers' understanding of the causes and consequences of poverty is a good start. The third way we could encourage educators to flip their thinking is in the area of parental involvement in school. Poor parents may be reluctant to become involved with the school or their child's education not because they are not interested in their child's success in school, but perhaps because they had poor experiences of school themselves. By flipping the thinking, teachers can question what may lie beneath parental reluctance: What were their own experiences of school like? Are they nervous? Do they lack confidence or social skills? Do they have low levels of numeracy or literacy that they are desperate to hide?

We need to explore why we allow individualistic attitudes to prevail and research what sustains existing approaches to poverty. It may be that there needs to be equality guidelines in place for the media, to prevent them portraying poor people as feral and feckless. This leads to stigma, shame and the demonisation of children living in poverty. In flipping the thinking on this, it is not enough to reduce discrimination and stigma; there ought to be an active promotion of dignity and respect. This is not as unattainable as it might sound. In Scotland, new legislation on social security has dignity and respect as a core thread running through it, a change that was instigated through the policy and research work I and others have done. From the perspective of the UK, we should all look at Scotland's divergence from the UK and what it is aiming to achieve in relation to children poverty. We should also raise the question as to why things have to be different in other parts of the UK.

The unemployed and the underemployed are held in the lowest esteem across societies today. In the UK in particular, there is a very potent and toxic discourse on strivers versus skivers. Even those undertaking other forms of unpaid work, for example caring, are held in scant regard. If we could flip the thinking on this, we would see that carrying out unpaid work in relation to the care of children, the elderly and the disabled is valuable and valid. We would appreciate how much money is saved by people carrying out unpaid work for friends and family, and we would wish to support them in these endeavours. To flip the thinking on those who are unemployed who are not carrying out caring responsibilities, we could consider the very strong desire they have to find work, the shame and grief it causes them when they cannot find work, and appreciate that the current state of the labour market makes it extremely difficult for people to find secure, sustainable employment.

Continuing with being in and out of work, employment in the UK is at its highest and unemployment is at its lowest for many years. Yet, two thirds of all children living in poverty live in a household where someone is working. This shows that not all work is working as a route out of poverty. Wages are too low and there is an overdependence on in-work benefits, which are being continually contracted by the UK government, adding to working families' financial worries. Furthermore, the work activation activities are focusing on 'fixing' the supply side, that is the behaviours and characteristics of the unemployed, with little focus on improving the demand side, that is increasing job quality and availability. To flip the thinking on this, it would be useful to look behind the statistics to understand (1) who is out of work and who is cycling between low-pay and no pay, and to work out how this could change; and (2) what type of employment opportunities are being created, for whom and to what effect. To flip our thinking, we should flip our understanding that the problem lies not in those without work, or in low-paid or precarious work, but in the systems governing employment, for example government management of the labour market and the actions of employer that perpetuate poverty.

Young people, and ethnic minority young people, are especially disadvantaged in the labour market in spite of their superior educations. This disadvantage holds when all other factors are accounted for, leaving the only explanation as conscious and unconscious bias and discrimination. How do we flip the thinking on this? The answer lies in dedicated, targeted policy responses to provide a platform from which to promote a shared understanding, ensure access to the full range of the employment market, and to reduce discrimination against the young. Another seriously disadvantaged group in the labour market are lone parents, especially lone mothers. Lone mothers are constructed in the mind of society as being dependent, undeserving and work avoiding. What is little considered is that they too are providing society with its future citizens and they desire that their children's lives are stable and secure. They too wish their children to achieve happiness and success in adulthood. To flip the thinking, it is worth considering that a lone mother's contribution to reproductive labour and social stability deserves to be more fully recognised.

In more extreme discourses, lone mothers are seen as deficient parents, feral parents even, as sexually promiscuous and as denying their children a normal childhood. In flipping the thinking, it is worth considering that this type of discourse, which is without factual foundation, serves only to demonise lone mothers and their children, and perpetuate their disadvantage. By affording them dignity and respect, and securing their and their children's financial wellbeing, lone mothers can be appreciated for the difficult jobs they do in the most difficult circumstances. In flipping the thinking on policies to lift lone mothers out of poverty, it is worth rejecting those that seek to change the behaviours of lone mothers but instead promote those that instead seek equity with other parents. For example, child maintenance is not often used as a social policy for lone mothers but is actually the most useful.

Lone mothers are seen as a threat to their own children's wellbeing. Yet, my research shows that it is not the state of lone motherhood that is detrimental to child wellbeing, but the impoverished and materially deprived conditions that lone mothers find themselves living in. In flipping the thinking, it is worth considering that, rather than being responsible for their children's deprivation, lone mothers actually suffer from the same, or worse, poverty and deprivation as their children and that the experience is felt and shared together.

Problem behaviours in childhood, but especially in adolescence, are strongly related to parental mental health problems. To flip the thinking, instead of thinking of children and young people's behaviour as proactive, think of it as *reactive*, as a response to their parent(s) mental wellbeing. Child social, emotional and behavioural wellbeing is 'malleable and that children are emotional barometers responding to and corresponding with their mothers' wellbeing' (Treanor, 2016a: 691). This indicates that were parental mental health conditions to improve, child mental health might too.

To improve the lives of children living with disability we need to flip our thinking on people's disabilities. Instead of believing that people's disability is exaggerated or fictional, we could flip our thinking if, instead of seeing them as unwilling, those in receipt of disability benefits were seen as unable. What is also needed, is for the government to change the benefit system to make it less stressful for claimants, especially those experiencing ill health and disability: there ought to be more support for disabled people who claim benefits to help them claim benefits.

This brings us on to the final factor in flipping the thinking, and that is in relation to money; that is, the increased cost of living, or of participation, for particular groups. Families where there is a disabled child, or a disabled parent, require a higher level of income than nondisabled families. As we have learned in this book, many factors on children's lives are interconnected and we need to look at the whole. As regards increasing funding to and for particular groups, there should be increased funding per capita for schools for particular groups of children as some children do present with additional difficulties that have resource implications on teachers and schools. For example, in Scotland that is the pupil premium awarded to individual schools of £2,500 for each pupil in receipt of free school meals, which is an out-of-work benefit. While this is a positive step to support schools and pupils with high levels of poverty, the similar premium in England extends beyond children living in poverty to children who are also adopted as there is an understanding that such pupils may present with difficulties that have resource implications for schools. From the findings in this book the pupil premium should be extended to other groups of pupils who have resource implications for school, for example those with a disability, refugee and asylum-seeking children, as well as those in state care, not just those who have been adopted or who are living in poverty.

Notes

Chapter 1

[1] www.bsa-data.natcen.ac.uk/#welfare.

Chapter 2

[1] While housing is an extremely important factor in the story of child poverty, it is not directly addressed in this book due to space restrictions.

Chapter 3

[1] www.trusselltrust.org/news-and-blog/latest-stats/end-year-stats/ (accessed 30 October 2018).

Chapter 6

[1] www.ohchr.org/EN/NewsEvents/Pages/DisplayNews.aspx?NewsID= 23881&LangID=E (accessed 20 November 2018).

Chapter 7

[1] www.scotpho.org.uk/population-dynamics/recent-mortality-trends/ (accessed 20 June 2019).

References

ACEVO 2012. *Youth unemployment: The crisis we cannot afford*. London, Association of Chief Executives of Voluntary Organisations.

ACMD 2011. Hidden harm: Report on children of drug users. London: Advisory Council on the Misuse of Drugs.

Adamsons, K. 2018. Quantity versus quality of nonresident father involvement: Deconstructing the argument that quantity doesn't matter. *Journal of Child Custody*, 15: 26–34.

Adamsons, K. & Johnson, S.K. 2013. An updated and expanded meta-analysis of nonresident fathering and child well-being. *Journal of Family Psychology*, 27: 589–99.

Adler, M. 2018. *Cruel, inhuman or degrading treatment? Benefit sanctions in the UK*. London: Palgrave MacMillan.

Ainge Roy, E. 2016. New Zealand's most shameful secret: 'We have normalised child poverty'. *The Guardian*, 16 August 2016.

Alcock, P. 2006. *Understanding poverty*. Basingstoke: Macmillan.

Alcock, P. 2008. Poverty and social exclusion. In: Ridge, T. & Wright, S. (eds.) *Understanding inequality, poverty and wealth: Policies and prospects*. Bristol: Policy Press.

Aldridge, J. 2006. The experiences of children living with and caring for parents with mental illness. *Child Abuse Review*, 15: 79–88.

Allen, K. 2014. 'Blair's children': Young women as 'aspirational subjects' in the psychic landscape of class. *The Sociological Review*, 62: 760–79.

Alston, P. 2018. Statement on visit to the United Kingdom, by Professor Philip Alston, United Nations Special Rapporteur on extreme poverty and human rights. London: United Nations.

Alston, P. 2019. Visit to the United Kingdom of Great Britain and Northern Ireland: Report of the special rapporteur on extreme poverty and human rights. In: Assembly, U.N.G. (ed.). United Nations Human Rights Council.

Anderson, L., Jacobs, J., Schramm, S. & Splittgerber, F. 2000. School transitions: Beginning of the end or a new beginning? *International Journal of Educational Research*, 33: 325–39.

Apouey, B. & Geoffard, P.-Y. 2013. Family income and child health in the UK. *Journal of Health Economics*, 32: 715–27.

Asenova, D., McKendrick, J.H. McCann, C. and Reynolds, R. 2015. *Redistribution of social and societal risks: the impact on individuals, their networks and communities in Scotland*. York: Joseph Rowntree Foundation.

Ayre, D. 2016. *Poor mental health: The links between child poverty and mental health problems*. London: The Children's Society.

Bailey, N. 2015. Exclusionary employment in Britain's broken labour market. *Critical Social Policy*, 36: 82–103.

Baker, A.J.L., Creegan, A., Quinones, A. & Rozelle, L. 2016. Foster children's views of their birth parents: A review of the literature. *Children and Youth Services Review*, 67: 177–83.

Barber, N. 2014. Blaming parents for their children's failings. *Psychology Today* (Online). https://www.psychologytoday.com/gb/blog/the-human-beast/201402/blaming-parents-their-childrens-failings (Accessed 4 September 2018).

Barnard, H. 2014. *Tackling poverty across all ethnicities in the UK*. York: Joseph Rowntree Foundation.

Barrett, W. 2018. Why I worry about the ACE-aware movement's impact (Online). www.tes.com/news/why-i-worry-about-ace-aware-movements-impact (Accessed 24 December 2018).

Barry, M. 2011. 'I realised that I wasn't alone': The views and experiences of young carers from a social capital perspective. *Journal of Youth Studies*, 14: 523–39.

BBC 2017. *Gender disparity report: TV licensing*. London: TV Licensing.

Bell, D.N.F. and Blanchflower, D.G. 2010. *Youth unemployment déjà vu?* Stirling: University of Stirling, Stirling Management School.

Bellis, M.A., Lowey, H., Leckenby, N., Hughes, K. and Harrison, D. 2013. Adverse childhood experiences: Retrospective study to determine their impact on adult health behaviours and health outcomes in a UK population. *Journal of Public Health*, 36: 81–91.

Bennett, J.E., Pearson-Stuttard, J., Kontis, V., Capewell, S., Wolfe, I. and Ezzati, M. 2018. Contributions of diseases and injuries to widening life expectancy inequalities in England from 2001 to 2016: A population-based analysis of vital registration data. *The Lancet Public Health*.

Berentson-Shaw, J. 2015. Child poverty: Stop blaming parents, read and understand the evidence. Morgan Foundation Blog Series (Online). http://morganfoundation.org.nz/child-poverty-stop-blaming-parents-read-and-understand-the-evidence/ (Accessed 4 September 2018).

Beveridge, W.H.B. 1944. *Full employment in a free society*. London: Allen & Unwin.

Blackburn, C.M., Spencer, N.J. and Read, J.M. 2010. Prevalence of childhood disability and the characteristics and circumstances of disabled children in the UK: Secondary analysis of the Family Resources Survey. *BMC Pediatrics*, 10.

Blum, L.M. 2015. Following Mother's Day, stop blaming mothers. Talk Poverty blog. https://talkpoverty.org/2015/05/14/blaming-mothers/ (Accessed on 5 September 2018).

Bodovski, K. 2010. Parental practices and educational achievement: Social class, race, and habitus. *British Journal of Sociology of Education*, 31: 139–56.

Booth, R. and Butler, P. 2018. UK austerity has inflicted 'great misery' on citizens, UN says. *The Guardian*, 16 November 2018.

Bourgonje, P. 2010. Education for refugee and asylum seeking children in OECD countries: Case studies from Australia, Spain, Sweden, and the United Kingdom, Brussels: Education Internationals.

Bradley, R.H. and Corwyn, R.F. 2002. Socio-economic status and child development. *Annual Review of Psychology*, 53: 371–99.

Bradshaw, J. 2006. Child support and child poverty. *Benefits*, 14: 199–208.

Bradshaw, J., Hoelscher, P. and Richardson, D. 2007. An index of child well-being in the European Union. *Social Indicators Research*, 80: 133–77.

Brady, D. 2009. *Rich democracies, poor people: How politics explain poverty*. New York, Oxford: Oxford University Press.

Brady, D. and Burroway, R. 2012. Targeting, universalism, and single-mother poverty: A multilevel analysis across 18 affluent democracies. *Demography*, 49: 719–46.

Bramley, G., Fitzpatrick, S., Edwards, J., Ford, D., Johnsen, S., Sosenko, F. and Watkins, D. 2015. *Hard edges: Mapping severe and multiple disadvantage in England*. London: Lankelly Chase Foundation.

Briant, E., Watson, N. and Philo, G. 2013. Reporting disability in the age of austerity: The changing face of media representation of disability and disabled people in the United Kingdom and the creation of new 'folk devils'. *Disability & Society*, 28: 874–89.

Browne, J., Hood, A. and Payne, J. 2016. *Living standards, poverty and inequality in the UK 2015–2016 to 2020–2021*. London: IFS.

Butterworth, P., Leach, L.S., Strazdins, L., Olesen, S.C., Rodgers, B. and Broom, D.H. 2011. The psychosocial quality of work determines whether employment has benefits for mental health: Results from a longitudinal national household panel survey. *Occupational and Environmental Medicine*, 68: 806.

Bywaters, P. 2016. *The relationship between poverty, child abuse and neglect: An evidence review*. York: Joseph Rowntree Foundation.

Bywaters, P., Scourfield, J., Jones, C., Sparks, T., Elliott, M., Hooper, J., McCartan, C., Shapira, M., Bunting, L. and Daniel, B. 2018. Child welfare inequalities in the four nations of the UK. *Journal of Social Work*: https://doi.org/10.1177/1468017318793479.

Calder, G. 2018. Social justice, single parents and their children. In: Nieuwenhuis, R. and Laurie, C.M. (eds.) *The triple bind of single-parent families*. Bristol: Policy Press.

Carers Trust 2016. *Invisible and in distress: Prioritising the mental health of England's young carers*. London: Carers Trust.

Carers Trust Scotland 2017. Child Poverty (Scotland) Bill: Evidence submission for Social Security Committee. Edinburgh: Scottish Parliament.

Catney, G. and Sabater, A. 2015. *Ethnic minority disadvantage in the labour market: Participation, skills and geographical inequalities*. York: Joseph Rowntree Foundation.

Children's Society 2012. *Hidden from view: The experiences of young carers in England*. London: The Children's Society.

Chorley, M. 2012. Problem families told – 'Stop blaming others'. *Independent on Sunday*, 10 June 2012.

City of Edinburgh Council 2018. *Making Education equal for all: Edinburgh's pupil equity framework*. Edinburgh: City of Edinburgh Council.

Claessens, E. and Mortelmans, D. 2018. Challenges for child support schemes: Accounting for shared care and complex families. *Journal of European Social Policy*, 28: 211–23.

Collins, S. 2016. Family First blames child poverty on divorce and single parents. *New Zealand Herald*, 30 May 2016.

Comeau, J. and Boyle, M.H. 2018. Patterns of poverty exposure and childrens trajectories of externalizing and internalizing behaviors. *SSMPH SSM – Population Health*, 4: 86–94.

Cooklin, A. 2009. Children as carers of parents with mental illness. *Psychiatry*, 8: 17–20.

Cooper, K. and Stewart, K. 2013. Does money affect children's outcomes? A systematic review. York: Joseph Rowntree Foundation.

Cooper, N. 2014. Below the breadline: The relentless rise of food poverty in Britain. Oxford: Church Action on Poverty and Oxfam.

Courea, E. 2018. MPs urged to consider voting down new rules on universal credit. *The Guardian*, 4 November.

CPAG NZ 2017. *Facts about child poverty*. Auckland: Child Poverty Action Group New Zealand.

Cree, V.E. 2003. Worries and problems of young carers: Issues for mental health. *Child & Family Social Work*, 8: 301–9.

Crompton, R. 2008. *Class and stratification*. Bristol: Polity Press.

Cross, M. 2013. Demonised, impoverished and now forced into isolation: The fate of disabled people under austerity. *Disability & Society*, 28: 719–23.

Crossley, S. 2016. 'Realising the (troubled) family', 'crafting the neoliberal state'. *Families, Relationships and Societies*, 5: 263–79.

Crowley, A. and Vulliamy, C. 2007. *Listen up!: Children and young people talk about poverty*. Cardiff: Save the Children.

Crowley, L., Jones, K., Cominetti, N. and Gulliford, J. 2013. *International lessons: Youth unemployment in the global context*. Lancaster: The Work Foundation, Lancaster University.

D'Arcy, C. and Finch, D. 2017. *The Great Escape? Low pay and progression in the UK's labour market*. London: Social Mobility Commission/The Resolution Foundation.

Davie, M. 2016. Children's mental health, poverty and life chances. In: Tucker, J. (ed.) *Improving children's life chances*. London: Child Poverty Action Group.

Davis, N. 2018. Life expectancy falling for women in poorest areas of England. *The Guardian*, 23 November.

De Benedictis, S. 2012. Feral parents: Austerity parenting under neoliberalism. *Studies in the Maternal*, 4: 1–21.

Dennell, B.L.L. and Logan, C. 2015. *Prejudice-based bullying in Scottish schools: A research report*. Edinburgh: Equality and Human Rights Commission.

Department for Work and Pensions 2019. *Households Below Average Income, 1994/95–2017/18*. 12th edn. London: UK Data Service.

Dermott, E. and Pomati, M. 2015. The parenting and economising practices of lone parents: Policy and evidence. *Critical Social Policy*, 36(1): 62–81.

Dermott, E. and Pomati, M. 2016. 'Good' parenting practices: How important are poverty, education and time pressure? *Sociology*, 50: 125–42.

Ditch the Label 2018. *The annual bullying survey 2018: The annual benchmark of bullying in the United Kingdom*. London: Ditch the Label.

Donkin, A. and Marmott, M. 2016. A standard of living sufficient for health, wellbeing and development. In: Tucker, J. (ed.) *Improving children's life chances*. London: Child Poverty Action Group.

Duncan, G.J. and Brooksgunn, J. (eds.) 1997. *Consequences of growing up poor*. New York: Russell Sage Foundation.

Dunn, J., Cheng, H., O'Connor, T.G. and Bridges, L. 2004. Children's perspectives on their relationships with their nonresident fathers: Influences, outcomes and implications. *Journal of Child Psychology and Psychiatry*, 45: 553–66.

Dwyer, P. and Wright, S. 2014. Universal credit, ubiquitous conditionality and its implications for social citizenship. *Journal of Poverty and Social Justice*, 22: 27–35.

Edwards, R., Gillies, V. and White, S. 2019. Introduction: Adverse childhood experiences (ACES) – implications and challenges. *Social Policy and Society*, 18: 411–14.

Edwards, R., McCarthy, J.R. and Gillies, V. 2012. The politics of concepts: Family and its (putative) replacements. *The British Journal of Sociology*, 63: 730–46.

EHRC 2015. *'Is Britain fairer?': Key facts and findings on ethnicity*. London: Equality and Human Rights Commission.

EHRC 2016. *Race report: Healing a divided Britain*. London: Equality and Human Rights Commission.

Elliott, I. 2016. *Poverty and mental health: A review to inform the Joseph Rowntree Foundation's anti-poverty strategy*. London: Mental Health Foundation.

Elsley, S. 2014. *Learning lessons: Young people's views on poverty and education in Scotland*. Edinburgh: Scotland's Commissioner for Children and Young, People, Save the Children.

Eriksson, U., Hochwalder, J., Carlsund, A. and Sellstrom, E. 2012. Health outcomes among Swedish children: The role of social capital in the family, school and neighbourhood. *Acta Paediatrica*, 101: 513–17.

Evangelou, M., Taggart, B., Sylva, K., Melhuish, E.C., Sammons, P. and Siraj-Blatchford, I. 2007. *Effective pre-school, primary and secondary education 3–14 project (EPPSE 3–14): What makes a successful transition from primary to secondary school?* Annesley: Department for Children, Schools and Families.

Evans, G. 2006. *Educational failure and working class white children in Britain*. Basingstoke, Palgrave Macmillan.

Evans, M. 2017. TV licence evaders could get off with slap on the wrist after new sentencing guidelines are introduced. *The Telegraph*, 24 January 2017.

Fanjul, G. 2014. Children of the recession: The impact of the economic crisis on child well-being in rich countries. New York; London: United Nations Children's Fund (UNICEF) Stationery Office.

Fazel, M. 2015. A moment of change: Facilitating refugee children's mental health in UK schools. *International Journal of Educational Development*. 41: 255–61.

Fazel, M. and Betancourt, T.S. 2018. Preventive mental health interventions for refugee children and adolescents in high-income settings. *The Lancet Child & Adolescent Health*, 2: 121–32.

Fazel, M., Reed, R.V., Panter-Brick, C. and Stein, A. 2012. Mental health of displaced and refugee children resettled in high-income countries: Risk and protective factors. *The Lancet*, 379: 266–82.

Felitti, V.J., Anda, R.F., Nordenberg, D., Williamson, D.F., Spitz, A.M., Edwards, V., Koss, M.P. and Marks, J.S. 1998. Relationship of childhood abuse and household dysfunction to many of the leading causes of death in adults: The adverse childhood experiences (ACE) study. *American Journal of Preventive Medicine*, 14: 245–58.

Finkelhor, D. 2018. Screening for adverse childhood experiences (ACEs): Cautions and suggestions. *Child Abuse & Neglect*, 85: 174–9.

Fitzpatrick, S., Bramley, G. and Johnsen, S. 2012. Pathways into multiple exclusion homelessness in seven UK cities. *Urban Studies*, 50: 148–68.

Fitzpatrick, S., Bramley, G., Sosenko, F., Blenkinsopp, J., Wood, J., Johnsen, S., Littlewood, M. and Watts, B. 2018. *Destitution in the UK 2018*. York: Joseph Rowntree Foundation.

Fitzsimons, E., Goodman, A., Kelly, E. and Smith, J.P. 2017. Poverty dynamics and parental mental health: Determinants of childhood mental health in the UK. *Social Science & Medicine*, 175: 43–51.

Fleming, J. 2016. *Evaluation report of young carers in focus champions – what have we found out?* London: Practical Participation.

Fletcher, D.R. and Flint, J. 2018. Welfare conditionality and social marginality: The folly of the tutelary state? *Critical Social Policy*, 38: 771–91.

Flouri, E., Midouhas, E. and Joshi, H. 2014. Family poverty and trajectories of children's emotional and behavioural problems: The moderating roles of self-regulation and verbal cognitive ability. *Journal of Abnormal Child Psychology*, 42: 1043–56.

Galton, M.J., Gray, J. and Ruddick, J. 1999. *The impact of school transitions and transfers on pupil progress and attainment*. Nottingham: DfEE.

Garey, A.I. and Arendell, T. 1999. *Children, work, and family: Some thoughts on 'mother blame'*. Working Paper No. 4. Berkeley: Center for Working Families, University of California.

Garfinkel, I. and McLanahan, S. 2003. Unwed parents in the US: Myths, realities and policy making. *Social Policy and Society*, 2: 143–50.

Garthwaite, K. 2011. 'The language of shirkers and scroungers?' Talking about illness, disability and coalition welfare reform. *Disability & Society*, 26: 369–72.

Garthwaite, K. 2016. *Hunger pains: Life inside foodbank Britain.* Bristol: Policy Press.

Garthwaite, K. 2017. Rethinking deservingness, choice and gratitude in emergency food provision. In: J. Hudson, C. Needham and E. Heins (eds.) *Social policy review 29: Analysis and debate in social policy, 2017.* Bristol: Policy Press.

Gewirtz, S. 2001. Cloning the Blairs: New Labour's programme for the re-socialization of working-class parents. *Journal of Education Policy*, 16: 365–78.

Ghate, D. and Hazel, N. 2002. *Parenting in poor environments: Stress, support, and coping.* London: Jessica Kingsley.

Ghoshray, A., Ordóñez, J. and Sala, H. 2016. Euro, crisis and unemployment: Youth patterns, youth policies? *Economic Modelling*, 58: 442–53.

Giddens, A. and Diamond, P. 2005. The new egalitarianism: Economic inequality in the UK. In: Giddens, A. and Diamond, P. (eds.) *The new egalitarianism.* Cambridge, UK; Malden, MA: Polity Press.

Gilchrist, A. and Kyprianou, P. 2011. *Social networks, poverty and ethnicity.* York: Joseph Rowntree Foundation.

Gillies, V. 2005. Raising the 'meritocracy': Parenting and the individualization of social class. *Sociology*, 39: 835–53.

Gillies, V. 2006. Working class mothers and school life: Exploring the role of emotional capital. *Gender and Education*, 18: 281–93.

Gillies, V. 2008. Childrearing, class and the new politics of parenting. *Sociology Compass*, 2: 1079–95.

Gillies, V. 2011. From function to competence: Engaging with the new politics of family. *Sociological Research Online*, 16: 11.

Gingerbread. 2018. Single parent statistics (Online). www.gingerbread. org.uk/policy-campaigns/publications-index/statistics/ (Accessed 21 September 2018).

Ginwright, S. 2018. The future of healing: Shifting from trauma informed care to healing centered engagement (Online). *Medium Psychology.* https://medium.com/@ginwright/the-future-of-healing-shifting-from-trauma-informed-care-to-healing-centered-engagement-634f557ce69c (Accessed 24 December 2018).

Goffman, E. 1990. *Stigma notes on the management of spoiled identity.* London, Penguin.

Goldthorpe, J.H. 2010. Analysing social inequality: A critique of two recent contributions from economics and epidemiology. *European Sociological Review*, 26: 731–44.

Goode, J., Callender, C., Lister, R. and Policy Studies Institute 1998. *Purse or wallet?: Gender inequalities and income distribution within families on benefits.* London: Policy Studies Institute.

Goodman, A. and Gregg, P. 2010. *Poorer children's educational attainment: How important are attitudes and behaviour?* York: Joseph Rowntree Foundation.

Green, M. 2007. *Voices of people experiencing poverty in Scotland.* York: Joseph Rowntree Foundation and the Poverty Alliance.

Green, M.J., Stritzel, H., Smith, C., Popham, F. and Crosnoe, R. 2018. Timing of poverty in childhood and adolescent health: Evidence from the US and UK. *Social Science & Medicine*, 197: 136–43.

Gregg, P. and Tominey, E. 2004. *The wage scar from youth unemployment.* Bristol: Department of Economics, University of Bristol.

Gregg, P. and Tominey, E. 2005. The wage scar from male youth unemployment. *Labour Economics*, 12: 487–509.

Gregg, P., Waldfogel, J., Washbrook, E. 2006. Family expenditures post-welfare reform in the UK: Are low-income families starting to catch up? *Labour Economics*, 13: 721–46.

Griggs, J. and Walker, R. 2008. *The costs of child poverty for individuals and society: A literature review.* York: Joseph Rowntree Foundation.

Grove, C., Riebschleger, J., Bosch, A., Cavanaugh, D. and Van Der Ende, P.C. 2017. Expert views of children's knowledge needs regarding parental mental illness. *Children and Youth Services Review*, 79: 249–55.

Grover, C. 2016. Social security and wage poverty: Historical and policy aspects of supplementing wages in Britain and beyond. London: Palgrave Macmillan.

Gutman, L.M. and Vorhaus, J. 2012. *The impact of pupil behaviour and wellbeing on educational outcomes.* London: Department for Education.

Hakovirta, M. 2011. Child maintenance and child poverty: A comparative analysis. *Journal of Poverty and Social Justice*, 19: 249–62.

Hamilton, M.G. and Adamson, E. 2013. Bounded agency in young carers' lifecourse-stage domains and transitions. *Journal of Youth Studies*, 16: 101–17.

Hanandita, W. and Tampubolon, G. 2014. Does poverty reduce mental health? An instrumental variable analysis. *Social science & medicine*, 113: 59–67.

Hancock, L. and Mooney, G. 2013. 'Welfare ghettos' and the 'broken society': Territorial stigmatization in the contemporary UK. *Housing, Theory and Society*, 30(1): 46–64.

Hands, C., Thomas, J. and John-Legere, S. 2016. Refugee children in the UK. *Paediatrics and Child Health Paediatrics and Child Health*, 26: 37–41.

Hanson, T.L., McLanahan, S. and Thomson, E. 1997. Economic resources, parental practices, and children's wellbeing. In: Duncan, G.J. and Brooksgunn, J. (eds.) *Consequences of growing up poor*. New York: Russell Sage Foundation.

Harkness, S. and Skipp, A. 2013. *Lone mothers, work and depression*. London: The Nuffield Foundation.

Harris, J., Treanor, M.C. and Sharma, N. 2009. *Below the breadline: A year in the life of families living in poverty*. London: Barnardos.

Hartas, D. 2019. Assessing the foundational studies on adverse childhood experiences. *Social Policy and Society*: 1–9.

Highet, G. and Jamieson, L. 2007. *Cool with change: Young people and family change*. Edinburgh: University of Edinburgh Centre for Research on Families and Relationships.

Hills, J. 2015. *Good times, bad times: The welfare myth of them and us*. Bristol; Chicago: Polity Press.

Hills, J., Brewer, M., Jenkins, S., Lister, R., Lupton, R., Machin, S., Mills, C., Modood, T., Rees, T. and Riddell, S. 2010. *An anatomy of economic inequality in the UK: Report of the National Equality Panel*. London: LSE.

Hirsch, D. 2007. *Experiences of poverty and educational disadvantage*. York: Joseph Rowntree Foundation.

Hirsch, D. 2008. *Estimating the cost of child poverty*. York: Joseph Rowntree Foundation.

Hirsch, D. 2013. *Estimating the cost of child poverty in 2013*. Loughborough: Centre for Research in Social Policy, Loughborough University.

HMRC 2017. *Child benefit, child tax credit and working tax credit take-up rates 2015–16*. London: HM Government.

Holloway, S.L. and Pimlott-Wilson, H. 2011. The politics of aspiration: Neo-liberal education policy, 'low' parental aspirations, and primary school. Extended Services in disadvantaged communities. *Children's Geographies*, 9: 79–94.

Hollywood, E., Egdell, V. and Mcquaid, R. 2012. Addressing the issue of disadvantaged youth seeking work. *Social Work and Society*, 10.

Hooper, C.-A. 2007. *Living with hardship 24/7: The diverse experiences of families in poverty in England*. London: Frank Buttle Trust.

Horgan, G. 2007. *The impact of poverty on young children's experience of school*. York: Joseph Rowntree Foundation.

Horgan, G. 2009. 'That child is smart because he's rich': The impact of poverty on young children's experiences of school. *International Journal of Inclusive Education*, 13: 359–76.

Horgan, G. 2011. The making of an outsider: Growing up in poverty in Northern Ireland. *Youth & Society*, 43: 453–67.

Hudson, J. and Kühner, S. 2016. *Fairness for children: A league table of inequality in child well-being in rich countries*. Florence: UNICEF Office of Research.

Hurrell, A. 2013. *Starting out or getting stuck?: An analysis of who gets trapped in low paid work – and who escapes*. London: Resolution Foundation.

IPPR 2018. *Prosperity and justice: A plan for the new economy*. London: Institute for Public Policy Research and the Commission on Economic Justice.

Irwin, S. and Elley, S. 2011. Concerted cultivation? Parenting values, education and class diversity. *Sociology*, 45: 480–95.

Ivinson, G., Beckett, L., Thompson, I., Wrigley, T., Egan, D., Leitch, R. and Stephen, M. 2016. *The research commission on poverty and policy advocacy*. London: British Educational Research Association.

Ivinson, G., Thompson, I., Beckett, L., Egan, D., Leitch, R. and McKinney, S. 2017. Learning the price of poverty across the UK. *Policy Futures in Education Policy Futures in Education*: https://doi.org/10.1177/1478210317736224.

Jans, M. 2004. Children as citizens: Towards a contemporary notion of child participation. *Childhood*, 11: 27–44.

Jenkins, S.P., Rigg, J.A., Devicienti, F. 2001. *The dynamics of poverty in Britain*. Leeds: Corporate Document Services for the Department for Work and Pensions.

Jones, R., Everson-Hock, E.S., Papaioannou, D., Guillaume, L., Goyder, E., Chilcott, J., Cooke, J., Payne, N., Duenas, A., Sheppard, L.M. and Swann, C. 2011. Factors associated with outcomes for looked-after children and young people: A correlates review of the literature. *Child*, 37(5): 613–22.

Joy, E. and Beddoe, L. 2019. ACEs, Cultural considerations and 'common sense' in Aotearoa New Zealand. *Social Policy and Society*, 18: 491–7.

JRF 2016. *UK poverty: causes, costs and solutions*. York: Joseph Rowntree Foundation.

JRF 2017. *UK poverty 2017: A comprehensive analysis of poverty trends and figures*. York: Joseph Rowntree Foundation.

JRF 2018a. *Budget 2018: Tackling the rising tide of in-work poverty.* York: Joseph Rowntree Foundation.

JRF 2018b. *UK poverty 2018: A comprehensive analysis of poverty trends and figures.* York: Joseph Rowntree Foundation.

Katikireddi, S.V., Molaodi, O.R., Gibson, M., Dundas, R. and Craig, P. 2018. Effects of restrictions to income support on health of lone mothers in the UK: A natural experiment study. *The Lancet Public Health*, 3: e333–e340.

Katz, I., Corlyon, J., La Placa, V. and Hunter, S. 2007. *The relationship between parenting and poverty.* York: Joseph Rowntree Foundation.

Kelly-Irving, M. and Delpierre, C. 2019. A critique of the adverse childhood experiences framework in epidemiology and public health: Uses and misuses. *Social Policy and Society*, 18: 445–56.

Khattab, N. 2009. Ethno-religious background as a determinant of educational and occupational attainment in Britain. *Sociology*, 43: 304–22.

Kiernan, K., McLanahan, S., Holmes, J. and Wright, M. 2011. *Fragile families in the US and UK.* Working Papers 1299. Princeton: Princeton University, Woodrow Wilson School of Public and International Affairs, Center for Research on Child Wellbeing.

Kiernan, K. and Mensah, F. 2010. Partnership trajectories, parent and child well-being. In: Hansen, K., Joshi, H. and Dex, S. (eds.) *Children of the 21st century: The first five years.* Bristol: Policy Press.

Kiernan, K.E. and Huerta, M.C. 2008. Economic deprivation, maternal depression, parenting and children's cognitive and emotional development in early childhood. *British Journal of Sociology*, 59: 783–806.

Kiernan, K.E. and Mensah, F.K. 2009. Poverty, maternal depression, family status and children's cognitive and behavioural development in early childhood: A longitudinal study. *Journal of Social Policy*, 38: 569–88.

Kim, J. 2012. Welfare reform and college enrollment among single mothers. *Social Service Review*, 86: 69–91.

Lansley, S. and Mack, J. 2015. *Breadline Britain: The rise of mass poverty.* London: Oneworld Publications.

Lareau, A. 1987. Social class differences in family-school relationships: The importance of cultural capital. *Sociology of Education*, 60: 73–85.

Leahy, M.A. 2015. Children of mentally ill parents: Understanding the effects of childhood trauma as it pertains to the school setting. *International Journal of Educational Research*, 71: 100–7.

Lehtonen, A. 2018. 'Helping workless families': Cultural poverty and the family in austerity and anti-welfare discourse. *Sociological Research Online*, 23: 84–99.

Lereya, S.T., Copeland, W.E., Costello, E.J. and Wolke, D. 2015. Adult mental health consequences of peer bullying and maltreatment in childhood: Two cohorts in two countries. *The Lancet Psychiatry*, 2: 524–31.

Levine, J. 2017. The plight of international child support enforcement. *Child & Family Social Work*, 22: 617–25.

Levitas, R. 2012. *There may be trouble ahead: What we know about those 120,000 'troubled' families*. Bristol: Poverty and Social Exclusion.

Levitas, R., Pantazis, C., Fahmy, E., Gordon, D., Lloyd, E. and Patsios, D. 2007. *The multidimensional analysis of social exclusion*. Bristol: Department of Sociology and School for Social Policy, Townsend Centre for the International Study of Poverty and Bristol Institute for Public Affairs, University of Bristol.

Lister, R. 2004. *Poverty*. Cambridge, UK; Malden, MA: Polity.

Lister, R. 2006. Children (but not women) first: New Labour, child welfare and gender. *Critical Social Policy*, 26: 315–35.

Lister, R. 2011. Social justice for children: Investigating and eradicating child poverty. In: Walker, A., Sinfield, A. and Walker, C. (eds.) *Fighting poverty, inequality and injustice: A manifesto inspired by Peter Townsend*. Bristol: The Policy Press.

Liu, C.H., Yasui, M., Giallo, R., Tronick, E. and Seidman, L.J. 2016. US caregivers with mental health problems: Parenting experiences and children's functioning. *Archives of Psychiatric Nursing*, 30: 753–60.

Lloyd, K. 2013. Happiness and well-being of young carers: Extent, nature and correlates of caring among 10 and 11 year old school children. *Journal of Happiness Studies*, 14: 67–80.

Loopstra, R., Fledderjohann, J., Reeves, A. and Stuckler, D. 2018. Impact of welfare benefit sanctioning on food insecurity: A dynamic cross-area study of food bank usage in the UK. *Journal of Social Policy*, 47: 437–57.

Lupton, R. 2005. Social justice and school improvement: Improving the quality of schooling in the poorest neighbourhoods. *British Educational Research Journal*, 31: 589–604.

Lupton, R. and Hempel-Jorgensen, A. 2012. The importance of teaching: Pedagogical constraints and possibilities in working-class schools. *Journal of Education Policy*, 27: 601–20.

Lyons, K. and Duncan, P. 2017. 'It's a shambles': Data shows most asylum seekers put in poorest parts of Britain. *The Guardian*, 9 April 2017.

MacDonald, R., Shildrick, T. and Furlong, A. 2014. In search of 'intergenerational cultures of worklessness': Hunting the Yeti and shooting zombies. *Critical Social Policy*, 34: 199–220.

Macnicol, J. 1987. In pursuit of the underclass. *Journal of Social Policy*, 16(3): 293–318.

Macnicol, J. 2017. Reconstructing the underclass. *Social Policy and Society*, 16: 99–108.

MacVarish, J. and Lee, E. 2019. Constructions of parents in adverse childhood experiences discourse. *Social Policy and Society*, 18: 467–77.

Magadi, M. & Middleton, S. 2007. *Severe child poverty in the UK*. London: Save the Children.

Main, G. & Bradshaw, J. 2012. A child material deprivation index. *Child Indicators Research*, 5: 503–21.

Manning, C. & Gregoire, A. 2009. Effects of parental mental illness on children. *Psychiatry*, 8: 7–9.

Mannion, G., Sowerby, M. & I'anson, J. 2015. *How young people's participation in school supports achievement and attainment*. Edinburgh: Scotland's Commissioner for Children and Young People.

Marmot, M. 2016. *The health gap: The challenge of an unequal world*. London: Bloomsbury.

Marmot, M. 2017. The health gap: Doctors and the social determinants of health. *Scandinavian Journal of Public Health*, 45: 686–93.

Marmot, M., Allen, J., Goldblatt, P., Boyce, T., McNeish, D. & Grady, M. 2010. Fair society, healthy lives. *The Marmot Review*, 14.

Marryat, L. & Frank, J. 2019. Factors associated with adverse childhood experiences in Scottish children: A prospective cohort study. *BMJ Paediatrics Open*, 3.

Marsh, A., Barker, K., Ayrton, C., Treanor, M. & Haddad, M. 2017. *Poverty: The facts*. London: Child Poverty Action Group.

Mayer, S. 2002. *The influence of parental income on children's outcomes*. Wellington: Ministry of Social Development.

Mazza, J.R.S.E., Lambert, J., Zunzunegui, M.V., Tremblay, R.E., Boivin, M. and Côté, S.M. 2017. Early adolescence behavior problems and timing of poverty during childhood: A comparison of lifecourse models. *Social Science & Medicine*, 177: 35–42.

McCarthy, J.R., Gilles, V. and Hooper, C.-A. 2018. Introduction. *Sociological Research Online*, 23: 153–9.

McEwen, C.A. and Gregerson, S.F. 2019. A critical assessment of the adverse childhood experiences study at 20 years. *American Journal of Preventive Medicine*, 56: 790–4.

McGee, C., Ward, R., Gibbsons, J. and Harlow, A. *Transition to secondary school: A literature review*. Hamilton: University of Waikato.

McGuinness, F. 2018a. *Poverty in the UK: Statistics*. London: House of Commons Library, UK Parliament.

McGuinness, F. 2018b. *Unemployment by ethnic background*. London: House of Commons Library.

McKendrick, J.H., Cunningham-Burley, S., Backett-Milburn, K. 2003. *Life in low income families in Scotland: Research report*. Edinburgh: Scottish Executive Social Research.

McKendrick, J. H., Mooney, G., Scott, G., Dickie, P. and McHardy, F. (eds) 2016. *Poverty in Scotland 2016: Tools for Transformation*, London: CPAG.

McKie, L. and Callan, S. 2012. *Understanding families: A global introduction*. London: SAGE.

McKinney, S. 2014. The relationship of child poverty to school education. *Improving Schools*, 17: 203–16.

McKnight, A., Duque, M. and Rucci, M. 2017. *Double trouble: A review of the relationship between UK poverty and economic inequality*. London: Oxfam/Centre for Analysis of Social Exclusion LSE.

McLanahan, S. 2007. Should government promote marriage? *Journal of Policy Analysis and Management*, 26: 951.

McLoyd, V.C. 1998. Socioeconomic disadvantage and child development. *American Psychologist*, 53: 185–204.

McMaugh, A. 2011. En/countering disablement in school life in Australia: Children talk about peer relations and living with illness and disability. *Disability & Society*, 26: 853–66.

Mensah, F.K. and Kiernan, K.E. 2009. Parents' mental health and children's cognitive and social development: Families in England in the Millennium Cohort Study. *Social Psychiatry and Psychiatric Epidemiology*, 45: 1023–35.

Mercer, P. 2018. How New Zealand is trying to take on child poverty. BBC News, 16 October. www.bbc.com/news/world–asia–45819681.

Mesie, J. 2018. *A better relationship with learning: An evaluation of the Young Carers in Schools Programme*. London: Coram.

Metzler, M., Merrick, M.T., Klevens, J., Ports, K.A. and Ford, D.C. 2017. Adverse childhood experiences and life opportunities: Shifting the narrative. *Children and Youth Services Review*, 72: 141–9.

Meyer, D.R. and Skinner, C. 2016. Privileging biological or residential obligations in separated families: Child maintenance policy approaches in 12 countries. *Families, Relationships and Societies*, 5: 79–95.

Meyer, D.R., Skinner, C. and Davidson, J. 2011. Complex families and equality in child support obligations: A comparative policy analysis. *Children and Youth Services Review*, 33: 1804–12.

Middleton, S., Ashworth, K. and Braithwaite, I. 1997. *Expenditure on children in Great Britain*. York: Joseph Rowntree Foundation.

Millar, J. and Bennett, F. 2017. Universal credit: Assumptions, contradictions and virtual reality. *Social Policy and Society*, 16: 169–82.

Millar, J. and Ridge, T. 2013. Lone mothers and paid work: The 'family–work project'. *International Review of Sociology*, 23: 564–77.

Ministry of Justice 2018. *Statistics on women and the criminal justice system 2017*. London: Ministry of Justice.

Morris, M. 2015. *Supporting ethnic minority young people from education into work*. York: Joseph Rowntree Foundation.

Mooney, G. 2011. *Stigmatising poverty? The 'broken society' and reflections on anti-welfarism in the UK today*. Oxford: Oxfam.

Nandi, A. and Platt, L. 2010. *Ethnic minority women's poverty and economic well being*. Colchester: Institute for Social and Economic Research, University of Essex.

Nazroo, J. and Kapadia, D. 2013. *Ethnic inequalities in labour market participation?* Manchester: Joseph Rowntree Foundation and Centre on Dynamics of Ethnicity (CoDE) at the University of Manchester.

Netto, G. 2011a. Identity negotiation, pathways to housing and "place": The experience of refugees in Glasgow. *Housing, Theory and Society*, 28: 123–43.

Netto, G. 2011b. Strangers in the city: Addressing challenges to the protection, housing and settlement of refugees. *International Journal of Housing Policy*, 11: 285–303.

New Statesman 2012. George Osborne's speech to the Conservative party conference. www.newstatesman.com/blogs/politics/2012/10/george-osbornes-speech-conservative-conference-full-text.

NHS Health Scotland 2017. *Tackling the attainment gap by preventing and responding to adverse childhood experiences (ACEs)*. Edinburgh: NHS Health Scotland.

NICHD 2005. Duration and developmental timing of poverty and children's cognitive and social development from birth through third grade. *Child Development*, 76: 795–810.

Nieuwenhuis, R. and Maldonado, L.C. 2018. *The triple bind of single-parent families*. Bristol: Policy Press.

Noonan, K., Burns, R. and Violato, M. 2018. Family income, maternal psychological distress and child socio-emotional behaviour: Longitudinal findings from the UK Millennium Cohort Study. *SSM – Population Health*, 4: 280–90.

Nussbaum, M. 2011. Foreword. In: Young, I.M. (ed.) *Responsibility for justice*. Oxford: Oxford University Press.

O'Higgins, N. 2015. *Youth unemployment, Policy Paper No.* 103. Bonn: Institute for the Study of Labor.

O'Connor, A. 2001. Poverty knowledge: Social science, social policy, and the poor in twentieth-century US History. Princeton: Princeton University Press.

OECD 2009. Is work the best antidote to poverty? In: OECD (ed.) *Employment outlook.* Paris: OECD.

OECD 2011. *Taxation and employment.* OECD Tax Policy Studies, No. 21. Paris: OECD Publishing. https://doi.org/10.1787/9789264120808-en (Accessed on 7 November 2018).

OECD 2018. *The future of social protection: What works for non-standard workers?* Paris: OECD Publishing. https://doi.org/10.1787/9789264306943-en (Accessed on 7 November 2018).

OECD 2018. *OECD Employment Outlook 2018.* Paris: OECD Publishing. https://doi.org/10.1787/empl_outlook-2018-en (Accessed on 8 November 2018).

ONS. 2018a. Ethnicity facts and figures: Employment (Online). www.ethnicity-facts-figures.service.gov.uk/work-pay-and-benefits/employment/employment/latest (Accessed 21 November 2018).

ONS. 2018b. Ethnicity facts and figures: Unemployment (Online). www.ethnicity-facts-figures.service.gov.uk/work-pay-and-benefits/employment/employment/latest (Accessed 21 November 2018).

ONS. 2019. *Labour Force Survey Household Data Set: April 2019.* https://www.eui.eu/Research/Library/ResearchGuides/Economics/Statistics/DataPortal/EU-LFS (Accessed 1 July 2019).

Osborne, C. and McLanahan, S. 2007. Partnership instability and child well-being. *Journal of Marriage and Family,* 69: 1065–83.

Pahl, J. 1999. *Family finances in the electronic economy.* York: Joseph Rowntree Foundation.

Pahl, J.M. 1989. *Money and marriage.* New York: St Martin's Press.

Paterson, L. 2015. *Social radicalism and liberal education.* Exeter: Imprint Acad.

Patrick, R. 2012. Work as the primary duty of the responsible citizen: A critique of this work-centric approach. *People Place and Policy Online,* 6: 5–15.

Patrick, R. 2014. Working on welfare: Findings from a qualitative longitudinal study into the lived experiences of welfare reform in the UK. *Journal of Social Policy,* 43: 705–25.

Patrick, R. 2016. Living with and responding to the 'scrounger' narrative in the UK: Exploring everyday strategies of acceptance, resistance and deflection. *Journal of Poverty and Social Justice,* 24: 245–59.

Pemberton, S., Fahmy, E., Sutton, E. and Bell, K. 2015. Navigating the stigmatised identities of poverty in austere times: Resisting and responding to narratives of personal failure. *Critical Social Policy*, 36: 21–37.

Platt, L. 2009. *Ethnicity and child poverty*. London: Department for Work and Pensions.

Portes, J. and Reed, H. 2018. *The cumulative impact of tax and welfare reforms*. Manchester: Equality and Human Rights Commission, Aubergine Analysis and Kings College London, Landman Economics.

Pruett, M.K., Pruett, K., Cowan, C.P. and Cowan, P.A. 2017. Enhancing father involvement in low-income families: A couples group approach to preventive intervention. *Child Development*, 88: 398–407.

Quilgars, D. and Pleace, N. 2016. Housing, living environments and life chances for children. In: Tucker, J. (ed.) *Improving children's life chances*. London: Child Poverty Action Group.

Raissian, K.M. and Bullinger, L.R. 2017. Money matters: Does the minimum wage affect child maltreatment rates? *Children and Youth Services Review*, 72: 60–70.

Raphael, D. 2011. Poverty in childhood and adverse health outcomes in adulthood. *Maturitas*, 69: 22–6.

Reay, D. 2018. *Miseducation: Inequality, education and the working classes*. Bristol: Policy Press.

Reay, D. and Lucey, H. 2003. The limits of 'choice': Children and inner city schooling. *Sociology*, 37: 121–42.

Reiss, F. 2013. Socioeconomic inequalities and mental health problems in children and adolescents: A systematic review. *SSM Social Science & Medicine*, 90: 24–31.

Reutter, L.I., Stewart, M.J., Veenstra, G., Love, R., Raphael, D. and Makwarimba, E. 2009. 'Who do they think we are, anyway?': Perceptions of and responses to poverty stigma. *Qualitative Health Research*, 19: 297–311.

Ribbens McCarthy, J. and Gillies, V. 2017. Troubling children's families: Who is troubled and why? Approaches to inter-cultural dialogue. *Sociological Research Online*, 23: 219–44.

Ribbens McCarthy, J., Gillies, V. and Hooper, C.-A. 2013. *Family troubles?: Exploring changes and challenges in family lives of children and young people*. Bristol: Policy Press.

Ridge, T. 2002. *Childhood poverty and social exclusion: From a child's perspective*. Bristol: Policy.

Ridge, T. 2007. It's a family affair: Low-income children's perspectives on maternal work. *Journal of Social Policy*, 36: 399–416.

Ridge, T. 2009a. *Living with poverty: A review of the literature on children's and families' experiences of poverty*. London: Department for Work and Pensions.

Ridge, T. 2009b. *Living with poverty: A review of the literature on children and families*. London: Department for Work and Pensions.

Ridge, T. 2011. The everyday costs of poverty in childhood: A review of qualitative research exploring the lives and experiences of low-income children in the UK. *Children & Society*, 25(1): 73–84.

Ridge, T. 2017. The 'go-between': Low-income children negotiating relationships of money and care with their separated parents. *Children & Society*, 31: 87–97.

Ridge, T. and Millar, J. 2011. Following families: Working lone-mother families and their children. *Social Policy & Administration*, 45: 85–97.

Ridge, T. and Wright, S. 2008a. State approaches to poverty and social exclusion. In: Press, P. (ed.) *Understanding inequality, poverty and wealth: Policies and prospects*. Bristol: Policy Press.

Ridge, T. and Wright, S. (eds.) 2008b. *Understanding inequality, poverty and wealth: Policies and prospects*. Bristol: Policy Press.

Rigg, J. and Sefton, T. 2006. Income dynamics and the life cycle. *Journal of Social Policy*, 35: 411–35.

Robison, O., Egan, J. and Inglis, G. 2017. *Young carers in Glasgow: Health, wellbeing and future expectations*. Glasgow: Centre for Population Health.

Runnymede Trust 2015. *The budget 2015. Effects on black and minority ethnic people*. London: Runnymede Trust.

Russell, M., Harris, B. and Gockel, A. 2008. Parenting in poverty: Perspectives of high-risk parents. *Journal of Children and Poverty*, 14: 83–98.

Saffer, J., Nolte, L. and Duffy, S. 2018. Living on a knife edge: The responses of people with physical health conditions to changes in disability benefits. *Disability & Society*: 1–24.

Sahoo, R. and Suar, D. 2009. Do young carers deserve justice? Young caring in the context of illness. *Psychology and Developing Societies*, 21: 133–50.

Santos-Pais, M. 1999. *A human rights conceptual framework for UNICEF*. Florence: UNICEF International Child Development Centre.

Savage, M. 2018. Complex rules for universal credit see one in five claims fail. *The Observer*, 12 May 2018.

Save the Children 2011. *Making work pay: The childcare trap*. London: Save the Children.

Sayer, A. 2017. Responding to the troubled families programme: Framing the injuries of inequality. *Social Policy and Society*, 16: 155–64.

Schoon, I., Cheng, H. and Jones, E. 2010a. Resilience in children's development. In: Hansen, K., Joshi, H. and Dex, S. (eds.) *Children of the 21st century*. Bristol: Policy Press.

Schoon, I., Hope, S., Ross, A. and Duckworth, K. 2010b. Family hardship and children's development: The early years. *Longitudinal and Life Course Studies*, 1(3): 209–22.

Schoon, I., Jones, E., Cheng, H. and Maughan, B. 2012. Family hardship, family instability, and cognitive development. *Journal of Epidemiology & Community Health*, 66(8): 716–22.

Scottish Government 2015. *Scotland's carers*. Edinburgh: Scottish Government.

Scottish Government 2017. *Young carers: Review of research and data*. Edinburgh: Scottish Government Social Research.

Scourfield, J. and Drakeford, M. 2002. New Labour and the 'problem of men'. *Critical Social Policy*, 22: 619–40.

Shaw, K.M., Goldrick-Rab, S., Mazzeo, C. and Jacobs, J.A. 2009. *Putting poor people to work: How the work-first idea eroded college access for the poor*. New York: Russell Sage Foundation.

Shildrick, T., Garthwaite, K., MacDonald, R. and Webster, C. 2013. *Poverty and insecurity: Life in low-pay, no-pay Britain*. Bristol: Policy Press.

Shildrick, T. and MacDonald, R. 2013. Poverty talk: How people experiencing poverty deny their poverty and why they blame 'the poor'. *The Sociological Review*, 61: 285–303.

Shildrick, T., MacDonald, R. and Furlong, A. 2016. Not single spies but in battalions: A critical, sociological engagement with the idea of so-called 'troubled families'. *Sociological Review*, 64: 821–36.

Shildrick, T., MacDonald, R., Webster, C. and Garthwaite, K. 2010. *The role of the lowpay, no-pay cycle in recurrent poverty*. York: Joseph Rowntree Foundation.

Shildrick, T., MacDonald, R., Webster, C. and Garthwaite, K. 2012. *Poverty and insecurity: Life in low-pay, no-pay Britain*. Bristol: Policy Press.

Shirani, F., Henwood, K. and Coltart, C. 2011. Meeting the challenges of intensive parenting culture: Gender, risk management and the moral parent. *Sociology*, 46: 25–40.

Sigle-Rushton, W., Hobcraft, J. and Kiernan, K. 2005. Parental divorce and subsequent disadvantage: A cross-cohort comparison. *Demography*, 42: 427–46.

Sime, D. and Sheridan, M. 2014. 'You want the best for your kids': Improving educational outcomes for children living in poverty through parental engagement. *Educational Research*, 56: 327–42.

Simpson, D., Lumsden, E. and Mcdowall Clark, R. 2015. Pre-school practitioners, child poverty and social justice. *International Journal of Sociology and Social Policy*, 35: 325–39.

Skinner, C. 2013. Child maintenance reforms: Understanding fathers' expressive agency and the power of reciprocity. *International Journal of Law, Policy and the Family*, 27: 242–65.

Skinner, C., Cook, K. and Sinclair, S. 2017a. The potential of child support to reduce lone mother poverty: Comparing population survey data in Australia and the UK. *Journal of Poverty and Social Justice*, 25: 79–94.

Skinner, C., Meyer, D.R., Cook, K.A.Y. and Fletcher, M. 2017b. Child maintenance and social security interactions: The poverty reduction effects in model lone parent families across four countries. *Journal of Social Policy*, 46(3): 495–516.

Slater, T. 2014. The myth of broken Britain: Welfare reform and the production of ignorance. *Antipode Antipode*, 46(4): 948–69.

Smith, J.R., Brooksgunn, J. and Klebanov, P.K. 1997. Consequences of living in poverty for young children's cognitive and verbal ability and early school achievement. In: Duncan, G.J. and Brooksgunn, J. (eds.) *Consequences of growing up poor*. New York: Russell Sage Foundation.

Smith, N. and Middleton, S. 2007. *A Review of Poverty Dynamics Research in the UK*. York, Joseph Rowntree Foundation.

Smith, S.R. 1999. Arguing against cuts in lone parent benefits: Reclaiming the desert ground in the UK. *Critical Social Policy: A Journal of Theory and Practice in Social Welfare*, 19.

Smyth, B.M., Vnuk, M., Rodgers, B. and Son, V. 2014. Can child support compliance be improved by the introduction of a 'fairer' child support formula and more rigorous enforcement? The recent Australian experience. *Journal of Family Studies*, 20: 204–20.

Sosu, E. and Ellis, S. 2014. *Closing the attainment gap in Scottish education*. York: Joseph Rowntree Foundation.

Sosu, E.M. 2014. Predicting maternal aspirations for their children's education: The role of parental and child characteristics. *International Journal of Educational Research*, 67: 67–79.

Spencer, S. 2015. *The cost of the school day*. Glasgow: Child Poverty Action Group in Scotland.

Spohrer, K. 2011. Deconstructing 'aspiration': UK policy debates and European policy trends. *European Educational Research Journal*, 10: 53–63.

St Clair, R. and Benjamin, A. 2011. Performing desires: The dilemma of aspirations and educational attainment. *British Educational Research Journal*, 37: 501–17.

St Clair, R., Kintrea, K. and Houston, M. 2013. Silver bullet or red herring? New evidence on the place of aspirations in education. *Oxford Review of Education*, 39: 719–38.

Steptoe, A., Marteau, T., Fonagy, P. and Abel, K. 2019. ACEs: Evidence, gaps, evaluation and future priorities. *Social Policy and Society*, 18: 415–24.

Stewart, K. 2016. Why we can't talk about life chances without talking about income. In: Tucker, J. (ed.) *Improving children's life chances*. London: Child Poverty Action Group.

Stewart, K., Sefton, T. and Hills, J. 2009. Introduction. In: Hills, J., Sefton, T. and Stewart, K. (eds.) *Towards a more equal society?: Poverty, inequality and policy since 1997*. Bristol: Policy Press in association with the Joseph Rowntree Foundation.

Stewart, T. 2009. *Counting on credit*. London: Barnardo's.

Strand, S. 1999. Ethnic group, sex and economic disadvantage: Associations with pupils' educational progress from baseline to the end of key stage 1. *British Educational Research Journal*, 25: 179–202.

Strand, S. 2011. The limits of social class in explaining ethnic gaps in educational attainment. *British Educational Research Journal*, 37: 197–229.

Strand, S. 2012. The white British–black Caribbean achievement gap: Tests, tiers and teacher expectations. *British Educational Research Journal*, 38: 75–101.

Sutton, L., Smith, N., Dearden, C. and Middleton, S. 2007. *A childs-eye view of social difference*. York: Joseph Rowntree Foundation.

Sylvester, J., Donnell, N., Gray, S., Higgins, K. and Stalker, K. 2014. A survey of disabled children and young people's views about their quality of life. *Disability & Society*, 29: 763–77.

Tackey, N.D., Barnes, H. and Khambhaita, P. 2011. *Poverty, ethnicity and education*. York: Joseph Rowntree Foundation.

Taulbut, M., Mackay, D.F. and McCartney, G. 2018. Job seeker's allowance (JSA) benefit sanctions and labour market outcomes in Britain, 2001–2014. *Cambridge Journal of Economics*, 42: 1417–34.

Tawney, R.H. 1913. 'Poverty as an industrial problem'. Inaugural lecture, reproduced in *Memoranda on the Problems of Poverty*. London: William Morris Press.

Taylor-Robinson, D., Wickham, S. and Barr, B. 2015. Child health at risk from welfare cuts. *British Medical Journal*, 351.

Teese, R. and Lamb, S. 2007. *Social inequalities in education: Enlarging the scope of public policy through reflection on context*. Dordrecht: Springer.

Terkel, S. 1989. *The Great Divide: Second Thoughts on the American Dream*, London: Hamilton.

Thompson, I., McNicholl, J. and Menter, I. 2016. Student teachers' perceptions of poverty and educational achievement. *Oxford Review of Education*, 42: 214–29.

Thompson, S. 2015. *The low-pay, no-pay cycle*. York: Joseph Rowntree Foundation.

Tilly, C. 1998. *Durable inequality*. Berkeley; London: University of California Press.

Townsend, P. 1964. *The last refuge*. London: Routledge and Kegan Paul.

Townsend, P. 1979. *Poverty in the United Kingdom: A survey of household resources and standards of living*. Harmondsworth: Penguin.

Townsend, P. 1987. Deprivation. *Journal of Social Policy*, 16: 125–46.

Townsend, P. and Walker, A. 2010. *The Peter Townsend reader*. Bristol, UK; Policy Press.

Treanor, Morag C. 2012, *The impacts of poverty on children's outcomes*. Stirling: Scottish Child Care and Protection Network (SCCPN).

Treanor, M. 2016a. The effects of financial vulnerability and mothers' emotional distress on child social, emotional and behavioural well-being: A structural equation model. *Sociology*, 50: 673–94.

Treanor, M. 2016b. Social assets, low income and child social, emotional and behavioural wellbeing. *Families, Relationships and Societies*, 5: 209–28.

Treanor, M. under review. Can we put the 'poverty of aspirations' myth to bed now?

Treanor, M.C. 2014. Deprived or not deprived? Comparing the measured extent of material deprivation using the UK government's and the Poverty and Social Exclusion surveys' method of calculating material deprivation. *Quality & Quantity*, 48: 1337–46.

Treanor, M.C. 2018a. Falling through the cracks: The cost of the school day for families living in in-work and out-of-work poverty. *Scottish Affairs*, 27: 486–511.

Treanor, M.C. 2018b. Income poverty, material deprivation and lone parenthood. In: Nieuwenhuis, R. and Laurie, C.M. (eds.) *The triple bind of single-parent families*. Bristol: Policy Press.

Tunstall, R., Lupton, R., Green, A., Watmough, S. and Bates, K. 2012. *Disadvantaged young people looking for work: A job in itself?* York: Joseph Rowntree Foundation.

UN 1989. Convention on the rights of the child: Text as adopted by the General Assembly of the United Nations, United Nations General Assembly.

UN General Assembly 1989. Convention on the Rights of the Child.

Ungar, M. 2015. Practitioner review: Diagnosing childhood resilience – a systemic approach to the diagnosis of adaptation in adverse social and physical ecologies. *Journal of Child Psychology and Psychiatry*, 56: 4–17.

UNICEF 2010. *The children left behind: A league table of inequality in child wellbeing in the world's rich countries.* Florence: Innocenti Research Centre.

Van Der Linden, B. 2016. *Do in-work benefits work for low-skilled workers?* IZA World of Labor: 246. doi: 10.15185/izawol.246.

Van Lancker, W. 2013. Putting the child-centred investment strategy to the test: Evidence for the EU27. *European Journal of Social Security*, 15: 4–27.

Van Lancker, W. 2018. Do reconciliation policies enable single mothers to work? In: Nieuwenhuis, R. and Maldonado, L.C. (eds.) *The triple bind of single-parent families: Resources, employment and policies to improve wellbeing.* Bristol: Policy Press.

Van Lancker, W. and Horemans, J. 2017. Into the great wide unknown: Untangling the relationship between childcare service use and in-work poverty. Working Papers 1704. Antwerp: University of Antwerp: Herman Deleeck Centre for Social Policy.

Walker, A. and Walker, C. 1997. Introduction: the strategy of inequality. *Britain divided: the growth of social exclusion in the 1980s and 1990s.* London: Child Poverty Action Group.

Walker, R. 2014. *The shame of poverty.* Oxford: Oxford University Press.

Walsh, D., Mccartney, G., Smith, M. and Armour, G. under review. The relationship between childhood socio-economic position and Adverse Childhood Experiences (ACEs): A systematic review.

Washbrook, E., Gregg, P. and Propper, C. 2014. A decomposition analysis of the relationship between parental income and multiple child outcomes. *Journal of the Royal Statistical Society*: Series A (Statistics in Society), 177: 757–82.

Wassell, C., Preston, P. and Jones, H. 2007. Transition: A universal issue. *Pastoral Care in Education*, 25: 49–53.

Watson, S. 2014. Does welfare conditionality reduce democratic participation? *Comparative Political Studies*, 48: 645–86.

Watt, G., Ibe, O., Edginton, E. and Whitehead, R. 2017. *'Coping is difficult, but I feel proud' Perspectives on mental health and wellbeing of youngcarers.* Edinburgh: Children and Young People's Commissioner Scotland, Carers Trust Scotland and Scottish Young Carers Services Alliance.

Watts, B., Fitzpatrick, S., Bramley, G. and Watkins, D. 2014. *Welfare sanctions and conditionality in the UK*. York: Joseph Rowntree Foundation.

Weekes-Bernard, D. 2017. *Poverty and ethnicity in the labour market*. York: Joseph Rowntree Foundation.

Welch, V. 2018. Talking back to 'family', 'family troubles', and 'the looked-after child'. *Sociological Research Online*, 23: 197–218.

Welshman, J. 2007. *From transmitted deprivation to social exclusion: Policy, poverty and parenting*. Bristol: Policy Press.

Welshman, J. 2013. *Underclass: A history of the excluded since 1880*. London, Bloomsbury.

West, P., Sweeting, H. and Young, R. 2010. Transition matters: Pupils' experiences of the primary-secondary school transition in the West of Scotland and consequences for well-being and attainment. *Research Papers in Education*, 25: 21–50.

White, S., Edwards, R., Gillies, V. and Wastell, D. 2019. All the ACEs: A chaotic concept for family policy and decision-making? *Social Policy and Society*, 18: 457–66.

Whitworth, A. and Griggs, J. 2013. Lone Parents and Welfare-to-work Conditionality: Necessary, Just, Effective? Ethics and Social Welfare, 7: 124–40.

WHO 2001. *The world health report 2001: Mental health: New understanding, new hope*. Geneva: World Health Organization.

WHO 2012. *Adolescent mental health: Mapping actions of nongovernmental organizations and other international development organizations*. Geneva: World Health Organization.

WHO 2013. *Mental health action plan 2013–2020*. Geneva: World Health Organization.

Wickham, S., Whitehead, M., Taylor-Robinson, D. and Barr, B. 2017. The effect of a transition into poverty on child and maternal mental health: A longitudinal analysis of the UK Millennium Cohort Study. *The Lancet Public Health*, 2: e141–e148.

Wilkinson, R.G. and Marmot, M.G. 2003. *The solid facts: Social determinants of health*. Copenhagen: Centre for Urban Health, World Health Organization.

Wilkinson, R.G. and Pickett, K. 2010. *The spirit level: Why equality is better for everyone*. London; New York: Penguin Books.

Williams, R. 1961. *The long revolution*. London: Chatto & Windus.

Winter, L.A. 2018. Relational equality in education: What, how, and why? *Oxford Review of Education*, 44: 338–52.

Wlodarczyk, O., Pawils, S., Metzner, F., Kriston, L., Klasen, F., Ravens-Sieberer, U. & Group, B.S. 2017. Risk and protective factors for mental health problems in preschool-aged children: Cross-sectional results of the BELLA preschool study. *Child and Adolescent Psychiatry and Mental Health*, 11: 12–12.

Wolff, J. and De-Shalit, A. 2007. *Disadvantage*. Oxford: Oxford University Press.

Young-Hwan, B. 2018. Middle-class single parents. In: Nieuwenhuis, R. and Laurie, C.M. (eds.) *The triple bind of single-parent families*. Bristol: Policy Press.

Young, I.M. 2001. Equality of whom? Social groups and judgments of injustice. *Journal of Political Philosophy*, 9: 1–18.

Zagel, H. and Hübgen, S. 2018. A life-course approach to single mothers' economic wellbeing in different welfare states. In: Nieuwenhuis, R. and Laurie, C.M. (eds.) *The triple bind of single-parent families*. Bristol: Policy Press.

Zeedyk, M.S., Gallacher, J., Henderson, M., Hope, G., Husband, B. and Lindsay, K. 2003. Negotiating the transition from primary to secondary school: Perceptions of pupils, parents and teachers. *School Psychology International*, 24: 67–79.

Zipin, L., Sellar, S., Brennan, M. and Gale, T. 2015. Educating for futures in marginalized regions: A sociological framework for rethinking and researching aspirations. *Educational Philosophy and Theory*, 47: 227–46.

Index

Note: page numbers in *italic* type refer to Figures; those in **bold** type refer to Tables.